The Victorian church

Chris Brooks & Andrew Saint

editors

The Victorian church

Architecture and society

Manchester University Press

Manchester and New York

distributed exclusively in the USA and Canada
by St Martin's Press

Published by Manchester University Press
Oxford Road, Manchester M13 9NR, UK
and Room 400, 175 Fifth Avenue, New York, NY 10010, USA

Distributed exclusively in the USA and Canada
by St Martin's Press, Inc., 175 Fifth Avenue, New York,
NY 10010, USA

British Library Cataloguing-in-Publication Data
A catalogue record is available from the British Library
Library of Congress Cataloging-in-Publication Data

The Victorian church / edited by Chris Brooks and Andrew Saint.
p. cm.
Includes index.
ISBN 0–7190–4019–1. 88 ISBN 0–7190–4020–5 (pbk.)
1. Great Britain – Church history – 19th century. I. Brooks,
Chris. II. Saint, Andrew.
BR759.V491994
274,1081–dc20 94–26465
CIP

ISBN 0 7190 4019 1 *hardback*
0 7190 4020 5 *paperback*

Designed by Max Nettleton

Photoset in Clearface
by Northern Phototypesetting Co. Ltd, Bolton

Printed in Great Britain
by Bell & Bain Limited, Glasgow

Contents

List of figures

Preface and acknowledgements

The essays in this book stem from a lecture-series held by the Victorian Society in London during the autumn of 1992 on building the Victorian church. It was high time, the Society felt, to take a fresh and full look from a wide perspective at this great and challenging subject. So precarious is the state of the whole Victorian ecclesiastical heritage today that it seemed ever more urgent to take stock of the forces that created it.

Churches are at the centre of Victorian culture and architecture. In our mental map of Victorian life, religion and religious observance figure large. We imagine a society secured at middle-class level upon the rock of church-going and chapel-going, with priests and ministers presiding over thronged, respectful and believing congregations. Likewise, when we think in the abstract about the architecture of the Victorians, our thoughts soon turn to the pointed arch and the runaway success of the Gothic Revival — a style developed first and foremost for churches.

The prolific church-building of the Victorians provided the greatest single source of the energy which fuelled their architectural styles, in a way that is quite different from preceding and succeeding periods. It follows that the reputation of Victorian churches is bound up with that of Victorian architecture as a whole. When that architecture fell out of fashion, nothing was so much derided as the Gothic Revival. Its dark and pedantic churches, packed with stained glass and pitchpine pews, became objects first of contempt and then of amusement. Even more ludicrous, people found, was the Victorians' attempt to translate forms and styles originated for churches into country houses, hospitals or station hotels. Aesthetics apart, it suggested a culture so obsessed with the paraphernalia of ancient religious observance that it could not face the challenges of its own times.

Soon, certain architects and amateurs began to take a kindlier view. The first of H. S. Goodhart-Rendel's persuasive pieces on Victorian Gothic appeared in 1924; Kenneth Clark published *The Gothic Revival* in 1928; John Summerson's earliest essay, on a Victorian church in Streatham, was written a year later. By the 1930s there was a coterie of enthusiasts for the subject. They approached it with different degrees of seriousness, and by no means agreed with one another. But they all recognised that the study of churches offered a key towards understanding what mattered about Victorian architecture as a whole. The inspired rhetoric of Pugin, the bloody-mindedness of Butterfield, the Greek-Presbyterian obsessiveness of Alexander Thomson were, they saw, much more than curiosities. The churches of the Victorians, indeed, were among the most creative and imaginative forms of expression in their age. So much could hardly be said of church architecture in other European countries during the nineteenth century. And despite the backward-looking nature of their styles, these British churches and the energy they represented turned out, as scholars traced the story back, to be forces for the universal reform of architecture.

Since the Victorian Society was founded in 1958, there has been a surge of discovery and scholarship about Victorian architecture in Great Britain and Ireland. Much of this has concerned churches. Books or theses have been written about most of the great church-building architects; their work is now well documented and respected. But whether it is so well loved, whether indeed Victorian church architecture as a whole is so well comprehended as its place in nineteenth-century British culture deserves, is doubtful. What are the reasons for this?

The obvious answer is that we live in an irreligious age. There may be no less 'belief' around in Britain than there was a hundred or a hundred and fifty years ago. But theological and sectarian differences have ceased to have anything like a consuming interest. A convergence has taken place in the ways in which people worship. The style, arrangement and very meaning of churches which were built to affirm particular religious standpoints and encourage particular patterns of liturgy have lost their significance, even for observant Christians. At the same time, Victorian churches and chapels have still not yet been around long enough to command the affection reserved for old parish churches, particularly in the countryside. They lack the full effect of layering and the sentimental patina of age.

There are other reasons as well. One is what might be called the problem of Gothic — the dominant language of the Victorian church. Gothic, or at least the Gothic of the Gothic Revival, had strong literary, archaeological and moral streaks to it. But the architectural culture of today is largely visual and functional. We cannot hope fully to understand or assess the quality of a Victorian Gothic church without a good deal of complex historical baggage. This is far less true for a Victorian building in the functional tradition. Some of the same difficulties apply to classicism. But the classical language of architecture enjoys visual rules and precedents which are quite easy to grasp. This, together with classicism's richer secular history, has given it a cultural and international status which Gothic, or at any rate the Gothic Revival, has never managed to achieve. You cannot crib from Street or Butterfield or Waterhouse in the way you can from Palladio, Inigo Jones or even Charles Barry.

Nor does the growing consumerism of our society help create a climate of sympathy towards Victorian churches. Many of us live in Victorian houses whose layout and looks we admire. The pride we take in them encourages us, as they grow older, to respect their character. The upsurge of interest now taken in the Victorian secular crafts has been fuelled by the urge people feel to buy appropriate objects for furnishing and restoring their homes. The same factors do not operate where churches are concerned. Priests, parsons, ministers and congregations find Victorian liturgical arrangements and fittings a hindrance to their ambitions. Money for spending on an ill-endowed and under-maintained fabric is hard to come by. When it does become available, the incentive is not to restore or enhance but to simplify, equalise and reduce.

For all these reasons, then, the Victorian church is still little loved. Indeed it may be less loved than it was a generation ago, when the process of rediscovery seemed new and the struggle for the recognition of Victorian architecture was still sharp. Yet the crisis which currently besets these exceptional buildings is even bigger than it then was. Church closures are taking place on an ever greater scale; the pace of liturgical change has increased across the denominations. Church after Victorian church in our towns and cities is reduced in size and 'reordered', or has its crumbling steeple chopped off, or is sold and cut up for warehousing or studios or flats with intrusive rooflights, or is simply knocked down. Few of these churches are of the highest artistic importance; but several that are sit empty, decaying and vandalised, because resources and a dignified destiny cannot be found for them. The spectacle of even the most humdrum chapel or church in dereliction or converted is always a sad one, because it is redolent of abandoned aspiration.

The Victorian church offers no answers to these pressing problems. Instead, it endeavours to enrich our understanding of these buildings — so vital to the society which created them, in so grave a plight today. Without the historical perspective, the rise and fall of the Victorian church cannot properly be charted. It was and is important to know who designed and crafted these churches, how their styles developed and which are the best of them. This we can now just about do. But we have little understanding of how church-building was organised in different parts of the country, not least in Scotland, Wales and Ireland. We know little about who paid for churches, how, and why; whether they were built in answer to proven need or were more often instruments of personal ambition; or how well they were attended. Our grasp is slight of the demands of different sects, or of the way in which church-planning responded to changes in Anglican or Catholic worship. And we have only the vaguest sense of how the vast industry of Victorian church-building and church-restoration influenced the development of the professions.

All these questions are addressed by contributors to this volume. Their answers will not save churches. What they set out instead is a less one-dimensional picture of Victorian church architecture. Strictly speaking, this is not a book about Victorian architecture but about Victorian society, and the way in which the building of churches and chapels fulfilled its demands. The predicament of so many of these buildings today suggests that the Victorians succeeded in taking only a short-term view of its needs. Given the pace of social change, it could hardly have been otherwise. The Victorians put their hearts, their souls and the best of their creative endeavours into their religious buildings, intending and believing that they would last for ever. We have inherited the artistic fruits and the social shortcomings of that endeavour. Unless we understand what motivated them, we cannot hope to sustain their legacy in times no less restless and turbulent than theirs.

It remains for the editors to thank the contributors to the volume, who volunteered to deliver the original lectures on behalf of the Victorian Society, wrote their essays up without payment or further incentive, and have since been patient in awaiting the fruits of their labours. The original lecture series, flawlessly organised by Beata Reynolds and Maya Donelan, was very well attended, proving that churches and church architecture are as important as they ever were to members of the Victorian Society. We are grateful to everyone who came and to all those who have expressed enthusiasm for this project, as well as to the Activities and Publications Sub-Committees of the Victorian Society. At Manchester University Press, Katharine Reeve, Vanessa Graham and Jane Hammond Foster have been helpful and sympathetic editors; the index was expertly prepared by Kim Latham.

Introduction · Chris Brooks

The building of the Victorian Church was an enterprise of heroic proportions undertaken in response to social and cultural changes on an unprecedented scale and of an unprecedented nature. In 1801, the year of the first census, the total population of the United Kingdom was around 16,000,000. It had passed 25,000,000 by the time the young Victoria came to the throne in 1837. When she died in 1901, the number of her subjects living in the British Isles had risen to 41,500,000. In the course of the century the national economy had been transformed from one that was predominantly agrarian to one that was overwhelmingly industrial and commercial, and Britain had become an urban nation.[1] Only about 20 per cent of the population lived in cities or urban concentrations in 1801; a hundred years later 75 per cent did. At the beginning of the century there was no city other than London that had more than 100,000 inhabitants; by 1901 there were eighteen, of which Glasgow, Liverpool, Manchester and Birmingham all had populations in excess of half a million.[2]

Over the same period, feeding and fed by the process of urbanisation, the emergence first of agrarian, then of industrial capitalism as the dominant modes of production effected the most profound alteration in the relationships between the social groups that made up the burgeoning population. The traditionary patterns of work and social relations that characterised the old rural community were supplanted by the horizontal cleavages of class.[3] Contract replaced custom, though agricultural workers were slow to recognise their new identity as a rural proletariat. In the raw cities, by contrast, customary structures vanished more quickly and more completely, abolished by the logic of *laissez-faire* and the factory system. Although Carlyle wrathfully denounced the inhumanity of the cash-nexus, he saw only anarchy in the working-class movement of Chartism.[4] Although Ruskin condemned the moral irresponsibility of Ricardian economics,[5] he could only occasionally glimpse the future as other than a return to the settled hierarchies of the past. Neither understood that it would be from the cities, and particularly from their characteristic relations of production, that the social, political, and cultural structures of a new Britain would emerge. Meanwhile, the Victorian city both astonished and appalled, its problems seemingly as boundless as its energy and productivity, its labyrinthine fabric increasingly compelling to the imaginations and anxieties of social enquirers, statisticians, novelists, artists and poets; and, of course, to men and women of religion, from sisterhoods to salvationists.

As the balance between town and country changed and class stratification became normative, so also did Britain's regions become more socially and culturally uniform, less autonomous. In part this was a function of increasing central government intervention in economic and social life, regulating factory conditions and hours of work, establishing mechanisms for the relief — or at least the management — of poverty, legislating for public health and the disposal of the dead, making provision for elementary education and artisan housing. More immediately felt in the lives of most people in mainland Britain, however, were the effects of cultural diffusion, a process of which London was the centre[6] and the railway the principal agent. For professional men, for businessmen of all descriptions, for middle-class and upper-class families, the Victorian railway system gave an unprecedented mobility. But it also opened up rural Britain,[7] bringing the pleasures and perils of the city within range of country folk, and, through excursion rates and cheap fares, carrying working people out from the crowded cities to the countryside and the coastal resorts. Along with passengers and freight came letters, newspapers, popular magazines, professional journals, sample books, trade catalogues and fashion plates — all the paraphernalia of a new national culture.

These, then, were the dynamics of the world in which the Victorian Church was built and to which it sought to address its ministry: a rapidly expanding population increasingly concentrated in cities; a shift from agriculture to industry and commerce as the basis of the economy; a fundamental change in the relations of production, the end of the pre-capitalist community and, as a consequence, the establishment of a rigidly tiered class system; the emergence of urban working-class institutions and organisations; growing state regulation; the urbanisation of experience and the increasing diffusion of a commercial, essentially urban culture.

At the beginning of the nineteenth century the Church of England, by law established, was by far the largest church and, as the spiritual arm of the secular authorities, was the nation's most powerful cultural and ideological institution.[8] Its hegemony was extended colonially through the Church of Wales and the Church of Ireland; in the latter case the Anglican establishment was a foreign power in a hostile land. In Scotland, by an odd quirk of ecclesiastical history, the established church was Presbyterian while the Episcopal church was only just beginning to recover from the state repression its Jacobitism had incurred. In theory at least the Church of England constituted an *ecclesia*,[9] a church claiming the allegiance of the whole nation, and though legal penalties for non-attendance at divine service were no longer imposed they had been within living memory. In a society that still retained much of the old pattern of deference and dependency, the authority of the Anglican establishment was prodigious: the monarch stood at the head of the Church; bishops lived like the lords they were and concerned themselves much with their landed estates; members of the gentry and aristocracy occupied the pulpits. The system of parishes that covered the kingdom formed the principal agency for local government, particularly in rural areas — which comprised most of the country. The parish vestry, chaired by the incumbent and with the principal ratepayers as its members, could boast an imposing range of social responsibilities: the relief of the poor, apprenticeship schemes, schools, the upkeep and lighting of roads, the appointment of parish constables, removing nuisances to public health, keeping down vermin. Outside the purely parochial structure, clergy also took a major part in the maintenance of law and order: in the first decades of the nineteenth century about a quarter of the magistrates in England and Wales were clergymen.[10] And in addition to all this, of course, the incumbent and his vestry made provision for maintaining the services and fabric of the parish church in pursuit of Anglicanism's spiritual responsibility for the cure of souls.

The legal strength, the practical machinery, the social authority of the Church of England were palpable and potent. But in reality early nineteenth-century Anglicanism was facing critical problems, and was poorly equipped to respond to the forces that were already in the process of reshaping the nation.[11] The Reformation had brought about a massive transfer of church patronage and thus of income from ecclesiastical to lay hands. Tithes which were intended to support parish priests were impropriated by non-resident rectors, usually laymen, who then paid the parish clergyman a stipend — often an inadequate one. By the time of Elizabeth's death in 1603, 43 per cent of the 9,284 livings in the Church of England had already been impropriated.[12] Even without impropriation, many livings in the Church were poor, particularly in the north of England, in many parts of Wales, and in the far south-west: by the 1830s, of benefices with over 300 inhabitants in the dioceses of Chester and Durham, over 50 per cent were identified as needing augmentation; in the dioceses of York and Lichfield and Coventry, the figure was between 35 per cent and 50 per cent.[13] The number of poor or impropriated benefices encouraged clergy to hold livings in plurality, with duty in the parishes being done by curates: in 1810 an extraordinary 47 per cent of the 10,261 beneficed clergy were non-resident.[14] Wealthy cathedral establishments and pluralist chapters with minimal spiritual duties did nothing to improve matters; the fleshy cleric enjoying his prebendal stall while he staffed his livings with curates on starveling wages became a familiar butt of late Georgian satirists. If the distribution of ecclesiastical wealth was a problem, so also was the geographical disposition of parishes. The Church of England was at its most effective in small parishes, amenable to the personal influence and control of the clergyman. At the beginning of the nineteenth century, for historical reasons, such parishes, averaging less than 3,000 acres, were characteristic of eastern and southern England. In the West Midlands and Cornwall, however, the average size of parishes was between 3,000 and 6,000 acres; in Yorkshire it was between 6,000 and 10,000; while in the north and north-west — Durham, Northumberland, Westmorland, Cumberland, Lancashire and Cheshire — the average parish was larger than 10,000 acres.[15]

All such factors, economic and geographical, had a direct effect upon the spiritual life of Anglicanism, as also had the very nature of Hanoverian worship. The dominance of the sermon, the enforcement of moral authority from the pulpit, the relegation of the sacramental element in worship, the distrust of emotional engagement, all tended towards impersonality.

Pew rents ensured that the physical arrangement of the church interior would replicate the class structure of the eighteenth-century parish. At the same time, the alliance that had been cemented between parson and squire — particularly in smaller parishes with their culture of dependency — meant that Anglicanism, rather than being responsive to the whole of the nation from which it claimed allegiance, was perceived as the morally coercive arm of the ruling élite. In many ways it was just that. The parson who dined and hunted with the squire, who owned land in the parish that had been enclosed from the commons, who handed down harsh sentences for poaching from the bench, and who preached the immutability of the status quo from the pulpit every Sunday, was unlikely to win either the hearts or the minds of labouring people.[16] But that status quo was changing under the accelerating pressure of industrialisation and urbanisation, particularly in the new manufacturing centres of the north of England and the north and west Midlands; that is, precisely in those areas where the Church of England had fewest clergy, where livings were poor and non-residence high, and where parishes were unmanageably large. The parish system, the control of parson and squire, the rule of the vestry, simply broke down in the face of the masses of people who packed into the industrial townships or into the sprawling conurbation of London's East End.

The Church of England initially perceived the crisis largely in terms of an external threat: the vigorous challenge that was being offered to its ascendancy by the dissenting churches.[17] That challenge had begun with the birth of Methodism in 1739. Its militant evangelicalism, soon adopted by Congregationalists and Baptists, was a conscious response to what adherents were already seeing as the failure of the established church to meet the religious needs of the population as a whole. Directed specifically at the labouring classes and the poor, evangelical nonconformity offered a dramatic alternative to Hanoverian Anglicanism: its emotional appeal was urgent and immediate; its overriding concern for personal salvation stressed the equality of all sinners and the irrelevance of rank; its open-air preaching created a forum for religious observance unfettered by the hierarchical arrangement that prevailed inside parish churches; its sectarianism offered self-definition and mutual support to its members; the autonomy enjoyed by each group of believers, each local cause, and the use of lay readers and lay preachers empowered people for whom the Church of England prescribed little more than passive obedience. From the 1750s through to the early decades of the nineteenth century, Methodist membership and membership of the New Dissent — the Particular Baptists and the Congregationalists — increased steeply and consistently. By the 1790s — after Wesley's death and the final separation of Methodists from the Anglican communion — these churches formed a powerful nonconformist bloc in competition with the established church. Much of their success came in those areas in which the Church of England, for the reasons already given, was weak; in south Wales, in Cornwall, in the north Midlands, in Yorkshire and Lincolnshire.[18] In general, evangelical nonconformity appealed more to social groups connected with manufacturing and commerce than to those associated with the land, and recruitment was particularly strong among skilled artisans.[19] Significantly, however, it drew relatively few adherents from the lower reaches of the working population, and its most characteristic successes were in areas of proto-industrialisation rather than in the solidly proletarian quarters of the cities.

The impact of Methodism and the New Dissent accelerated a long-term decline in allegiance to the Church of England. It seems clear that its membership had been falling in real terms from at least the middle of the eighteenth century, and by the early nineteenth century Anglicanism appeared to be fast losing its hold on the people it claimed to serve. Between 1801 and 1831 the proportion of the population aged fifteen and over taking communion on Easter Sunday slid from some 10 per cent to just over 7 per cent.[20] Over the same period and in the same section of the population, membership of the evangelical nonconformist churches doubled from 2.75 per cent to 5.5 per cent.[21] An obvious part of the problem was that Anglicanism simply did not have the buildings in the new urban centres. For dissenters, a meeting-room or a simply converted secular building was enough, and most early nineteenth-century nonconformist causes were carried on in such temporary accommodation. The very fact of the Church of England's establishment held it back in this respect, for a new Anglican parish church needed an Act of Parliament before it could be built. An important first step towards recovery was the establishment of the Church Building Commission in 1818, its initial government grant of £1,000,000 for the erection of new churches supplemented by a further £500,000 in 1824.[22] But these grants were to be the last direct assistance provided by the state to help its church redirect money and manpower towards the urban population. Through the 1820s, the twilight years of the Georgian Church, the Anglican Establishment came under increasing attack. In the *Black Book* of 1820 and its successor, the *Extraordinary Black Book* of 1831, radicals gleefully tore into pluralism, nepotism in preferment, sinecures, and the whole murky realm of financial abuse in the Church.[23] Dissenters began what would turn out to be a long campaign against compulsory church rates.[24] In both England and Wales there was growing resistance to the collection of tithes, while in Ireland the Roman Catholic majority simply refused to pay for the support of an alien Establishment.[25] In 1828 the repeal of the Test and Corporation Acts at last wiped from the statutes the provision for legal penalties against nonconformity — though for years annual acts of indemnity had nullified them in practice. This largely symbolic victory for religious tolerance paved the way for the Catholic Emancipation Act of 1829, which removed civil disabilities for Roman Catholics which were both real and in force. The Church of England was still by law established, but the two acts effectively ended the legislative basis for its claims to a religious monopoly. The state would no longer entertain legal sanctions against other churches; from its theoretical position as an *ecclesia* the Church of England was set on the path that would lead to its becoming one denomination among several. The reformed parliament that met after 1832, spurred on by radicals, utilitarians and the new representatives of the manufacturing districts, set its sights on reforming the Church, the largest corporation of state.[26] As a first step, the Irish Temporalities Act of 1833 reordered the finances of the Church of Ireland, abolishing ten bishoprics in the process. In 1836, after several years of commissions and reports, the Ecclesiastical Commission was established as a permanent body charged with reforming financial abuses in the Church of England and redistributing its revenues.

It was just at this period, when even churchmen were gloomily prophesying the end, that Anglicanism reasserted itself. Spiritual revival had been under way for a couple of decades as the impetus of evangelicalism began to make itself felt,[27] securing not only influence but also — crucially — patronage. The Clapham Sect in London, the group around Charles Simeon in Cambridge, the abolitionists led by Wilberforce, were all key centres of activity, and organisations like the Religious Tract Society and the Church Missionary Society, both founded in 1799, directed evangelical energy both at home and abroad. More pervasively, the habits of personal piety fostered by evangelicalism, the earnestness, the family prayers, came to influence the lives of thousands of Anglican laity and clergy. For the defence of the Church as an institution, however, a different ideological tack was needed. This came with the High Anglican revival of the 1830s. Keble's 'Sermon on National Apostasy', preached in 1833, was a militant response to the suppression of the Irish bishoprics, a refusal to accept the right of a mere parliament to interfere in the dispositions of a body that was ultimately Catholic and divine. In its wake came the Oxford Movement,[28] *Tracts for the Times*, a rediscovered theology of the Church, a stress upon the sacraments more emphatic than anything that had been heard since the Jacobean divines, and a reassertion of the sacred nature of the priesthood that cast the glamour of Apostolic Succession over even the humblest Anglican parson. As for the Ecclesiastical Commission, so often sneered down as Erastian by the zealots of the High Church, it also proved a means of Anglican revival, taken over as it was by the organisational genius of Charles Blomfield, Bishop of London. Genuinely committed to sorting out the tangled inequities of ecclesiastical revenues and to pushing forward the urban mission of Anglicanism, Blomfield understood that failure to reform would leave the Church open to the imposition of more radical measures. As an Ecclesiastical Commissioner he defined a new and distinctly nineteenth-century role for the episcopacy: the bishop as man of business. He became the Commission's driving force, effectively transforming it from an agent of state correction to a practical instrument for renewing the Church. Efficient and unflagging, Blomfield was one of the heroes of early Victorian administrative reform — an ironic but instructive parallel to that arch-utilitarian Edwin Chadwick, Secretary to the Poor Law Commissioners.

For Blomfield, the key to Anglican advance in the cities was the building and endowment of new churches: Anglicanism rested on its parochial structure, after all, so the way forward was through its extension and intensification.[29] He knew that the state grants of 1818 and 1824 would not be added to; expansion would thus have to be financed from the Church's own resources. But Blomfield also recognised that the redistribution of revenues would not be sufficient in itself. Also necessary was a massive and sustained voluntary effort from the Anglican laity. Accordingly, in 1836, the same year as that in which the Ecclesiastical Commission had become permanent, Blomfield launched a fund to build new churches in London; chapter 1 in this book discusses the outcome of this initiative. The Metropolis Churches Fund was a supplement to the voluntary effort that was already under way under the auspices of the Incorporated Church Building Society. Founded in 1818, the year of the Million Act, and incorporated in 1828, the national Society began to expand through diocesan societies after 1825, when the first such was established in Exeter. The development was a shrewd one, for as well as providing contributions to the central fund, diocesan organisation meant that monies raised locally could be directed to specifically local needs. In rural dioceses this appealed to old paternalist models of social organisation, to the traditions of regional leadership by gentry and aristocracy. In dioceses that included major urban populations county money could be mobilised for the cities, and the magic of aristocratic patronage might just charm the urban *nouveaux riches* into generosity on behalf of the established church.

The objective of the Church Building Societies, national and diocesan, was highly practical: the provision of sufficient church accommodation for the rapidly growing numbers of the rural and urban proletariat. The motivation was quite as much a fear of the revolutionary potential of the godless masses as a desire to save souls. What really energised the church-building efforts of Anglicanism, however, was the passionate conviction, not to say fanaticism, of the ecclesiological movement. The founding of the Cambridge Camden Society in 1839 and, even more, the appearance of *The Ecclesiologist* in 1841, brought the dogmatic theology of the Oxford Movement and the equally dogmatic architectural theory of Pugin to the design of Anglican churches.[30] Where church-building before had been a practical campaign, it now became a crusade, and *The Ecclesiologist* wielded prescription and proscription with formidable assurance. Georgian church design was 'the *ne plus ultra* of wretchedness'[31] and Hanoverian worship had turned God's temples into preaching-boxes: galleries, high pews and triple-deckers must all be swept away. Churches should again embody and symbolise Catholic principles, with the emphasis upon sacraments, not upon sermonising; chancels must be distinct and fully developed, discrete baptisteries must be created, and the whole physical focus of the interior shifted from the pulpit to the altar.[32] To celebrate their continuity with the medieval Catholic past, new churches should be designed in a historically correct Gothic — more precisely, as Pugin advocated, in the English Decorated style of the early fourteenth century. Medieval churches — suffering from neglect, makeshift repairs and crude alterations — should be restored. Like the campaign of the Incorporated Church Building Society, the ecclesiological crusade was helped forward by organisation at diocesan level; interestingly, it was again Exeter which was first in the field, its Diocesan Architectural Society established in 1841 as a sister society to the Cambridge Camden. Societies such as Exeter's — which is discussed in chapter 2 and chapter 8 — played a key role in bringing together like-minded patrons, clergy and architects, and giving regional shape to the lead which the ecclesiologists and the High Church seized nationally in Anglican church-building. Although the stylistic repertoire of the Camdenians expanded greatly in the 1850s and 1860s; although ritualism became ever more advanced and later liturgical thinking — explored in chapter 9 — developed away from medieval models; although attitudes towards restoration — considered in chapter 7 — changed from the 1870s, the impetus that ecclesiology gave to Anglican church-building lasted through most of the Victorian period. It determined the architectural conception, and much of the cultural identity, of the Anglican church until well into the twentieth century. Indeed, it froze the popular image of the English parish church — as witnessed by a thousand Christmas cards.

Identifying the successes of ecclesiology is easy; accounting for quite why ecclesiology took the form it did, and why it proved culturally so compelling for the early and mid-Victorians, is more difficult. A primary reason may have been generational. The Cambridge Camden Society was dreamed up by a small group of undergraduates: despite its august patrons, it was essentially a young man's venture. And the late 1830s and 1840s were very much a time for clever young men. Pugin, whose inspirational bigotry flared so brightly across the sober facades of late Georgian architecture, was only twenty-four when he published *Contrasts* in 1836. Dickens was the same age when *Pickwick Papers* appeared, also in 1836; by 1840 he was on his fifth book, was the best-known novelist in England, and was not yet thirty. A year later Gladstone became a privy councillor at the age of thirty-two. In 1843 the twenty-four-year-old John Ruskin brought out the first volume of *Modern Painters*, his *nom de plume*, 'a Graduate of Oxford', signalling both his youth and — less convincingly — his modesty. In Manchester in the following year, and a whole world away, *The Condition of the Working Class in England*[33] was written by a very different twenty-four-year-old, Friedrich Engels. He was a year younger than that other clever German, Albert, the Prince Consort, who had married his cousin Victoria in 1842 and who would be planning the Great Exhibition by the time he was thirty. All these — and the founders of ecclesiology, John Mason Neale and Benjamin Webb — were born as the visionary fire of Romanticism was dying into the light of common day. They were both its heirs and its critics; the idealism and subjective intensity they inherited strained in and against the social realities of the industrial England that was growing up with them. Their poet, somewhat older than any of them, was Alfred Tennyson, whose *Poems* of 1842 returns again and again to the collision between the cultural construction(s) of the past and the disorienting turmoil of the present.

In the lines which frame the 'Morte D'Arthur' fragment in the 1842 *Poems*, Everard Hall ponders the significance — or insignificance — of having written an Arthurian epic in the 1840s.

> Why take the style of those heroic times?
> For nature brings not back the Mastodon,
> Nor we those times; and why should any man
> Remodel models?[34]

Yet bringing back the style of heroic times, remodelling models, was precisely the enterprise upon which the young Camdenians were embarked. They confront us with the cultural paradox of an engagement with the present, the terms of which are wholly those of the past. The alternation, the transposition of now and then, articulates difference as it strives to create continuity, conjuring a rediscovered history both mentally to construct and physically to reconstruct the contemporary world. The strategy adopted by the ecclesiologists was wholly of its time: it was the same as Pugin's, particularly as shown in *Contrasts*' juxtaposition of a Catholic town in 1440 with the same town in 1840;[35] it was the same as Carlyle's in *Past and Present*,[36] where Abbot Samson of old St Edmondsbury is ushered forward as the pattern strong man for remedying England's woes; it was even the same as the fantasies of the Young England group who gathered, ineffectively aristocratic, around Disraeli.[37] Here was much more than a common nostalgia for a better-ordered past. Every model of society that was invoked idealised pre-capitalist community, hierarchically structured by the reciprocity of responsibility and deference, with religion functioning both to safeguard and to spiritualise the shared system of social values. Ecclesiology's model of community gave Anglicanism an ideological paradigm at a critical moment in its development and in its relationship to the economic forces shaping the larger society. In terms of practice, its influence can be detected in the new paternalism announced by the thousands of country parish churches restored and rebuilt by rural landowners, or by the reanimated alliance of parson and squire in the middle decades of the century, discussed in chapter 2. In the cities, it underpinned the settlements of High Church clergy associated with the great mission churches designed by architects like James Brooks and William Butterfield. It can be traced in the new role for cathedrals proposed by Beresford Hope in *The English Cathedral of the Nineteenth Century*,[38]

The achievements of the church-building programme that grew directly from the Anglian revival of the 1830s and 1840s are impressive. Between 1835 and 1875 3,765 new or rebuilt Anglican churches were consecrated, 1,010 of them in the peak decade of the 1860s; over the forty-year period an average of 96 consecrations took place each year.[39] After the mid-1870s the rate of work slackened somewhat, particularly in rural areas. In 1841 the Establishment had 12,668 churches and chapels, which increased to 15,867 by 1876, a rise of 25 per cent; in the following thirty-five years 2,159 churches and chapels were added to the total, an increase of 13.5 per cent.[40] Even so, the statistics compiled by the Home Office for the years from 1873 to 1891[41] show that £20,531,402 were expended on the building and restoration of churches and cathedrals in England and Wales during the period, almost all of it from private sources, helped out by the various Church Building Societies — which were themselves, of course, voluntarily funded. The Home Office returns, moreover, included only programmes that cost more than £500; the amount of money laid out in addition on individual fittings, decorative schemes and stained-glass windows is incalculable. This extraordinary expansion of Anglican churches, accompanied by a growth in the number of clergy from 14,613 in 1841 to 24,968 in 1911,[42] by the virtual elimination of non-residence, and by a proliferation of pastoral activity at parish level — everything from coal and clothing charities to church institutes and the Mothers' Union — produced a steady increase in the membership of the Church of England. Where there were 605,000 adult communicants on Easter Day in 1831, there were, 1,110,000 in 1871, and 2,293,000 in 1911.[43] Most importantly, this growth rate was higher than that of the population as a whole. In other words, from the 1830s through to the eve of the First World War, the Church of England grew in membership in absolute terms: a greater percentage of the population was Anglican in 1911 than had been the case in 1831. As far as it is possible to tell, this span of eighty years represents the only period of sustained growth in the Church of England from the Restoration to the present day.

The church-building drive of the Anglican Establishment was met by a nonconformist response of equivalent fervour. The nonconformist building effort — the subject of chapter 3 — shared many of the Anglican objectives; principally, to provide accommodation sufficient for the burgeoning population and to carry Christianity into the urban abyss of Darkest England. Such ambitions were conceived in conscious competition with the Church of England — a rivalry that was wholly reciprocated. If chapel-building was not often as confrontational — or as farcical — as Mr Puddleham's edification of Salem outside the vicarage garden gate in Bullhampton,[44] the building of dissenting chapels opposite or adjacent to parish churches was sufficiently common as to give competitive siting the look of deliberate policy. But giving nonconformity an architectural presence on the city streets and in the village squares had motives other than the undignified, if delightful, attractions of thumbing the nose at authority. Indeed, dignity, or at least respectability, had much to do with it. The success of evangelical nonconformity in the eighteenth and early nineteenth centuries was inseparable from its sectarian structure; that is, from the way in which it spread as a plethora of semi-autonomous causes, each one defining itself in opposition to the hostile world outside. Such causes, with their lay membership and strongly localised identity, took on the character of cults. While imposing severe restrictions on the lives of adherents — by means of such restrictions in fact — they offered a complete social, cultural and even economic context. In effect, these stubborn little gatherings of saints had all the components of what today we would call an alternative lifestyle. It was a lifestyle that, by the very nature of nonconformity, fostered individualism and — to use Tawney's phrase[45] — the economic virtues: diligence, thrift, sobriety, method. There is much evidence, indeed, that it was the more enterprising — both psychologically and economically — who were attracted to dissenting causes.

Such enterprise found its most spectacular reward, on earth at least, in the prizes of successful manufacturing and commerce, and much of the economic dynamism of the new cities was generated by nonconformity. From economic success came social status and political power, an eminence that organised dissent had not seen since the heady and heroic days of the seventeenth century. Prosperous Victorian nonconformist families formed local élites, dominated municipal government, fostered civic pride, got up subscription lists, built big villas around the still green edges of their cities. Nonconformists became councillors, aldermen and mayors; they sat as members of parliament in the liberal interest; eventually they became ministers of the crown and even peers of the realm.[46] All this was a long way from a Beulah on the margin of Bodmin Moor, or a Shiloh in the back courts of Sheffield. It was a particularly long way for dissent's construction of itself. From being encamped against the world, nonconformity had become, within a couple of generations, a power in the land. The idea of casting down the mighty in the name of the Lord might have appealed to the mechanic scrambling upwards, but was unlikely to commend itself to the magnate sitting on top of the heap. From the 1840s, after some seventy years of rapid expansion, the major evangelical nonconformist churches began to consolidate. Doctrinal diversity, an inevitable consequence of the way in which growth had taken place, began to be ironed out. The lay ministry, though remaining a vital part of the nonconformist tradition, was gradually subordinated to professional clergy. Colleges for their training were established — there was even one in Oxford by the end of the century. Sound, middle-class young men no doubt felt their vocation, but, with careers to make and families to keep, were unlikely to be attracted to the rigours of the missionary circuit. Security, a regular stipend and a decent house were the concomitants of professionalisation — just as they were the badges of respectability. Above all, consolidation expressed itself in building.[47] Chapels were needed to accommodate congregations that gathered in makeshift meeting-rooms and converted barns, to meet the expectations of the clergy who would minister to them, and, not least, to confront the challenge of renascent Anglicanism. But chapel-building was also symbolic, significant of newly-acquired status, brick-and-mortar proof of the social substance of nonconformity.

The organisational devolution characteristic of nonconformity means that reliable church-building figures are difficult to get. However, the statistics for the Wesleyan Methodist Original Connexion, the most centralised of the Methodist societies, show that between 1851 and 1909 the number of their churches in England, Scotland and Wales grew from 6,649 to 8,606, an increase of nearly 30 per cent.[48] This figure is for new foundations only, and does not include the large number of rebuildings that date from the second half of the century. The Congregationalists managed a significantly higher rate, though its precise calculation is problematic: even on the less impressive figures, their places of worship grew from 3,244 in 1851 to 4,652 in 1909, an increase of 43 per cent. The second total, moreover, does not include mission stations; in 1907, with these added in, there were 4,928 Congregationalist places of worship in mainland Britain.[49] The figures available for the various Baptist societies indicate a higher rate again, the complement of permanent Baptist churches in England, Scotland and Wales expanding from 2,082 in 1861 to 3,047 in 1911, an increase of 46 per cent.[50] Such rates compare well with that achieved by the Church of England: between 1851 and 1911, the number of Anglican churches and chapels of ease grew by 28 per cent from 14,077 to 18,026[51] — though it must be remembered that the establishment was starting from a much higher base and the figures do not include the huge number of restorations and refittings that formed such a major part of the Anglican campaign. In terms of new churches on new sites, however, it is quite clear that, in the second half of the nineteenth century, the nonconformists were in no way outbuilt by their establishment rivals. But their pattern of recruitment was different. As was noticed before, Anglicanism consistently increased its percentage share of the population over the whole period from the 1830s to the First World War. Not so nonconformity. In 1841, the peak year for membership, the Methodist societies could claim between them a membership of 4.5 per cent of the adult English population. This stabilised at around 4 per cent from the late 1850s through to the end of the 1880s; so, for some thirty years, growth kept pace with that of the general population. Then a steady decline began: from 3.8 per cent down to 3.2 per cent on the eve of the Great War. Taking the nineteenth and early twentieth centuries as a whole, Methodist recruitment gradually slowed down. In the heroic years of the first three decades, membership rose by over 200 per cent, while the population of England grew by 56 per cent; in the forty years between 1831 and 1871, membership virtually doubled from 288,000 to 571,000 as population increased by 63 per cent; in the forty years after 1871, the number of Methodists rose by 37 per cent, the number of people in England by 58 per cent.[52] Despite periodic boosts from the great revivals of Spurgeon or Sankey and Moody, the other churches of evangelical nonconformity show the same pattern of recruitment: steep progress, a period of levelling out, then gentle decline. It is of course no coincidence that the decade in which the churches' leadership decided on a policy of consolidation, the 1840s, should also be the point at which rapid expansion was checked. Building chapels gave dissent a physical stake in the country, and with it, institutional stability and enhanced social standing. But this was achieved at the cost of the evangelical impetus that had driven the saints. The alternative lifestyle, the enthusiasm that exhilarated and alarmed, mellowed into respectability: English nonconformity had paid the price of social and cultural assimilation.[53]

The Roman Catholic church in England was essentially a nineteenth-century creation.[54] The numbers of the 'Old Catholics' remaining at the beginning of the century were small, their social and cultural life marginalised: years of being on the receiving end of prejudice and discrimination had instilled self-effacement and insularity. The Catholic Emancipation Act of 1829 initiated a remarkable renaissance, what Newman was to call the 'Second Spring'.[55] Emancipation did not simply lift legally imposed disabilities: it changed the personality of Catholicism in England, brought the church and its adherents into the mainstream of religious activity. Headstrong young converts like Kenelm Digby, Ambrose Phillips de Lisle and — not least — Augustus Welby Pugin claimed a distinctive and highly Romantic cultural identity for the faith. Gothicising passions gave the buildings of the medieval church iconic status. In effecting a profound theological shift in the identity of the established church, the Oxford Movement also changed the perceived relationship between Anglicanism and the Church of Rome. The missionary efforts of Fathers Barberi and Gentili impressed even Propaganda. As early as 1840, Phillips de Lisle, writing to Montalembert, claimed that 'Catholicity in England is proceeding at a railroad pace'.[56] Newman's conversion in 1845 was followed by a flurry of others — actually quite a modest flurry, though heavily publicised by triumphant Catholics and outraged evangelicals alike. But above all, the industrial cities were attracting emigrant Irish workers, the vast majority of whom were Catholics, and the Great Hunger of the mid-1840s turned what had been a steady stream into a flood of the desperate and destitute. In 1850 Pope Pius IX re-established the hierarchy in England. The Prime Minister, Lord John Russell, posturing briefly as the champion of protestantism, passed some wholly ineffectual legislation against the 'Papal Aggression'; *Punch* tried to stir up fears of priestcraft; there were sporadic 'No Popery' riots — most of them directed at immigrant communities.[57] The hierarchy was set in place all the same; England and Wales were constituted as a single province comprising the metropolitan see of Westminster and twelve suffragan sees. The rest of the century saw the building of the physical fabric of English Catholicism in cathedrals, churches, religious communities and schools. The 1851 census recorded 570 churches and chapels in England and Wales; in 1870 there were 1,151, though this figure includes a number of private chapels; in 1900 there were 1,529, excluding the private establishments.[58] This was an increase over the fifty years of 168 per cent, and was achieved without the financial resources at the call of the Church of England and of much urban nonconformity. During the same period the estimated number of Roman Catholics in England had risen from about 700,000 to over 1,500,000.[59] Most of this growth, however, was exogenous, the result of Irish immigration and of the strong cultural bonds that kept Irish families together and kept them Catholic. Phillips de Lisle's mid-century predictions of mass conversion proved to be fantasies. Outside the constituency formed by the Irish and the 'Old Catholics', Roman Catholic recruitment from the wider English society was numerically negligible.

In Wales, Scotland and Ireland, building campaigns similar to those in England were initiated by the various churches, but were inflected differently by the social and religious circumstances peculiar to each of the three countries. Only some aspects of these differences can be noticed here; others are dealt with more fully in chapters 4, 5 and 6.

The torpor that affected the Church of England in the century before the 1830s lay even more heavily upon her sister Church of Wales. The rural parishes of much of the principality were large, poor and remote. In a scandalously large number of them the tithes were impropriated to laymen, many of whom lived in England — a state of affairs that was a contributory cause of the Rebecca Riots of 1842-43.[60] As a result there were many poor benefices, despite some efforts at amelioration by the Commissioners of Queen Anne's Bounty. In 1830, 59 per cent of Welsh livings were worth less than £200 per year; in England the equivalent figure was 37.5 per cent.[61] Non-residence was shockingly high and can only partly be blamed on poor benefices. In 1810, in the four dioceses of Wales, 60 per cent of the clergy were non-resident and did not do duty in their parishes; the ministers of the established church had virtually deserted the diocese of Llandaff, where a staggering 85 per cent of them were absentees.[62] Even had they been resident, few of them would have been able to minister adequately to their flocks, for the clergy were predominantly English-speaking, while a large part of the principality was monoglot Welsh. Unsurprisingly in this panorama of negligence, the physical condition of the parish churches, and even the Welsh cathedrals, was deplorable. Whereas the Church of England in the early decades of the nineteenth century was facing a crisis, the Church of Wales, to all intents and purposes, had failed. Its place as the principal provider of organised religion had been taken by Methodism and dissent[63] — perhaps the most dramatic success for evangelical nonconformity in Britain.

The 1851 religious census showed that in Wales as a whole only 9 per cent of the people who attended services on Easter Sunday did so in the Church of Wales; 87 per cent worshipped in nonconformist chapels.[64] That majority was especially strong among Welsh-speakers, and in the newly industrialised and urbanised areas of South Wales. By the middle of the nineteenth century, the deeply-held religious culture of the Welsh people expressed itself overwhelmingly through nonconformity, particularly through Calvinism. Moderate Calvinist protestantism was the Welsh religion, and the Calvinist Methodists and Calvinist Baptists the most successful churches.[65] In 1801 there were fifty nonconformist chapels in Llandaff, the most industrialised diocese; half a century later there were 550.[66] In Caernarfonshire, in the north-west, over the same period, the number of chapels increased from thirty to 224, of which 103, 46 per cent, were Calvinist Methodist.[67] Moreover, as the 1851 census revealed, not only did 71 per cent of all sittings in places of worship in the principality belong to the nonconformists,[68] but the total accommodation available provided a quarter of a million more seats than the population needed — the reverse of the situation in England. This 'excess of spiritual privileges', as Horace Mann put it,[69] may be ascribed to the efforts of working-class people themselves. The iron and steel areas were characterised by small towns and villages rather than by mass urban development, and industrialisation had grown without the emergence of that middle class which was the backbone of English nonconformity. The chapels were not the fruit of consolidation and newly-won respectability, paid for by middle-class subscription lists, but were expressions of a new sort of communal identity grown up to replace the old. Welsh nonconformity and its buildings were the authentic fruit of popular culture.[70]

Remarkably, from the 1840s the Church of Wales rallied, spurred on by the Anglican revival in England and led by a sequence of committed bishops: Connop Thirlwall at St David's (1840-74), Thomas Vowler Short at St Asaph (1846-70), Arthur Ollivant at Llandaff (1849-82), and James Colquhoun Campbell at Bangor (1859-90). Medieval parish churches, frequently semi-derelict, were restored, as were the four Welsh cathedrals, and new churches were built. In Llandaff, for example, sixty-nine churches were restored and forty-seven new ones erected during Ollivant's episcopate, and the reign of his successor, Richard Lewis (1883-1905), saw the building of over 150 new churches and mission halls.[71] By the beginning of the twentieth century, with disestablishment in prospect, supporters of the Church of Wales were even claiming to be able to match the nonconformists in the number of their adherents.[72] This seems unlikely. Although there was undoubtedly a striking improvement in the established church's position, it never attracted the level of support — most crucially, middle-class support — that was enjoyed in England. The Home Office returns on church-building expenditure, mentioned before, show that £1,127,500 were spent on building and restoration in the four Welsh dioceses between 1873 and 1891.[73] Impressive as this is, it represents a considerably lower rate than England: 14*s* 10*d* per head of the Welsh population in 1891, compared to £1 7*s* per head of the English — more than 80 per cent higher.

Popular nationalism in Wales, growing during the nineteenth century, came to identify the established church as an English imposition, though resentment was deflected to an extent by appointing Welshmen as bishops and by an increase in Welsh-speaking clergy. Across the Irish Sea popular feeling against the Anglican establishment was far more embittered. From the seventeenth century the Church of Ireland had been an instrument of colonial policy, a key element in the Ascendancy, committed to the reciprocal aims of converting the population to protestantism and eradicating Catholicism. The course followed by the Church was entirely in keeping with the whole sorry history of English misgovernment in Ireland. Institutional support for the Penal Code in the eighteenth century, endorsement of the systematic exploitation practised by Anglo-Irish landlords, similar rapacity by the landed magnates of the establishment itself, pluralism and absenteeism, nepotism and jobbery, the extraction of tithes from a peasantry whose indigence the church itself had helped to cause, contempt for native cultural and religious traditions — all these ensured that, by the early nineteenth century, the Church of Ireland was detested by the great bulk of the Irish people. The radicals who compiled the *Black Book* reserved a special loathing for the Irish episcopate:

> Without the claim of public services or superior mental endowments, they succeed to honours and vast revenues, obtained through intrigue, family connexion, or political interest, and die loaded with spoil, either on a foreign soil, or amidst the scorn and hatred of the people whom they have impoverished and oppressed.[74]

Needless to say, the Church of Ireland signally failed to convince the Irish population of the higher truth of reformed religion, let alone to effect a mass conversion to Anglican protestantism. Once Catholic Emancipation was conceded there were few reasons left for maintaining the established status of the Irish Church, yet the establishment survived for a further thirty years. The 1861 census proved decisive: of 5,799,000 inhabitants only 693,400 belonged to the Church of Ireland, whereas 4,505,300 were Catholics — 12 per cent of the population as against 78 per cent.[75] Gladstone identified the established church as one of the three branches of the Upas Tree that poisoned Ireland and determined to lop it off. He became Prime Minister in 1868 and the Act of Disestablishment followed in the next year.

As the Church of Ireland moved towards the loss of its privileges the Roman Catholic church was renewed, despite the poverty and cultural deprivation of its constituency. A programme of church-building got under way in the 1830s and was given further impetus by the organisational reforms introduced by Cardinal Cullen after 1850, discussed in chapter 6. In the century after Emancipation the Catholic church in Ireland built twenty-four cathedrals or pro-cathedrals and more than 3,000 churches, not including temporary chapels and missions.[76] After the repression of the penal years, the number of religious houses also grew, and with them a whole range of charitable activities. Alongside this expanding religious provision went a long campaign, often made difficult by the English government, to set up a Catholic educational system; primary schools, intermediate colleges, training colleges for teachers, seminaries, were all gradually built, and from 1854 Dublin had its own Catholic University. The physical fabric of Irish Catholicism was thus essentially a nineteenth-century creation, as it was in England. The institutional success of Irish Catholicism was qualified, however, by demographic processes over which none of the churches had any control. The famine-driven exodus of the 1840s settled into a steady pattern of depopulation during the rest of the century as emigration drained the countryside and poor Irish men and women sought some kind of economic future in the United States, the Empire and mainland Britain. As we saw earlier, the growth of the Roman Catholic church in England was fuelled from Ireland. In Ireland itself the population slid from 6,552,400 in 1851 to 4,458,800 in 1901. The Catholic share of the ever-declining total remained consistent at around 75 per cent, but emigration changed the age profile of Catholic congregations just as it changed that of Irish society as a whole: 82 per cent of those who left in the second half of the century were aged between fifteen and thirty-five.[77] Ironically, the position of the Church of Ireland improved. The financial provisions of the 1869 Act had been generous, and shrewd management in the decades after disestablishment placed the church and its clergy on a sound economic basis. Relative prosperity in the protestant community meant far less emigration, and by the early years of the twentieth century the Anglican share of Irish religious allegiance had edged up to 14 per cent from the 12 per cent that had stirred Gladstone into action.[78]

The position of institutional religion in nineteenth-century Scotland was wholly different from that in Wales or Ireland, principally because the religious settlement of the country bore a direct relationship to the cultural traditions of its people. The religious policy of the Stuarts in the second half of the seventeenth century had sought to repress Scotland's staunch Presbyterianism and had foisted an episcopal structure upon the country. After James II had been bundled off the throne, William III was prepared to accept Scottish episcopacy provided that the bishops would swear the Oath of Allegiance and could demonstrate that they had the support of the Scottish people. The first they refused on grounds of conscience; the second was a manifest impossibility. Accordingly, in the 1690s, the Church of Scotland was established with a Presbyterian system of government. Now outside the established kirk, the bishops were deprived of their territorial sees, and many non-juring clergy were ejected from their livings. The intermittent stubborness with which eighteenth-century episcopalianism clung to the Jacobite cause led to legal disabilities and, in the aftermaths of the '15 and the '45, direct state repression. The death of the Young Pretender in 1788 allowed the bishops to recognise George III, and the repeal of penal measures followed in 1792; but by this time the episcopal church was a remnant.[79]

Meanwhile, despite abiding anxieties about lay patronage and dependence upon the state, the kirk had settled firmly into support for the Hanoverian government. Thus, when the population began to grow steeply, and industrialisation and urbanisation started to spread across the central Lowlands, it was the Presbyterian Church of Scotland — by far the largest church in the country — that confronted the challenge. A church extension committee was appointed in 1828, concerning itself not only with the new townships but also with the deprived Highlands. Although government support was looked for at first, the doctrinal strength of the voluntary principle within Presbyterianism ensured that self-help would drive the church-building effort. Led by the organising ability of Thomas Chalmers, the kirk collected £305,750 between 1828 and 1841, and erected 222 new churches.[80] Then, in 1843, came the 'Great Disruption'. No longer willing to accept what were seen as establishment compromises over spiritual autonomy and the rights of individual presbyteries, a third of the ministers of the kirk seceded, taking most of their congregations with them, to form the Free Church of Scotland.[81] Because the free clergy renounced their temporalities and quit their churches, they had to find both new endowments and new buildings in which to worship — and the only source for both was voluntary donation. Presbyterianism's campaign for church extension was thus split in two and, in many areas, effectively duplicated: the minister and congregation who had walked out of their church had to put up a new one, while the established kirk had somehow to provide for the building and pulpit they had vacated.

The Free Church managed its half of the split with striking dispatch. The ingenious Chalmers, one of the principals of the Disruption, devised a sustentation fund from which clergy drew equal dividends by way of remuneration. At the same time a general building fund was organised, with parish funds set up wherever possible. By the summer of 1844 £227,800 had already been raised and 470 churches were either built or nearing completion. By 1847, a mere four years after its formation, the Free Church had erected more than 700 churches[82] — sufficient testimony to the vigour that rebellion can impart. The depleted kirk, still walking in conservative ways, took time to recover, but did so by virtue of a carefully planned and funded expansion of its parochial organisation — a policy which had its origins in the 'territorial principle' conceived, ironically enough, by Chalmers in the 1830s. It was realised that new parishes and their churches would only work if they were adequately endowed. Straightforward as this might seem, it was frequently forgotten by the establishment south of the border. Moreover, such endowment would have to be voluntarily funded: partly because secular patronage was contentious within Presbyterianism, and had been a root cause of the split of 1843; partly because it was clear that the government was not going to provide the money anyway. In the 1850s the kirk's church-building fund was converted into an endowment fund, and this shaped expansion in the second half of the nineteenth century. In 1843 there were 924 parishes, in 1909 there were 1,437: an increase of 55 per cent.[83]

Growth in membership of the established church was particularly marked after the Westminster parliament abolished secular patronage in Scotland in 1874, following a petition from the kirk's own assembly — telling evidence of the importance of independence in the traditions of Scottish institutional religion. Between 1881 and 1911 its membership grew by 35.2 per cent, against an increase in the total Scottish population of 27.4 per cent. By 1911 the kirk had 504,495 active communicants, 10.8 per cent of the Scottish population compared to an estimated 9.3 per cent thirty years before. The United Free Church, formed in 1900 by an alliance between the Free Church of Scotland and the United Presbyterians, whose secession dated from the eighteenth century, reckoned its communicants in 1911 at 504,672 — 10.6 per cent of the population. But this was only 19 per cent more than the combined total of its two constituent churches in 1881, when they had been able to claim 11.3 per cent of the Scottish people as communicants.[84] Thus the experience of Scottish Presbyterianism in the late Victorian and Edwardian periods seems to replicate that of the churches south of the border; the established church securing a gradually increasing share of the population as a whole while the growth-rate of denominations outside the establishment began to fall behind that of the overall demographic rate. This may indicate that, after the religious upheavals of the earlier nineteenth century in both countries, churchgoers by the end of the century were being swayed less by doctrinal complexion or the mode of church government and more by the social values pertaining to membership of the establishment. Such an interpretation is tellingly supported by the relative success of the Church of Wales during the same period.

Only one church in Scotland at this time could rival the numbers of the two major Presbyterian churches, and it was certainly growing faster than they: the Roman Catholic. The Catholic hierarchy had been re-established in Scotland in 1878, following an increase in the numbers of Scottish Catholics that had been maintained throughout the century. The growth was particularly rapid in the industrial conurbations of the Lowlands: in the forty years before 1845 the number of Catholics in Glasgow had mushroomed from 1,000 to 70,000. By 1909 there were 398 Roman Catholic churches in Scotland where there had been no more than twenty a century before, and 519,000 people, nominally at least, were Catholic — 375,000 of them in the single Archdiocese of Glasgow. Of the national total, a mere 25,000, less than 5 per cent, were of purely Scots extraction.[85] The rest, of course, were either Irish or of Irish parentage, immigrants who had arrived in the booming townships of the Clyde just as they had in Liverpool and Manchester, and for the same reasons of economic desperation. Even more than was the case in England, the growth of the nineteenth-century Roman Catholic church in Scotland was exogenous.

Finally, what of the little Episcopal Church of Scotland, that 'exotic religious body', as the *Catholic Encyclopedia* contemptuously referred to it in 1912?[86] Marginalised, fragmented, and numerically tiny after the penal years, the episcopal church was reinvented by the nineteenth century. In a period that was assiduously constructing Romantic Scotland,[87] the church's use of the Scottish Communion Office and its bishops' claim to continuity with the medieval church had undeniable antiquarian allure; the master mythopoeist himself, Walter Scott, became a convert. With the onset of the ecclesiological crusade in England, that allure took on the glamour of a historical martyrdom. Here was an ancient and unbroken episcopate that, alone in Britain, had refused to truckle to the Hanoverian settlement, that had suffered persecution for the sake of principle, and had remained resolutely non-juring until the last royal Stuart was under the earth. To Oxbridge zealots the Scottish bishops could be heroes of the inviolate church in a way that the trimmers of the Georgian episcopate could never be. Such admiration was invigorating: the Marchioness of Lothian became one of the co-founders of the Cambridge Camden Society and built the first ecclesiological church in Scotland, at Jedburgh in 1843; in Alexander Penrose Forbes, Bishop of Brechin from 1847 to 1876, Tractarians were happy to recognise 'the Scottish Pusey' — especially as he was soon agreeably involved in a row about the Real Presence. With the theological complexion of Anglicanism edging higher, legal penalties against episcopalian clergy were finally lifted in 1864; thereafter, priests could move between the Church of England and the Episcopal Church of Scotland, and the two, for most practical purposes, were united. While all this was happening there was considerable missionary work in the cities, and a major church-building effort that included half a dozen cathedrals — not least the Cathedral of the Isles at Cumbrae and St Ninian's in Perth, both designed by Butterfield. By 1911 there was a total membership of 142,464, which represented an increase of more than 150 per cent since the mid-1870s; communicants had risen from 25,460 in 1883 to 54,751 in 1911.[88] Though still relatively small, the Episcopal Church of Scotland certainly did not deserve the *Catholic Encyclopedia*'s sneer. In many ways, indeed, its members were far more integrated into the cultural life of the nation than were the ghettoised Irish Catholics who packed the tenements of Glasgow.

The great building campaigns of the Victorian churches had a profound impact, not only on the lives and habits of churchgoers, but also on the economic, cultural and physical composition of the larger society. Church-building was a key sector of the Victorian building industry as a whole. Indeed it became an industry in its own right, with its own characteristic structures of funding and organisation. Certainly, the complex enterprise of planning, building, equipping, decorating, repairing and maintaining churches and chapels employed thousands of people and involved an annual turnover of millions of pounds. Church-building grew in step with the expanding economy, and though its stylistic paradigms tended to avoid the new technologies of iron and steel, it used them both in its methods of production and, thanks to the railways, in its means of distribution. Through catalogues and trade journals it developed a sophisticated range of products targeted at the subtly gradated tastes and demands of its consumers — from High Church patricians to civic-minded Presbyterians. It created a market for new and often highly specialised craft skills. It helped to establish the professional status of architecture, and it invented that élite member of the profession, the ecclesiastical architect.

As chapter 7 makes clear, restoring medieval churches and designing new ones involved not only knowledge of construction, a practical and even artisan attainment, but also of archaeology and history, attainments that belonged indisputably to the realm of the gentleman. Expertise in stylistic development, liturgical planning and iconography contributed further to the corpus of specialist knowledge that defined the professional. Mastery of such privileged discourses changed the whole status of architects, and the cultural centrality of church-building charged their work(s) with a new ideological significance. Men like William Butterfield, George Gilbert Scott, G. E. Street, J. L. Pearson, William White and G. F. Bodley were the architects of Victorian Anglicanism in a far more profound sense than simply being its employees; they were the designers of Anglicanism's physical fabric, both the agents and the realisers of the visible church. Pugin, who in many ways had invented such a role, strove to fulfil it for Roman Catholicism, and was followed by his son E. W. Pugin, by William Wardell, George Goldie, Joseph Hansom and J. F. Bentley. Although nonconformity rejected high-flying notions of the architect's religious function, the dissenting churches had their uniquely qualified specialists as well: John Tarring, Paull and Ayliffe, Poulton and Woodman, John Wills, to mention only a few of the more prolific.[89] Architects who were able to develop their ecclesiastical specialism into a country-wide practice, usually based in London, could give something like a national architectural identity to the denominations for which they worked and in which they built. Local architects could establish church-building practices that had a similar significance at a regional level, particularly in relationship to Anglicanism (see chapter 8). Such was the case with John Hayward in the south-west between the 1840s and 1860s; with Paley and Austin in Lancashire from the 1870s to the 1890s; with C. E. Ponting in Wiltshire and Dorset around the turn of the century. Powerful regional practices such as these did not merely trail along in the metropolitan wake; the Victorian revolution in transport and communications meant that regionally-based architects could be just as well-informed, as stylistically *au fait*, as their London counterparts. Indeed, by the end of the nineteenth century, the designs of architects like Ponting were appearing regularly in the national professional journals. Such developments spelt the end of the genuinely local practitioner, the pre- or early Victorian builder/architect who worked at the level of, at most, ten or a dozen adjacent parishes. Ponting was no more 'local' to Dorset, or Hayward to north Devon, than was Pearson or Street, and once the railway had brought the one from Marlborough or Exeter, why should it not bring the others, or their assistants, from London? As, most famously, in 1870, the railway and the carrier brought the young Thomas Hardy from Blomfield's office in London to restore the church of St Juliot on the north coast of Cornwall.[90]

The provision of furniture and fittings — particularly all those esoteric items required by the advanced young men of the High Church — went in a precisely similar way. From the middle of the nineteenth century onwards, specialist firms of ecclesiastical stone-carvers, woodworkers and metalworkers supplied reredoses, choir stalls and lecterns that were beyond the scope of the village mason, carpenter and blacksmith. By the last decades of Victoria's reign ecclesiastical art manufactories like Farmer and Brindley, Cox and Buckley, Jones and Willis, or Harry Hems, distributed their church furnishings not just nationally, but internationally. Moreover, although they might concentrate on particular sectors of the market, their customers, unlike those of the specialist architects, often came from a number of different denominations, both at home and abroad. The great stained glass workshops of London and the regional workshops located in the cities were similarly organised, marketing and distributing their products — which came to include mural decoration — in the same way. Such specialist firms were the necessary complement to the professional ecclesiastical architect. Economically, they were organised, again necessarily, in terms of the dominant mode of production, which was industrial capitalism — one of the reasons why William Morris disliked them so much, even though his own company was structured along the same lines. By the end of the nineteenth century the designs of churches, chapels and fittings, though immensely various, derived from paradigms that were established at a national level. Despite their rhetoric, the Arts and Crafts movement and the kindred vernacular revival were confirmation of this; their advocacy of craft skills, local materials and regional styles was part of a national debate that had its origins in the city, and in London particularly.

The tens of thousands of churches and chapels which the Victorians and Edwardians built, rebuilt and restored are a decisive testimony to an extraordinary corporate effort. They were the result of the most intensive religious building drive in British history. Qualitatively, they were the creation of the finest architects, designers, builders and craftsmen. As a corpus of work, the religious architecture of the period can stand comparison with that of any other. Yet, ironically, as the physical fabric of Victorian Christianity raised itself triumphant in every British shire and city, its ideological substance shook and then, in the twentieth century, failed. The failure has been that of institutional religion itself. At the start of 1854 Horace Mann reported on the outcome of the great religious census that had been held in England and Wales on the Easter Sunday of 1851.[91] By way of some complicated statistical footwork and a few conjectural leaps, Mann arrived at the conclusion that 58 per cent of those people who could have attended a place of worship on Census Sunday had done so, 52 per cent of the attendants going to the established church, 38 per cent to the three largest nonconformist denominations. Non-attendance was highest in the cities, particularly in working-class districts — which was where the amount of accommodation, the number of seats in church or chapel, was at its most inadequate. As we have already seen, the response both of Anglicanism and of dissent was energetic and sustained. By the end of the century, it was not just the accommodation in places of worship that had grown significantly: there were also missions, revivals and salvationist crusades; social and charitable organisations had been developed by all denominations; there were dedicated priests and ministers, clergymen's wives, sisterhoods, laymen and laywomen. Yet by the 1890s, as was remarked earlier, recruitment to the nonconformist churches in England and the Presbyterian churches outside the establishment in Scotland was starting to decline. By the 1920s the memberships of the Church of England, the now disestablished Church of Wales, the Church of Scotland and the Episcopal Church of Scotland were all falling relative to the population as a whole. Erosion quickened in the second half of the twentieth century and began to affect even the Roman Catholic church, where strong cultural traditions had held congregations together for longest. In the last twenty years relative decline in membership has become absolute decline in all the major churches. The Church of England lost 21 per cent of its worshippers between 1975 and 1992; over the same period the Roman Catholics lost 19 per cent, the Methodists 23 per cent, and the Presbyterians 24 per cent.[92]

The reasons for the long-term deterioration in church membership lie with the socio-economic forces that have driven the development of modern Britain, forces that institutional religion could not contain and which it now seems unlikely to survive. The urban, industrial and technological culture that attained hegemony by the end of the nineteenth century was essentially secular. Functions of local government that, a hundred years previously, had been discharged most frequently by the Anglican parish church through its vestry, had become, in the course of the century, the responsibility of secular authorities. At the core of these changes were the needs and increasingly vocal demands of a mass workforce, that majority of the population that had been so conspicuously absent on Census Sunday in 1851. And absent, by and large, they remained.[93] Church extension was impelled principally by the middle and upper classes. The social gospel that Victorian Christianity developed, with its odd blend of charity and self-help, certainly managed to alleviate some of the misery and deprivation that industrial capitalism visited upon the labouring masses, and may have blunted the sharpness of class conflict.[94] But it never delivered the churches to the people themselves. The Victorian church was built, ideologically as well as physically, by an empowered minority. There were exceptions of course, such as the popular Calvinism of the Welsh people and of intense little denominations like the Bible Christians, while the social structures of Roman Catholicism, particularly in English and Scottish immigrant communities, were different again. Nevertheless, institutional religion in Victorian Britain generally operated from the top downwards. As the product of a class-structured and hierarchical society, and as a primary agent of social control within it, this was inevitable. The result was the eventual failure of the churches to secure the allegiance of working-class people. In the cities the victory of the cash-nexus, the replacement of the customary by the contractual, erased vertical social ties and with them the pattern of paternalism and deference upon which a substantial part of religious organisation had rested. In such a context the ecclesiological vision of paternalist community — a version of pastoral — was anachronistic, and looked particularly so to second-generation city-dwellers who had no memories of such pre-urban structures. In the countryside itself, agrarian labourers nursed a long resentment against the clerical magistrates who had dealt so savagely with the Captain Swing disturbances of 1830–32, and against the parsons who allied with the squires to root out agricultural trade unionism.[95] In the 1870s Richard Jefferies reckoned that village labourers 'were as oblivious of the vicar as the wind that blew'.[96] Writing in *The Nineteenth Century* in 1892, the wife of a country clergyman was more bitter: 'Our labourer hates his employer, he hates his squire, but, above all, he hates his parson.'[97] By the second half of the nineteenth century, moreover, the nonconformity that had provided an alternative religious structure at least for the artisanate was — as we saw earlier — increasingly settled into a respectability that had little interest in upsetting the class status quo.

In the end, organised religion, whether establishment or dissent, was simply rejected by the majority of working-class people. Only rarely was that rejection an act of deliberate opposition; Thomas Wright thought that there were very few atheists among the million Londoners who made up his 'Great Unwashed'.[98] Conscious atheism among the Victorians was largely the reserve of a tiny intellectual élite who had education and leisure sufficient to allow them to worry about the niceties of biblical criticism, the theories of Charles Darwin, or — at the end of the century — the distressing notions of Krafft-Ebing and Sigmund Freud.[99] For the proletariat, the failure of institutional religion was productive not of argument but of indifference. In the cities, in the last quarter of the nineteenth century, the growth of proletarian self-consciousness, the explicit awareness of class identity, was expressed through a distinct culture in which religious observance, so central to middle- and upper-class culture, was peripheral. It articulated a separate life:[100] trade unionism as the key political institution; cheap newspapers, from the shock-horror of *Reynolds' Weekly* to the knock-about of *Ally Sloper's Half Holiday*; a distinct food and drink culture in fish and chip shops and public houses; entertainment in the music halls; street games for the children, sports teams — especially football teams — for the men. Moreover, the people of the new culture also constituted a new market that, increasingly, would be exploited by the mass retailing both of consumer goods and of cultural products. Here indeed was the shape of things to come. The failure of the nineteenth-century churches to attract the working class, the emergence in the later Victorian city of a secular proletarian culture, and its twentieth-century metamorphosis into a mass market, were coextensive with the replacement of institutional religion by the state as the principal provider of education, social services and welfare support. For much of the nineteenth century the competition that confronted the churches was perceived as internal: Anglicans inveighed against the schismatic nature of nonconformity; dissenters railed at the monopolistic claims of the establishment. In the twentieth century it has been institutional religion itself that has had to compete for the allegiance of the population. The result may be seen in empty churches and chapels throughout Britain.

Notes

1 Of the many studies of Victorian urbanism published in the last thirty years, still fundamental are Asa Briggs, *Victorian Cities*, London, 1963, and H. J. Dyos and Michael Wolff (eds), *The Victorian City: Images and Realities*, 2 vols, London, 1973.

2 The most accessible digest of socio-economic statistics for the nineteenth century is John Langton and R. J. Morris (eds), *Atlas of Industrializing Britain 1780–1914*, London, 1986.

3 The sociological literature relating to these changes is vast and there are different analyses of the nature of the shift from pre-capitalist to capitalist, from a status society to a class society, from rural to urban, from *Gemeinschaft* (community) to *Gesellschaft* (association). For a useful summary of the positions see John C. McKinney's introduction to Ferdinand Tönnies, *Community and Society*, translated and edited by Charles P. Loomis, New York, 1963.

4 Thomas Carlyle, *Chartism*, London, 1839; *The Works of Thomas Carlyle*, Centenary Edition, 30 vols, London, 1897–99, XXIX.

5 John Ruskin, *Unto this Last: Four Essays on the First Principles of Political Economy*, London, 1862; E. T. Cook and A. Wedderburn (eds), *The Complete Works of John Ruskin*, 38 vols, London, 1903–09, XVII.

6 See 'Greater and greater London: metropolis and provinces in the nineteenth and twentieth centuries' in David Cannadine and David Reeder (eds), *Exploring the Urban Past: Essays in urban history by H. J. Dyos*, Cambridge, 1982, pp. 37–55.

7 See Philip S. Bagwell, 'The decline of rural isolation', in G. E. Mingay (ed.), *The Victorian Countryside*, 2 vols, London, 1981, I, pp. 30–42.

8 As Robert Hole has said in summary of Edmund Burke's position, 'The purpose of establishment was not to benefit the church ... [but] ... to support the state', *Pulpits, Politics and Public Order in England 1760–1832*, Cambridge, 1989, p. 56.

9 The term is from J. Milton Yinger's analysis of types of religious organisation in *Religion, Society and the Individual*, New York, 1957, pp. 147ff.; his definitions of 'cult' and 'denomination' are also particularly relevant to considerations of the development of religion in the nineteenth century.

10 See Alan D. Gilbert, *Religion and Society in Industrial England: Church, Chapel and Social Change, 1740–1914*, London, 1976, pp. 80–81.

11 For a survey of the crisis confronting the Church of England by the 1820s see Owen Chadwick, *The Victorian Church*, 2 vols, London, 1966 and 1970, I, pp. 7–100. Chadwick's work remains the most authoritative general study of organised religion in the Victorian period.

12 Gilbert, *Religion and Society*, p. 5.

13 These figures are extrapolated from the detailed statistics given by Gilbert, *Religion and Society*, p. 102.
14 Gilbert, *Religion and Society*, p. 131. See also Peter Virgin, *The Church in an Age of Negligence: Ecclesiastical Structure and Problems of Church Reform 1700–1840*, Cambridge, 1989, pp. 191–214.
15 For detailed figures and discussion see Gilbert, *Religion and Society*, pp. 98–101.
16 See R. A. Soloway, *Prelates and People: Ecclesiastical Social Thought in England, 1783–1852*, London, 1969, chapter 2, 'Inequity and Poverty, 1783–1815'.
17 For a detailed and balanced history of the competition between Anglicanism and dissent in the eighteenth century see John Stoughton, *History of Religion in England from the Opening of the Long Parliament to 1850*, 8 vols, London, 1867–84, V, *Church of the Revolution*, and VI, *Church in the Georgian Era*; for the geographical pattern of nonconformist development see John D. Gay, *The Geography of Religion in England*, London, 1971; for the sociology of nonconformist encroachment see Gilbert, *Church and Society*, pp. 51–121.
18 The classic regional study of competition between nonconformity and the establishment in the nineteenth century is James Obelkevich, *Religion and Society: South Lindsey 1825–1875*, Oxford, 1976.
19 The relationship between dissent, especially Methodism, and the artisanate is a central theme in E. P. Thompson, *The Making of the English Working Class*, London, 1963.
20 Gilbert, *Religion and Society*, p. 28.
21 This calculation is based on statistics given by Gilbert, *Church and Society*, pp. 36–9.
22 See M. H. Port, *Six Hundred New Churches: a Study of the Church Building Commission, 1818–56, and its Church-Building Activities*, London, 1961.
23 [John Wade], *The Black Book: an Exposition of Abuses in Church and State, Courts of Law, Municipal Corporations, and Public Companies* ..., new edition, London, 1835.
24 The compulsory church rate was eventually abolished in 1868.
25 For the agitation against tithes and the workings of the 1836 Tithe Commutation Act see Eric J. Evans, *The Contentious Tithe. The tithe problem and English agriculture, 1750–1850*, London, 1976.
26 See E. R. Norman, *Church and Society in England 1770–1970*, Oxford, 1976, chapter 3, 'Constitutional Adjustments of Church and State, 1828–1846'.
27 The best account of Anglican evangelicalism is still G. R. Balleine, *A History of the Evangelical Party in the Church of England*, London, 1908; new edition, 1951.
28 There is a vast literature on the Oxford Movement and the Anglican Revival; perhaps the fullest bibliography is by S. L. Ollard in F. W. Bateson (ed.), *The Cambridge Bibliography of English Literature*, 4 vols, Cambridge, 1940 and suppl. 1957. Ollard also wrote one of the best historical studies, *A Short History of the Oxford Movement*, London, 1915. All general histories of the Victorian Church include more or less substantial accounts of the Movement; see particularly S. C. Carpenter, *Church and People, 1789–1889*, London, 1933, pp. 110–74, and *Chadwick, Victorian Church*, I, pp. 167–221. For a succinct account of the Movement's place in the Victorian development of Anglicanism see Gerald Parsons, 'Reform, revival and realignment: the experience of Victorian Anglicanism', in Gerald Parsons and James R. Moore (eds), *Religion in Victorian Britain*, 4 vols, Manchester, 1988, I, *Traditions*, pp. 17–66. Owen Chadwick, *The Mind of the Oxford Movement*, London, 1960, is a substantial selection of extracts from contempory theological writings and has an important introduction; Elisabeth Jay (ed.), *The Evangelical and Oxford Movements*, Cambridge, 1983, usefully brings together writings by the Tractarians and by representatives of the other major movement in the Victorian churches.
29 For the early nineteenth-century response of the bishops to the need for more urban churches see Soloway, *Prelates and People*, chapter 8, 'People, Towns and Churches'.
30 The standard history of the ecclesiologists is J. White, *The Cambridge Movement: the Ecclesiologists and the Gothic Revival*, Cambridge, 1962.
31 John Mason Neale and Benjamin Webb, *The Symbolism of Churches and Church Ornaments: a Translation of the First Book of the 'Rationale Divinorum Officiorum', written by William Durandus, sometime Bishop of Mende*, Leeds, 1843, p. cxxvii.
32 The most detailed account of the developing impact of ecclesiology upon church fittings and furniture is Peter F. Anson, *Fashions in Church Furnishings 1840–1940*, London, 1960. For its effect upon liturgical planning see Nigel Yates, *Buildings, Faith and Worship: The Liturgical Arrangement of Anglican Churches 1600–1900*, Oxford, 1991.
33 *Die Lage der arbeitenden Klasse in England*, Berlin, 1845; the first English translation was not published until 1887 in America and 1892 in Britain.
34 Alfred Tennyson, *Poems*, London, 1842, 'The Epic', 11, 35–8.

35 The pair of plates was added for the second edition of *Contrasts or, a Parallel between the Noble Edifices of the Fourteenth and Fifteenth Centuries, and Similar Buildings of the Present Day* ... in 1841.
36 Thomas Carlyle, *Past and Present*, London 1843, *Works*, X.
37 For a nicely wry account of Young England see Mark Girouard, *The Return to Camelot: Chivalry and the English Gentleman*, New Haven, 1981, pp. 82–5. 'Young England's liveliest achievements', as Girouard rightly says, were Benjamin Disraeli's two novels *Coningsby*, 1844, and *Sybil*, 1845.
38 A. J. B. Beresford Hope, *The English Cathedral in the Nineteenth Century*, London, 1861; Hope was the dominant figure in the Ecclesiological Society from the mid-1840s, and the leading spokesman for the High Church party in the House of Commons.
39 The figures are based on the five-yearly totals given in Gilbert, *Church and Society*, p. 130.
40 These figures are drawn from those given in Robert Currie, Alan Gilbert and Lee Horsley, *Churches and Churchgoers: Patterns of Church Growth in the British Isles since 1700*, Oxford, 1977, pp. 213–15. This book is the most impressive sociological summary of church development in Britain over the last three centuries and contains a wealth of statistical information, particularly relating to church membership, recruitment and staffing, but also to church- and chapel-building. Many of its conclusions, along with those of Gilbert in *Church and Society*, underpin this Introduction.
41 *Return showing the Number of Churches (including Cathedrals) in every Diocese ... which have been Built or Restored at a Cost exceeding £500 since the Year 1873 ...*, London, 1892.
42 Alan Haig, *The Victorian Clergy*, London, 1984, p. 3.
43 Gilbert, *Church and Society*, p. 28.
44 Anthony Trollope, *The Vicar of Bullhampton*, London, 1870.
45 In his classic study *Religion and the Rise of Capitalism*, London, 1926.
46 In *A Popular History of the Free Churches*, London, 1903, C. Silvester Horne particularly stresses — and celebrates — the national political eminence of nonconformists like John Bright and Edward Miall, and the local power of ministers such as the Congregationalist Robert William Dale in Birmingham. 'Starting from such small and obscure origins', Horne concludes, '[nonconformity] had come to wield a quite extraordinary influence in the State' (p. 416).
47 A. Peel, *These Hundred Years: a History of the Congregational Union of England and Wales, 1831–1931*, London, 1931, p. 149, quotes John Angell James, Robert Dale's predecessor in Birmingham, urging his fellow Congregationalists in 1839, 'We must catch the building spirit of the age. We must *build, build, build*'.
48 The figures are based on the statistical summary of the findings of the 1851 religious census given in Currie, Gilbert and Horsley, *Churches and Churchgoers*, pp. 216–19; on those given in W. J. Townsend, H. B. Workman and George Eayrs (eds), *A New History of Methodism*, 2 vols, London, 1909; and on J. A. Vanes's article, 'Methodism' in *Encyclopædia Britannica*, 11th edition, 29 vols, New York, 1910–11, XVIII, pp. 293–4.
49 The total from the 1851 religious census includes Independents along with Congregationalists; other statistics are drawn from the entry on 'Independents' in Benjamin Vincent (ed.), *Haydn's Dictionary of Dates*, 25th edition, London, 1910; and J. V. Bartlet's article 'Congregationalism' in the 11th edition of *Encyclopædia Britannica*. In *Churches and Churchgoers*, pp. 213–15, the authors base their figures on the Congregationalist *Yearbooks*, which give 2,337 places of worship in 1861 and 4,910 in 1911 — a massive 110 per cent increase. How far the 1911 total incorporates churches calling themselves Independent in 1861, and thus not included in the figure for that year, is unclear.
50 As with the Congregationalists, calculations are problematic: a number of different societies come under the heading Baptists, and there are difficulties in interpreting the figures given at various times for the total of their places of worship. The figures used here are for churches, and are taken from Currie, Gilbert and Horsley, *Churches and Churchgoers*, pp. 213–15. However, the 1851 religious census gives a total of 2,908 Baptist places of worship in mainland Britain, and, in 1911, there were 4,120 Baptist chapels in addition to the 3,047 churches. If the 1851 figure really includes all Baptist places of worship, then this represents an increase of 146 per cent. Unfortunately for any statistical purposes, the 1851 census also lumps together 589 'Isolated Congregations' without further denominational identity: it is certain that many of these were Baptists. Taking account of such uncertainties, it seems likely that the number of places in which Baptists were worshipping regularly rather more than doubled in the sixty years after 1851; many of these places, however, would not have been permanent or purpose–built.

51 Currie, Gilbert and Horsley, *Churches and Churchgoers*, pp. 213–14,
52 The rates given here for Methodist growth are based on those in Gilbert, *Church and Society*, pp. 30–2; there are more detailed statistics in Currie, Gilbert and Horsley, *Churches and Churchgoers*, pp. 139–46, as well as an important discussion of the relationships between church growth, national population, and recruitment constituencies (pp. 46–74).
53 For a useful summary of nonconformist experience in the period see Gerald Parsons, 'From Dissenters to Free Churchmen: the transitions of Victorian nonconformity', in Parsons and Moore, *Religion in Victorian Britain*, I, *Traditions*, pp. 67–116.
54 For the most accessible account of Roman Catholicism in Victorian Britain see Edward Norman, *The English Catholic Church in the Nineteenth Century*, Oxford, 1984, which also has an excellent bibliography.
55 The two books by Bernard Ward, *The Eve of Catholic Emancipation*, London, 1911, and *The Sequel to Catholic Emancipation*, London, 1915, are still standard; see also Denis Gwynn, *The Second Spring 1818–1852: A Study of the Catholic Revival in England*, London, 1942.
56 Quoted by Norman, *Catholic Church in the Nineteenth Century*, p. 201.
57 Public interest was sufficient to merit the serial publication of *The Roman Catholic Question: a copious series of important documents, of permanent historical interest, on the re-establishment of the Catholic Hierarchy in England, 1850–1*; published by James Gilbert of London, it ran for twenty-four numbers in 1851.
58 The 1870 and 1900 figures are given by Norman, *Catholic Church in the Nineteenth Century*, p. 203, and are taken from *The Catholic Directory*. In Britain as a whole, excluding Ireland, the total number of Catholic places of worship went up from 737 in 1851 to 2,179 in 1911 — a rise of 195 per cent over sixty years.
59 See Norman, *Catholic Church in the Nineteenth Century*, pp. 205–6, and Currie, Gilbert and Horsley, *Churches and Churchgoers*, p. 153.
60 Evans, *Contentious Tithe*, p. 157.
61 See Virgin; *Church in an Age of Negligence*, pp. 277–8.
62 These figures are extrapolated from the detailed statistics given by Virgin, *Church in an Age of Negligence*, pp. 293–4.
63 Edward Jones, harpist to George IV, in *The Bardic Museum*, London, 1802, blamed the rise of nonconformist culture for turning Wales from 'one of the merriest, and happiest countries in the World' into 'one of the dullest' (p. xvi). See Prys Morgan, 'From a Death to a View: the Hunt for the Welsh Past in the Romantic Period', in Eric Hobsbawm and Terence Ranger (eds), *The Invention of Tradition*, Cambridge, 1983, pp. 43–100.
64 Ieuan Gwynedd Jones, *Explorations and Explanations: Essays in the Social History of Victorian Wales*, Llandysul, 1981, 'Religion and society in the first half of the nineteenth century' (p. 227).
65 See Jones, *Explorations and Explanations*, 'Religion and society', pp. 227–30.
66 F. L. Cross and E. A. Livingstone (eds), *The Oxford Dictionary of the Christian Church*, second edition, Oxford, 1974, 'Christianity in Wales'.
67 See Ieuan Gwynned Jones' detailed discussion 'Denominationalism in Caernarfonshire in the mid-nineteenth century as shown in the religious census of 1851', *Explorations and Explanations*, pp. 17–52.
68 Anglican accommodation amounted to 236,650 sittings, that of the nonconformist churches to 524,250; see Currie, Gilbert and Horsley, *Churches and Churchgoers*, p. 218, where the other 1851 census figures for Wales are also disaggregated.
69 Horace Mann, *Census of 1851: Religious Worship, England and Wales, Report and Tables, Parliamentary Papers*, LXXXIX, 1852–53, p. cxxvii.
70 The argument is Ieuan Gwynned Jones's in 'Religion and Society'.
71 E. C. Morgan Willmott, *The Cathedral Church of Llandaff: A Description of the Building and a Short History of the See*, London, 1907, p. 90.
72 See, for example, J. E. de Hirsch-Davies, *A Popular History of the Church in Wales*, London, 1912, pp. 308–35.
73 *Churches ... Built or Restored ... since ... 1873*, 'Summary', p. 254.
74 [John Wade], *Black Book*, 1835, p. 143.
75 See J. H. Bernard's article 'The Church of Ireland', *Encyclopædia Britannica*, 11th edition, XIV, pp. 789–91.
76 Cross and Livingstone, *Dictionary of the Christian Church*, 'Christianity in Ireland'.
77 E. A. D'Alton, 'Ireland', *The Catholic Encyclopedia*, 15 vols, London, 1907–12, VIII, p. 114.
78 The calculation is based upon figures for 1901 given in Bernard, 'Church of Ireland'.

79 See F. Goldie, *A Short History of the Episcopal Church in Scotland from the Reformation to the Present Time*, London, 1951.
80 See A. Menzies, 'Church of Scotland', *Encyclopædia Britannica*, 11th edition, XXIV, pp. 460–7.
81 According to W. L. Mathieson, *Church and Reform in Scotland: a History from 1797–1843*, Glasgow, 1916, p. 371, between 351 and 374 ministers seceded, out of a total of 1,203, along with some 38 per cent of the kirk's members.
82 See J. S. Black and A. Menzies, 'Free Church of Scotland', *Encyclopædia Britannica*, 11th edition, XI, pp. 71–5. By the time of the 1851 religious census the Free Church had 889 places of worship; Currie, Gilbert and Horsley, *Chuches and Churchgoers*, p. 219.
83 Menzies, 'Church of Scotland', p. 465.
84 All the calculations here are based on the statistics for members and communicants of the Scottish churches given in Currie, Gilbert and Horsley, *Churches and Churchgoers*, pp. 132–3; see also pp. 136–8 for their outline of the problems of interpretation involved.
85 Statistics are drawn from D. O. Hunter-Blair, 'Scotland', *Catholic Encyclopedia*, XIII, pp. 613–22, and Currie, Gilbert and Horsley, *Churches and Churchgoers*, pp. 153–5.
86 Hunter-Blair, 'Scotland', p. 621.
87 See Hugh Trevor-Roper, 'The Invention of Tradition: the Highland Tradition of Scotland', in Hobsbawm and Ranger, *Invention of Tradition*, pp. 15–41.
88 Currie, Gilbert and Horsley, *Churches and Churchgoers*, pp. 128–31.
89 Although a considerable amount of work has been published on the major Anglican and Roman Catholic architects, very little has been done on the leading nonconformist practices.
90 The whole episode is fictionalised in Hardy's *A Pair of Blue Eyes*, London, 1873. Less well known, and far more highly dramatised in its representation of architectural practice, is John Meade Falkner's *The Nebuly Coat*, London, 1903, in which the young Edward Westray is sent down to Dorset from the office of Sir George Farquhar — clearly based on Scott — to restore the church of Cullerne Minster.
91 Horace Mann, *Census of 1851: Religious Worship, England and Wales, Report and Tables, Parliamentary Papers*, LXXXIX, 1852–53. The voluminous statistics gathered by the census, particularly those relating to attendance, are notoriously difficult to interpret – a fact which led, on their publication, to the so-called 'arithmetical war' between Anglicans and nonconformists. The seminal modern study of the census is K. S. Inglis, 'Patterns of Religious Worship in 1851', *Journal of Ecclesiastical History*, XI, 1960, pp. 74–86, and there is additional discussion in D. M. Thompson, 'The 1851 Religious Census: Problems and Possibilities', *Victorian Studies*, XI, 1967–68, pp. 87–97. In recent years there have been several valuable regional studies based on the census. Ieuan Gwynedd Jones's 'Religion and Society in the first half of the nineteenth century' and 'Denominationalism in Caernarfonshire' have already been referred to, and to them should be added his 'Denominationalism in Swansea and District: a study of the Ecclesiastical Census of 1851', in *Explorations and Explanations*, pp. 53–80. See also Bruce Coleman, 'Southern England in the Census of Religious Worship, 1851', *Southern History*, V, 1983; Kate Tiller, 'Church and Chapel in Oxfordshire 1851', *Oxfordshire Record Society*, LV, 1987; J. A. Vickers, 'The Religious Census of Sussex 1851', *Sussex Record Society*, LXXV, 1987.
92 The figures are given in P. Brierley *et al.* (eds), *The United Kingdom Christian Handbook 1994–95*, Christian Research Association, 1993.
93 See K. S. Inglis, *Churches and the Working Classes in Victorian England*, London, 1963, and Hugh McLeod, *Class and Religion in the Late Victorian City*, London, 1974.
94 This is one of the central arguments of Desmond Bowen, *The Idea of the Victorian Church: A Study of the Church of England 1833–1889*, Montreal, 1968.
95 See J. P. D. Dunbabin, *Rural Discontent in Nineteenth-Century Britain*, New York, 1974, chapter 4, 'The Rise and Fall of Agricultural Trades Unionism'; Pamela Horn, *Labouring Life in the Victorian Countryside*, Dublin, 1976, chapter 6, 'Agricultural Wages, Trade Unionism and Politics'; and Pamela Horn, 'Labour Organizations' in G. E. Mingay (ed.), *The Unquiet Countryside*, London, 1989, pp. 99–110.
96 Richard Jefferies, 'A modern Country Curate', in *Hodge and his Masters*, London, 1880; reprinted, 2 vols, London, 1966, I, p. 165.
97 Mrs Stephen Batson, 'Hodge at Home', *The Nineteenth Century*, XXXI, 1892, p. 178.
98 [Thomas Wright], *The Great Unwashed by The Journeyman Engineer*, London, 1868, pp. 79–96, 'The Working Classes and the Church'.
99 Although there was a tradition of radical and popularist infidelism; see Edward Royle, *Radical Politics 1790–1900: Religion and Unbelief*, London, 1971.

100 See Standish Meacham, *A Life Apart. The Working Class in Britain 1885–1914*, London, 1984. For a European perspective see Dietrich Mühlberg, *Proletariat: Culture and Lifestyle in the Nineteenth Century*, translated by Katherine Vanovitch, Leipzig, 1988, pp. 187–256, 'Workers' Leisure and Proletarian Culture'.

Chapter 1 · Andrew Saint

Anglican church-building in London, 1790–1890: from state subsidy to the free market

This essay is about the ways in which the nineteenth-century Church of England built and paid for its new urban churches, and about the growth of these methods and their consequences. Anglican church-extension in Britain's cities, the argument runs, was always a hopeful rather than a rational activity. It was undertaken to meet a potential rather than a real demand for accommodation which in the long term could not be forced into existence, and to solve social problems which the mere proliferation of churches in itself could never have answered. In the early decades of the nineteenth century, church-extension was indeed long overdue because of the expansion of the urban population. It could be quite soundly financed out of local taxation or government grants, because Church and State were more or less one. But after the tacit semi-disestablishment of the Church of England in the Age of Reform, Victorian private enterprise had to take over the burden of church-extension. There followed a rash of fashionable, competitive church-building with little regard for demand, reaching a perilous climax in the 1860s and 1870s. The upshot we see today in the mass of redundant and uncared-for churches in our cities. Many of them are splendid as architecture. But few ever fulfilled the hopes they were built with.

Though the case could be made for any city in Britain, it assumes its starkest form in London. London and its spiritual destitution exerted an early and enduring hold over the religious reformers of the nineteenth century. The outward causes of the Anglican revival — the migration to the cities, the competition of dissent and enthusiasm, and the moral and political challenge of the French Revolution — affected everyone, everywhere. But they were at their most conspicuous in London. Because of its pre-eminent size, status and problems, the capital was always before the eyes of the bishops, archbishops, peers, commoners, theologians, clergy and plain, concerned churchgoers. It especially concerned the constitutional loyalists of the Church of England, for whom the renewal of religious institutions counted for as much as the rebirth of spirituality.

To understand nineteenth-century church-building in London, it may help to start with the 'Clapham Sect' and the 'Hackney Phalanx'. These were the facetious sobriquets invented by Sydney Smith for the two loose groups of suburban merchants and intellectuals, largely laymen, who did so much to reawaken Anglican religious life around 1800 and after.

The Claphamites were low churchmen. Influenced by Wesley, they sought a renewed spiritual life through personal and family example. Their great public success was the crusade against slavery, led by Wilberforce. The men of Hackney, by contrast, are remembered as organisers. They belonged to the 'high and dry' party; in other words, they were sacramentarians, but they did not anticipate the coming clamour for ritual and the reordering of churches. Rather, they saw the established Church of England as a 'visible society', with its own renewed social and hegemonic role within the national body politic. From their activity, notably the lobbying and committee work of the indefatigable Joshua Watson of Hackney and his friends, emerged three key institutions of reform within the Church: the state-supported National Society for Educating the Poor, the Church Building Commission of 1818, and — indirectly — the permanent Ecclesiastical Commission of 1836, which furnished the administrative framework within which the Victorian Church operated.[1]

Both the Clapham Sect and the Hackney Phalanx sprang up in prosperous London suburbs whose churches had just been rebuilt, Clapham's in 1774–76, Hackney's in 1793–97. This can hardly be fortuitous; it shows, in middle-class ideal, how a fresh start and a new building could help to animate parish life. The Claphamites are not usually connected with new churches, though Wilberforce did promote an abortive church-building bill in 1800. Hackney's case is different. It was the Phalanx that did most to secure the Church Building Acts of 1818 and 1819, in particular through the influence of well-connected Hackney gentlemen (the vicar's brother, Joshua Watson, and the curate, H. H. Norris) upon the Prime Minister, Lord Liverpool.

But in planning that grand programme of state-financed church-building, the case of St John-at-Hackney [**1**] must have been a lesson of what to avoid.[2] The consent of the parishioners had not been a problem. Hackney's existing church was too small for the swelling population, and its vestry was rich and proud enough to commission a fine building, designed by James Spiller. There were several strong and articulate local independent congregations who would have had no interest in the project: Richard Price, Burke's radical bugbear, and the scientist Joseph Priestley both occupied dissenting pulpits in Hackney during the 1790s. But the bond between secular and religious administration was still then taken for granted. If a parish opted to rebuild its church, it was assumed that local people would be taxed to provide it, whatever their beliefs, just as they would be taxed for lighting, paving or care of the poor.

The problem at Hackney, and for that matter in the case of many other churches rebuilt before 1818, had been managerial. A special and costly yet narrowly framed Act of Parliament had to be applied for in order for the parish to raise the funds to build the church, which was done by means of annuities guaranteed by a sixpenny church rate. When things went wrong and the carpenting contractor went bankrupt, there was nothing for the cumbersome body of trustees to do but go back and get another Act. This happened twice at Hackney, causing much delay. In this the parish was by no means unique. It was the price paid by the Church of England in the eighteenth century for being locked into the privileges of the State.

For reasons like this, the typical form of Anglican church-extension in prosperous parts of London all through the Georgian period had been the 'proprietary chapel', raised in a newly built-up district of an existing parish. These chapels were usually private ventures promoted by landlords and developers to add tone to surrounding property, and thus keep up its rental value; sometimes speculating clergymen were also involved. They depended upon pew rents and the attractions of the preacher, had little status or responsibility, and their religious vigour was intermittent. The buildings tended to be basic, without any pretension of accommodating anything like the whole of the local population.

So many of the London proprietary chapels have disappeared or been transformed that we forget now how many there once were. St Marylebone, for instance, had eight; and the private interests of their owners and preachers were among the reasons why the parish took forty-five years and three Acts of Parliament before it finally managed to rebuild its church in 1813–17.[3] Neighbouring St Pancras, embarking on its campaign for a new parish church a little later, in 1812, ran into similar problems. In the climate of Tory reform which developed after Waterloo they were more rapidly resolved, allowing the Inwoods' great Greek Revival fane to be erected in 1819–22.[4] The grandeur, vast cost and landmark status of these two sumptuous Regency parish churches, built at key points along the New Road, reasserted the secular and religious authority of the London parish over the drab proprietary chapels. But they belonged to an old way of doing things, soon to be overtaken by events.

The Church Building Acts of 1818 and 1819 provided more than a million pounds of public money for new churches. They were in many ways a fluke of the moment — an unanticipated victory for the 'high and dry' party, won against a background of deep social unrest. Urban church-extension, the Government and many others piously imagined, might help to pacify the people:

> ... the time
> Is conscious of her want; through England's bounds,
> In rival haste, the wished-for Temples rise!

sang Wordsworth, insipidly hopeful.[5]

1] James Spiller, St-John-at-Hackney, 1792–97; tower and porticoes 1812. Erected by private Act of Parliament, authorising loans secured on the parish rates

The new state-subsidised churches were in the main justified by arguments about London. The evidence that Joshua Watson, H. H. Norris and John Bowdler had put to Lord Liverpool was largely based on the dearth of metropolitan church accommodation; the subsidy limits of £20,000 per church and the directions for style and arrangement contributed by Soane, Nash and Smirke were also framed with London in mind. During the 1820s, the capital got something like 35 of the 214 churches built nationally under the terms of the Acts. These were district churches, under the full control of the vestry, vicar and churchwardens of the parish as a whole; their function was religious only, and each had a proportion of free seats. Effectively, they put paid to the proprietary-chapel system.[5]

Yet even while this great state-subsidised effort of church-extension was going forward, the roof was falling in upon the ramshackle administrative structure on which it depended for support. By the end of the 1820s, the old compact between Church and State was in tatters. Catholics had been emancipated, radicals and dissenters were up in arms over the payment of church rates, and wedges had been inserted between the parochial exercise of secular and of religious powers. The Great Reform and, in the towns, the Municipal Corporations Act of 1835 completed the rout. The outcome was that all Anglican urban churches — old parish churches as well as the new district churches — were henceforward more or less confined to religious functions.

Such was the temporal threat, a threat tantamount to disestablishment, that confronted the Church of England in the 1830s. The collapse of the Church's secular authority was the most direct cause of the Oxford Movement, spiritual and theological though that movement became in its orientation. And the man who above all others met the challenge of virtual disestablishment head on and raced to set up an alternative framework within which the Church could operate was not an Oxford Movement enthusiast at all, but someone of the previous generation: Charles James Blomfield, Bishop of London from 1828 to 1856. Blomfield saw that if the Church was to survive in recognisable form, there had to be a complete overhaul of church functions and emoluments. 'It is impossible that the Church (in so far as it is of human institution) can go on as it is now', he told Archbishop Howley in 1832.[7] Hence the permanent Ecclesiastical Commission, set up by Blomfield with Peel's political help in 1835–6.

Efficient, ambitious, somewhat impersonal, Blomfield usually gets an indifferent press. He had the misfortune to tangle with Sydney Smith, who respected him ('The original Commission, excluding the Ministers of State and the Archbishops, was the Bishop of London, diluted with some watery additions') but mocked him as a 'holy innovator' bedevilled by 'an ungovernable passion for business and a constitutional impetuosity'.[8] The cause of their quarrel was Blomfield's campaign to redistribute the inflated incomes of the canons of St Paul's Cathedral, among whom Smith was numbered. Smith lost, deservedly, but posterity prefers his nimble pamphleteering to Blomfield's reformist logic.

Blomfield was an indefatigable London church-builder. The thirty-five-odd Commissioners' churches of the 1820s still seemed wholly inadequate to London's needs; some districts had hardly been touched by them. The mere proliferation of churches was a good thing, he at first felt. During the 1830s, the Church-Building Commissioners were still giving money, though their hand-outs were on a reduced scale. To these the Bishop was able to add sizeable sums culled from his reforms of London diocesan finance. Given the political climate of the 1830s, he was unable to interest Parliament in a new church-building subsidy. Instead, Blomfield in 1836 set up the Metropolis Churches Extension Fund.[9] The key factor in this was private giving. While Church and State were indissoluble, it had hardly occurred even to the devoutest Anglicans to pay for their local urban parish church — as opposed to proprietary chapel — out of their own pocket. Rural landowners might build a church, but in Georgian London the practice was unknown. London landlords now became the primary target of Blomfield's forcible fund-raising rhetoric.[10] So effective were the results that by the 1840s and 1850s most of the big landowners, such as the Grosvenors, were giving sites for churches in developing districts, and often contributed substantially towards their fabric as well.

Nevertheless, the fund-raising campaign of 1836 was far from a complete success. The Metropolis Churches Fund never reached anything like its target of fifty churches. Some interesting ones were built — notably Christ Church, Albany Street, by Pennethorne, and Christ Church, Streatham, by Wild. But on the whole, the incidence of private donation was disappointing.

Blomfield had one stalwart supporter, however: William Cotton, a rich banker and East End cordage manufacturer whose support for church-building went back to the initiatives of the 1810s. It was Cotton who in 1837–38 built London's first privately given district church on the new model, St Peter's, Stepney. He went on to pay for two further complete East End churches, St Thomas's, Bethnal Green, and St Paul's, Bow Common.[11] All three churches, alas, have been demolished. But Cotton's wider fame was as the father of the 'Bethnal Green scheme'.

Blomfield and Cotton's Bethnal Green Fund of 1839–50 was a semi-independent offshoot of the Metropolis Churches Fund.[12] It was perhaps the first structured programme of intervention in the moral and social condition of the East End, and ushered in the whole tradition of middle-class involvement in the area. For the first time, the reformed Church of England systematically tried to target an urban area in distress. The collapse of the Spitalfields and Bethnal Green silk industry at the end of the 1820s and the degradation that rapidly ensued had set off the long downward social spiral of the East End. For the next 125 years, the very name of Bethnal Green in reformist circles meant somewhere that needed outside study and help, whether from the Church of England, Baroness Burdett-Coutts, the London County Council, the architects of the Mars Group, or the intellectual planners and sociologists of the 1940s and 1950s.[13]

If none of these interventions was an unqualified success, the first and most innocent of them, the Blomfield-Cotton campaign, came close to disaster. Ten churches were built under the Bethnal Green scheme [**2**]. Of these, just two, St Peter's and St James the Less, still function as places of worship — and St James the Less has been largely rebuilt after war damage.

This failure is by no means a modern perception; it was articulated at the time. The simplest indictment came from Charles Booth, writing at the end of the century: there was, he remarked, 'wasted effort to such an extent that even now "remember Bethnal Green" is apt to be thrown in the teeth of those who try to inaugurate any great movement in the City on behalf of the Church'.[14] Earlier, when the last of the new churches was consecrated in 1850, the churchwardens felt compelled to apologise to Blomfield: 'My Lord, it has been significantly said, that the churches of Bethnal Green have not answered. We are here to testify that they do answer.'[15] But the most devastating indictment is a private letter written in 1859 by Gibson, the Vicar of St Matthew's, the parish church, to H. J. Mackenzie, who had been secretary of the Bethnal Green Fund.[16] With savage candour, Gibson goes through the whole ten churches cataloguing the sins and errors of their successive incumbents, running the gamut of adultery, apostasy, assault, simony, humbug and sheer idleness. Here are the choicest extracts:

> St Peter still retains Mr Packer as Incumbent — who is a worthy man, without much energy — the Church about half filled on Sundays — whilst the Schools are flourishing.
>
> St Andrew's ... The present incumbent, Mr Parker ... has become a great Politician and tells the very few people who attend him — that they should read nothing but the Bible and the newspaper — the destinies of the French Empire form the perpetual theme of his Sermons ... His Schools are shut up — his Church almost empty.
>
> St Philip ... was for years, the scene of Mr Alston's vagaries, who annoyed the Bishop — and tormented and defrauded the Clergy by marrying for 2*s* 6*d* (including all charges) thus he brought people from all parts of London to be married at his Church — and used frequently to join together 50 couples *per diem*. Mr Trevitt, his successor, is a most amiable man ... very lax and liberal in his Notions — stating that being obliged to sign and swear conformity to — or agreement with the Articles and Liturgy is one of the greatest curses of our Church. He also marries at a lower price (not so low as 2*s* 6*d*) than any of the rest of us — and hence carries on a successful trade in that way — but his Church is very poorly attended.
>
> St James the Less, Victoria Park, has proved a uniform failure till recently — the first incumbent, Mr Coghlan, was a most extravagant and wordy man — and after being there some years to the injury and disgrace of the Church — left over head and ears in debt ... He was succeeded by a Mr Haughton ... he had an aversion to coming in contact with poor people — had boxes affixed to the inner doors of the Church — as watering places for the morning and evening contributions for the congregation in lieu of pew rents ... he would have no schools built ... he was a sort of perpetual blister to good Mr Cotton and to our late good Bishop.

St James the Great ... Mr James proved a very inefficient and immoral man — his Wife and children being in the country — and he remaining at home he went to bed with his servant maid — this was, in some sort hushed up — but the matter was so well known in the Parish, that his usefulness was at an end here — therefore he exchanged livings with the present Incumbent, Mr Coke

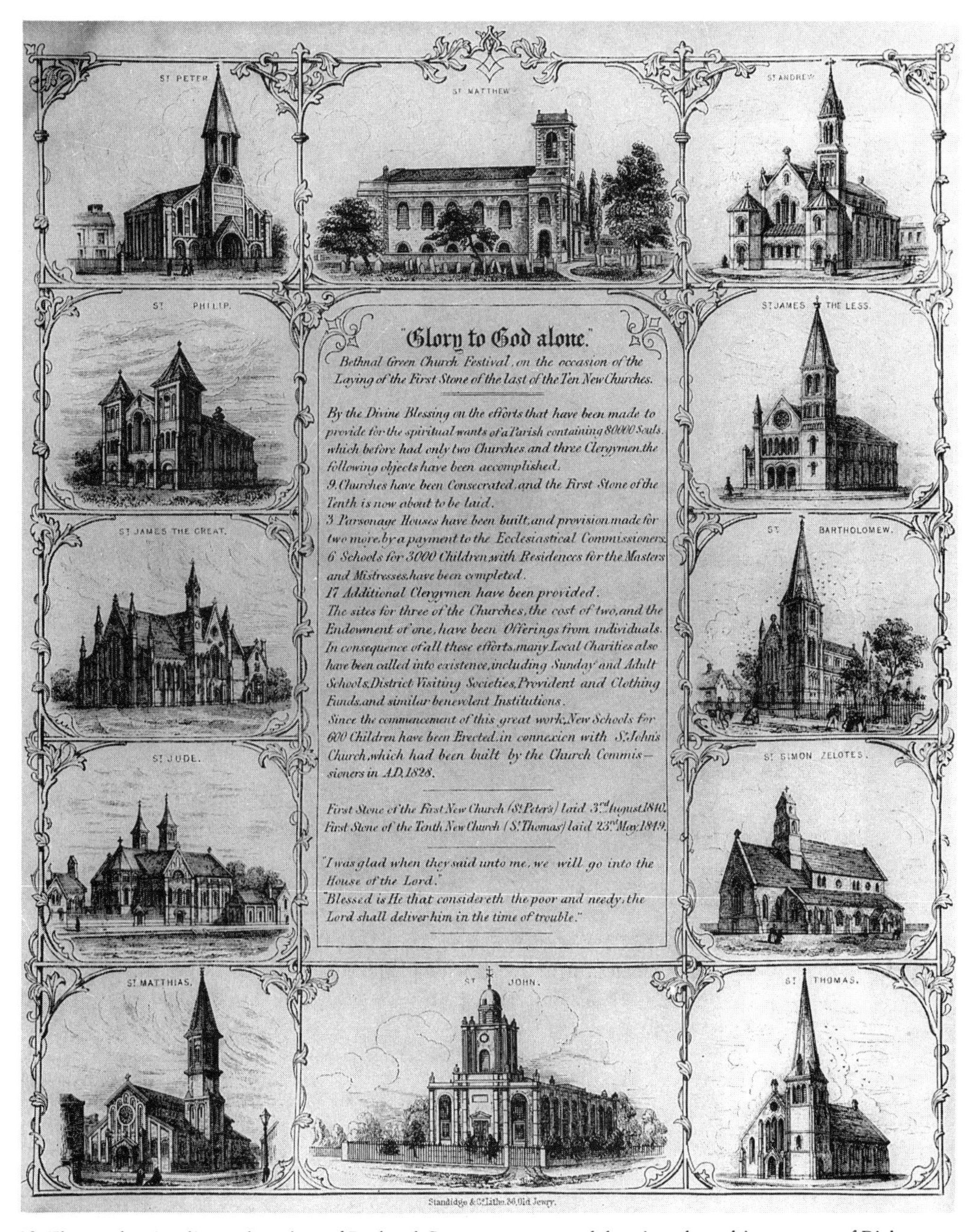

2] The twelve Anglican churches of Bethnal Green: a poster celebrating the achievements of Bishop Blomfield's Bethnal Green Fund. Top centre, the parish church; bottom centre, Soane's St John's, a Commissioners' church; along the sides, the ten churches erected between 1836 and 1850

> ... Mr Coke out Herods Herod ... he has shut up his Schools — although they have an endowment of £1,000 — having bought a house for his wife and family at Tottenham he is seldom in residence: every winter, and all through the year he collects for the poor large sums by Advertisements — and no one knows what becomes of the money. About four weeks ago he knocked down a pauper in his hall who asked him for a receipt for some shillings he had been sent with from the Chairman of our Board of Guardians ... He told me a year ago that he is a Roman Catholic at heart — he seldom has twenty people in his Church — and I am sorry to be compelled to say that at St James the Great it is indeed 'death in the pot'.

> St Simon Zelotes had for the first Incumbent, Mr Ansted — a truly excellent man — but he was so out of health — that for the most part he was compelled to be from home — and when in residence his illness destroyed all his energies — and his wife was a forward, meddling and quarrelsome person — who by her frequent indiscretions did great injury to the District ... The present Incumbent Mr Christie is only a slug in the Lord's Vineyard — consequently there is scarcely any congregation and the Schools are in a languishing state.

Among all the new churches, Gibson gives only two a clean bill of health.

What then had gone wrong at Bethnal Green? The answers, implicit in Gibson's letter, tally with modern urban experience. In an area where habits of churchgoing were weak or non-existent, there were too many separate small churches and parishes. The clergy found themselves operating in impecunious isolation, outside the middle-class cultural milieu natural to them and to received Anglican habits of church life. As a result they took to gimmickry or became lonely, eccentric and perverse. The parishes that did best seem to have been those that had good schools, which Blomfield tried to provide at the same time through the National Society. Churches, indeed, were not what was primarily wanted in the East End or other working-class areas of the Victorian inner city. They were the icing on the cake, only to be built once an infrastructure of parish life was in place.

The lessons of Bethnal Green took a long time to digest. This was in part because they clashed with the powerful, 'private enterprise' church-building movement that gathered pace in the early Victorian era and found mutual enthusiasm among clergy and architects. There were some changes. The Shoreditch and Haggerston churches designed by James Brooks in the 1860s and 1870s, for instance, were less isolated. There was a team feeling to parochial organisation, with clergy living 'in community' in a capacious vicarage next to the church, on the model of All Saints', Margaret Street. But everything was still staked on the great, glorious church building and the events that took place in it — whether the sacrament or the sermon. Only with Toynbee Hall and the other missions of the 1880s and 1890s did the 'architecture' lose its primacy as the focus of urban Anglican activity.

At the other end of the social spectrum, in the freshly developed, higher-class districts of London, new Anglican churches had a much better chance of finding a congregation and prospering. But here the seeds of difficulties to come — difficulties which are still having an impact today — were sown by the 'privatisation' of early Victorian church-building; a phenomenon which led in the 1860s and 1870s to those concomitants of private enterprise, rampant competition and an excess of supply over demand.

Kensington is the best part of London in which to see this process at work. The Vicar of Kensington from 1842 to 1875 was John Sinclair, a wealthy Scot, a trusted lieutenant of Blomfield's, and an efficient ecclesiastical administrator of the new breed. 'Called to the charge of Kensington', wrote Archbishop Tait of Sinclair, 'he at once began the work of subdividing it into manageable districts; and he allowed no personal interest to stand in his way when a partition of his pastoral authority seemed right'.[17] Sinclair's monument in St Mary Abbots adds: 'In his time through his self-denying efforts fourteen ecclesiastical districts were formed out of the mother parish of Kensington.' In other words, Sinclair could afford the parcelling-up of his territory which less privileged parsons could not.

How was this done? Before the 1840s, taking completely independent smaller parishes out of big urban parishes had been administratively difficult; there were problems of compensation, among others. The Commissioners' churches, of which Kensington had two, therefore started life as district churches. But Peel's Act of 1843, followed by Blandford's Act of 1856, transformed the parish-making system. Thereafter if anyone, clergyman or layman, volunteered to found a church and could get the consent of the vicar, archdeacon and bishop, he could do so. Once the building was up and running, a district would almost automatically be lopped off the existing parish and assigned to it. In this way parishes were subdivided again and again, into areas sometimes almost as small as the ancient parishes of the City of London; with this difference, that the size of the projected churches was invariably greater, and their endowment usually trivial.

The commonest motive for church-building in Victorian Kensington remained, as it had been in Georgian London, to lend tone and respectability to residential development. Most of South Kensington's new churches were 'estate churches', at least partly backed by landowners. In view of the fast-growing population, there were good arguments for providing many of them. But after the first battles over ritual around 1850, this motive became overlaid by that of competition between High Church and Low Church factions. London landlords and developers of course held views of their own on these issues, tending usually towards the 'low' end of the spectrum. C. J. Freake, for instance, ensured that the two churches he built to bolster his developments, St Paul's, Onslow Square [**3**] and St Peter's, Cranley Gardens, were evangelical in religious observance and arrangement.[18]

Anglican church-building peaked in Kensington, as it did nationally, in the decade 1865-75. It is illuminating to see how this worked in more detail.[19] First the 'low' churches.

Two such foundations, less than half a mile apart but on different freehold estates, were St Stephen's, Gloucester Road (1866–67) and St Jude's, Courtfield Gardens (1870). In neither case was the landowner much

3] C. J. Freake, St Paul's, Onslow Square, Kensington, 1859–60. A fashionable estate church, conforming to the Low Churchmanship of its developer and builder

involved. St Stephen's sprang from Archdeacon Sinclair's initiative. Sinclair seems to have found both the patron, John Cator, who put up most of the money, and the first incumbent, J. A. Aston. Subscriptions made up the rest and allowed the body of the church to be built in one go, but did not stretch far enough to allow Joseph Peacock, the architect, to erect the rugged Rhenish tower he had designed. A district for St Stephen's was then duly carved out from the main parish of Kensington.

No sooner had this been done than Aston began to promote a second new church, the eventual St Jude's, on Gunter land south of the Cromwell Road, in an area of 'cabbage gardens' hardly yet reached by development. Again the first thing was to secure a patron and a promising incumbent, in this case R. W. Forrest, a strenuous preacher who had occupied the pulpit of the Lock Chapel. Subscriptions were expected to come in on the strength of Forrest's name, but failed to do so. So Forrest approached the glove manufacturer J. D. Allcroft, a stranger to Kensington but well known as a munificent benefactor of evangelical church-building (he had just paid for the whole of E. B. Lamb's costly St Martin's, Gospel Oak). Allcroft relieved the St Jude's promoters of their commitments to the tune of £16,000. This allowed the whole church to be built to Henry Godwin's designs in 1870 (except the tower and spire, which followed in 1879). St Stephen's parish was therefore subdivided within five years of its creation;

but not without strife, as Aston had by this time fallen out with Forrest. He lost, and soon left St Stephen's.

In this way, with outside help and slim evidence of 'demand', two ambitious Kensington churches were built very close to each other. In the event both of them flourished, at any rate until the First World War. St Stephen's in due course switched to Anglo-Catholicism, and enjoyed a palmy Edwardian heyday. St Jude's, under Forrest, became the evangelical stronghold of South Kensington. Its chic congregational atmosphere and the floridity of Forrest's preaching ('great *copia verborum*, but there were frequent repetitions and no very logical arrangement') are mordantly sketched by that eloquent sermon-taster C. Maurice Davies in his entertaining book, *Orthodox London*.

Kensington's 'low' churches like St Stephen's, St Jude's and Freake's two foundations were saved from utter precariousness by the pew-renting system, to which they still adhered. Pew rents had been standard for centuries in Anglican tradition. Renting a seat in a newly-built church was not so different from taking a lease of a local house; the two things went respectably together. The pew rent, paid usually in advance by the year, offered regular income and potential endowment for the church. In the new evangelical churches, as in fashionable dissenting chapels, rents were fixed in proportion to the class of clergyman and standard of sermon anticipated; hence the importance of a figure like Forrest at St Jude's, who was literally a box-office draw.

Pew rents had hardly been questioned by the 'high and dry' party during the first phase of nineteenth-century Anglican church-building. The Church Building Commissioners had institutionalised the system in 1818, by stipulating that only one fifth of the seats in the churches they subsidised need be free, and fixing a scale for the rentals. Some argued that pew-renting encouraged family churchgoing; and Bishop Blomfield, always sensitive to financial issues, believed the system provided crucial support for the clergy. But after 1840, there was a fervent High Church reaction against pew-renting, and indeed against pews themselves, 'the wooden walls within which selfishness encases itself', as one churchman dubbed them.[20] With the influential Broad-Church support of F. W. Farrar, this campaign climaxed in the 1860s and 1870s, the peak years of church-building. The arguments were several: legal (no Act of Parliament permitted pew rents generally), scriptural (the Bible implied that churches and temples should be open to all), social (pew-renting kept the working classes out of churches) and financial (offertories yielded more money than pew rents). Within ten years of its foundation in 1866, the London Free and Open Church Association succeeded in bumping up the percentage of churches in the capital and its suburbs where all seats were free from less than 10 per cent to 30 per cent and the incidence of the weekly offertory from under 20 per cent to nearly 50 per cent. Many more London churches also began to be open on weekdays.[21]

The veto on pew rents made it doubly difficult for the High Church party to finance urban church-building soundly, unless there was a rich benefactor behind the scene. That is proved by their experience in Kensington, in particular by the messy story of the foundation of St Matthias', Warwick Road and its two daughter churches, the abortive St Patrick's, Kenway Road and the better-known St Cuthbert's, Philbeach Gardens.

St Matthias' (1869–72) was the child of Samuel Haines, a clergyman often in trouble with his bishop for ritualist excesses. It was an offshoot of St Philip's, Earl's Court Road, where High Church traditions had developed, and took its parish from that church. But because Archdeacon Sinclair was suspicious of Haines, he was allowed only a small and unpromising district. Haines started building before he had collected enough money. He followed what had become a Kensington tradition. First a temporary iron church was erected, then the permanent chancel, then the nave; usually a tower was also intended, though at St Matthias', designed by J. H. Hakewill, this may not have been the case. Such was the state of the church finances that the builders of the nave obtained a bond guaranteeing payment from twenty prominent supporters; and at some point, as collateral for debts owing to contractors, Haines took out a life-insurance policy, the premiums for which were met out of church-building funds. Nothing could better articulate the dependence of these new foundations on individual charisma and ambition. Safeguards of this kind were not excessive. Close by, at St Luke's, Redcliffe Square (1872–73), the zeal of the first incumbent, W. F. Handcock, to build nave, chancel and tower all in one go on money borrowed from the local developers, Corbett and McClymont, seems to have been a powerful factor in the latters' eventual bankruptcy.[22] With clergymen, you could not be too careful, especially when they had no pew rents to look forward to.

St Patrick's was a daughter church of St Matthias', projected by Haines in 1872 within his own tiny parish but provocatively close to St Jude's, Courtfield Gardens. He simply took the discarded iron church from St Matthias' and re-erected it at the end of Kenway Road, then commissioned an elaborate but fantastic design [**4**] for a permanent church from a member of his flock, Henry Conybeare. This time, Bishop Jackson stood firm against further competition and subdivision, thus quashing effective fund-raising for Conybeare's design. Haines eventually sold the temporary St Patrick's for others to make a go of. By 1879 it had passed to Maxwell Ben-Oliel, a High Church clergyman who had previously been in difficulties in Croydon. In that year, the iron church burnt down. Ben-Oliel tried to resurrect the church, but was firmly suppressed by the Bishop: 'I have distinctly told him, as the two previous owners of the chapel, that I have no intention of consecrating, or of consenting to the assignment of a district to, any permanent church built on that site.' Ben-Oliel himself admitted that the Kenway Road site was 'on the verge of four different parishes, and three of these have their own churches very near this particular spot'.[23] But he did not give up; instead, he looked for another site, the one eventually to become St Cuthbert's.

Even St Cuthbert's (1884–87), famous though it became, was a precarious enough foundation. Without the fund-raising genius, even cunning, of its originator, Haines's former curate Henry Westall, it would never have succeeded. Westall took over the project of a daughter church for St

4] Henry Conybeare, design for St Patrick's, Kenway Road, Kensington, 1873. Owing to boundary disputes with neighbouring parishes, it had no hope of being built

Matthias' from Ben-Oliel in about 1881. The new site was to be in Philbeach Gardens, then in St Philip's parish, not St Matthias'; and to this the vicar of St Philip's, Walter Pennington, raised strong objection. The issue was simple. Pennington ('commonly spoken of in the neighbourhood as a disgrace in his sacred office'[24]) was poor, and depended wholly on his pew rents. So indebted had he become by 1880 that St Philip's and its pew rents were actually sequestrated under ecclesiastical law, and Pennington was paid an income by the sequestrator. The prospect of the loss of a chunk of his parish was the last thing he could contemplate. The result was a two-year delay, during which Westall explored alternative legal ways of getting his church. Not indeed until Pennington had gone and Frederick Temple had succeeded the more cautious John Jackson as bishop in 1885 was the future of St Cuthbert's secure. By starting on the permanent vicarage and church before then, Westall was taking enormous risks, justified only by his persuasiveness.

Over the ensuing thirty years Westall managed to turn H. R. Gough's austere, Cistercian-style fabric into one of London's most richly ornamented churches. But this was done at the expense of basic endowment, and relied on outsiders. With such small parishes, fashionable London churches were beginning by the end of the century to rely for their congregations on non-parishioners — a development helped by improvements in transport during the last thirty years of the Victorian period. The success of idiosyncratic churches like St Cuthbert's — or indeed the rather earlier St Jude's — foreshadowed a breakdown in the old parish tradition of local attendance and loyalties in London. The Methodists, with their Edwardian emphasis on central halls, learnt to accept this. Anglicans never did so, because the district system of churches and parishes was ingrained in the Church of England's history.

How typical is the example of Kensington? It is hard to say. But in St Pancras, one of the few parts of London where — thanks to the railway historian, the late Charles E. Lee — the pattern of Anglican church-building has been studied, the same story of irrational, competitive, mid-Victorian church-extension emerges.[25]

St Pancras remained one vast administrative parish until 1847, though with a proliferating number of district churches as its population surged towards 150,000. In the previous year, Thomas Dale replaced the conservative James Moore as vicar. He immediately set about implementing Peel's Act of 1842, which allowed him to appoint clergy before a church was built. He set up the St Pancras Church Extension Fund, picked four clergymen, and gave them autonomous districts in which to form parishes and build churches. One of his appointments Dale described thus:

> I had an unexpected visit from the Rev. David Laing, who at once with his characteristic frankness and decision said to me, 'I hear that you are meditating the formation of several districts in your great parish; if you are disposed to appoint me to one of them, I will work it.' My answer, based on previous knowledge of the person with whom I had to deal was, 'If you will work it, I will certainly appoint you to a district.'[25]

The upshot was that Laing took on the Chalk Farm district, and promptly built most of Holy Trinity, Haverstock Hill (1849–50). Unable to complete it, and having 'incurred personal responsibility for a very considerable sum of money', he had to resign in 1857 and accept a more lucrative, less onerous, City living.

As in Kensington, further churches were in due course built and smaller parishes lopped off and then subdivided out of Dale's original four districts of St Pancras. Some were officially promoted from the mother church; others (like St Mary Magdalene's, Munster Square, and St Martin's, Gospel Oak) were the fruits of individual initiative. Once autonomy had been granted to a district, what happened within it was hard for the old parish church to control. Before about 1875, no attempt to limit the number of new foundations or impose a realistic system seems to have been made. It was largely a matter of chance and whim. No wonder, therefore, that of the twenty-seven new Anglican churches built in St Pancras during the nineteenth century, only ten survive in their original use, many by the skin of their teeth.

Sometimes, indeed, the frenetic church-building of the 1860s and 1870s impeded other work, such as the relief of the poor. In Greenwich, for instance, three evangelical clergymen banded together in 1864 to build the church of St Paul's, Devonshire Drive. W. M. Teulon produced the requisite pretty drawing [**5**] and the works began, minus the tower. By the time of completion there was a heavy debt, for the clearance of which insistent appeal was made to the locality. Among the arguments used was that the 'chronic distress' from which working-class Greenwich was suffering during the slump of 1866 could only be addressed once the church-building liabilities had been met.[27] As so often, the tower was never built. Contemplating the redundant ragstone lump in Devonshire Drive today, one is bound to wonder whether all the earnest effort was worth while.

A well-documented instance of the 'go-it-alone' spirit that pervaded Anglican church-extension in London at this time is the case of St Jude's, Mildmay Grove, on the border between Islington and Stoke Newington. A small, pew-renting church and schools had been efficiently built here in 1854–55 as offshoots of St Paul's, Balls Pond Road. Then a charismatic evangelical, Revd William Pennefather, bumped up the congregations in the late 1860s. There began to be talk of an enlargement. The seatholders met and debated how it might be financed; they were divided between a subscription list which should go to regular attenders and visitors alike, or a 'weekly offertory from pew to pew', or some other form of 'systematic giving'. A self-financed enlargement on a handsome scale, Pennefather and his flock hoped, would help cut the increasingly irksome links with the mother church in Balls Pond Road. Yet the truth was that local money was not remotely available to the amount required, and Pennefather was very choosy about accepting grants. The 'Bishop of London's Fund' (one of Blomfield's inventions) was the obvious place to apply. But Pennefather would have none of it, objecting that

> they gave to all churches indiscriminately. A grant had just been made of £1,000 for a new church in St Matthias district and they had subscribed to two churches in Shoreditch, where the most extreme ritual was practised. Many subscribers had paid towards building churches to have the Gospel privileges preached and taught when virtually it was the doctrines of the Church of Rome. On a previous occasion he had ... waited on the then Bishop of London, when

5] W. M. Teulon, design for St Paul's Devonshire Drive, Greenwich. Advertisement for a fund-raising bazaar, 1866. Characteristically, the tower was never built

> the Bishop had requested him to have a collection in the church on the same day as at all the other churches, and he told him he could not ask his congregation to subscribe, neither did he want to have Romish doctrines circulated.[28]

So the fund-raisers were obliged to fall back on the device of exploring a loan from an insurance company secured, as at St Matthias in Kensington, on their much-esteemed pastor's life. The parish embarked in 1870 upon a virtual rebuilding of St Jude's with less than half the cost promised and no formal guarantees. They were saved from difficulties only because, with the work well advanced, Pennefather himself agreed to give £1,000 — at much 'personal sacrifice'. From today's standpoint, it is hard to appreciate the sacrifice, for the enlarged St Jude's was principally a monument to the ambitious vicar himself, who died soon afterwards, in 1873. The church still flourishes, but its aisles have been taken out of use, leaving it about the same size as it was before the overweening reconstruction was undertaken [**6**].

After 1875 there was some return all over London to a more thoughtful programme of church-extension. South of the river, the lack of a diocesan focus on London made things difficult; most of south London was in the Diocese of Winchester and was then transferred to Rochester, before ending up in the new Diocese of Southwark, only formed in 1905 when metropolitan church-building was on the wane. North of the river, the Diocese of London, in partnership with the Ecclesiastical Commissioners, went back to Blomfieldian efforts at redistributing resources. In particular, there was the anomaly of the City churches. The policy of closing City churches, inaugurated in 1860, was increasingly tied in with attempts to use their wealth to build churches in less favoured suburbs. Several such new churches were designed by Ewan Christian and retained the old dedications.[29] Regrettable though the closures may have been from the antiquarian standpoint, the campaign represented a certain rationality and a return to the idea of centrally guided church-extension. The previous generation of churchmen and architects, who had done well out of the private enterprise church-building system, opposed it not so much on grounds of vandalism but because it meant, in G. E. Street's words, 'making our ancestors' piety and liberality pay for building and endowing churches which we, with all our increased wealth, think we cannot afford to erect.'[30]

The basic free-enterprise system of parochial subdivision continued in London down to the First World War, but it was pursued with greatly decreased zeal. New in the last years of the century were the semi-secular mission buildings, built (often by outside middle-class institutions like public schools, Oxbridge colleges and Inns of Court) not only in the East End but also in the centre, south and west of London, and the growing number of parish halls. Their considerable social success was proof, if proof were still needed, that a church by itself was a weak lure for the urban masses. By the end of the century, it was common knowledge that church attendances, never as high as had been hoped — even in middle-class districts and in the peak period of the Anglican revival — were permanently down. The church-building boom was over. The years of

6] St Jude's, Mildmay Grove, Islington. Interior in 1993. The church has now shrunk back almost to its original size of 1855, the aisles added by the ambitious Revd William Pennefather in 1871 having been sealed off

difficulty for the copious and grand churches created over the previous eighty years had set in.

The Victorian Church of England is too often thought of, most of all perhaps by those who see it through the lens of its architectural masterpieces, as robust, expansive and assured. In truth, even the most spendid of its urban monuments were raised against a background of frailty, sometimes almost of fantasy. This was especially true during the mid-Victorian years, when private-enterprise methods of financing multiplied the number of London's churches far beyond ascertainable demand. The ambitious architecture of so many of these churches stands for more than a heroic Puginism, a public endorsement of renewed Christian faith and values. Consciously or not, their assertiveness was also competitive. But it was purchased at the expense of a secure future.

By building all these new urban parish churches, the Victorians hoped to emulate their medieval forebears. It is true that the old churches which they admired were as many, even more, in number. But they were accretive, evolutionary and — with exceptions — externally more restrained. Most important, they were the products of a polity in which the Church played an integrated role that could not be re-established in the nineteenth century. Endowments, donations, the compulsion of attendance and the proliferation of the religious orders gave the medieval parish church a function and a social plausibility which the nineteenth-century Church of England simply could not match.

Compared to the urban church-builders of medieval London, the Victorians enjoyed greater wealth, clearer professional organisation, better technology for building fast, and more settled social conditions in which to do so. They can hardly be censured for careering ahead with such speed. London and our other towns and cities would be immeasurably impoverished without the money, energy and artistry lavished upon the new churches. But that work was done against the backdrop of a dubious and divided religious present — Matthew Arnold's ebbing 'sea of faith' — and a wholly uncertain future. 'Will the restoration of the body of the Church to its original possessors really win back the alienated masses to the Church?', asked the Free and Open Church Association in the 1870s. 'The reply is, Firstly, *time will show* ... Secondly, even if the *Remedy* does not succeed, it is the proper one to use.'[31] On such imprudent assumptions was Victorian urban church-building premised. From their different perspectives, churchmen and those who care about architecture are still trying to pick up the pieces today. They will do so successfully only if they understand that fragmentation, competition and free enterprise are no more the answer now than they ever have been. As our urban churches decay and the future of the Church of England looks bleaker, an enlightened national system for dealing with these buildings is more than ever required.

Notes

1 A. B. Webster, *Joshua Watson: The Story of a Layman*, London, 1954.
2 A fuller account of the rebuilding of St John-at-Hackney appears in *Hackney Terrier*, no. 28, Autumn 1992.
3 F. H. W. Sheppard, *Local Government in St Marylebone 1688–1835*, London, 1958, pp. 245–74.
4 Charles E. Lee, *St Pancras Church and Parish*, London, 1955, pp. 37–43.
5 William Wordsworth, *Ecclesiastical Sketches*, London, 1822, 'Ecclesiastical Sonnets', XXXVIII, 'New Churches'.
6 Webster, *Joshua Watson*, chapter 5, and M. H. Port, *Six Hundred New Churches*, London, 1961, especially appendix 1; see also Gerald Lawrence Carr, *The Commissioners' Churches of London 1818–1836*, unpublished Ph.D. thesis, University of Michigan, 1976.
7 Alfred Blomfield (ed.), *A Memoir of Charles James Blomfield*, 2 vols, London, 1863, I, pp. 206–7; see also Geoffrey Best, *Temporal Pillars*, Cambridge, 1964, pp. 297ff.

8 Blomfield, *Blomfield*, I, pp. 217–18.
9 *Metropolis Churches Fund Report*, London, 1854; Best, *Temporal Pillars*, pp. 400–3.
10 Blomfield, *Blomfield*, I, p. 237.
11 James Sutherland Cotton, 'William Cotton', in *DNB*, Blomfield, *Blomfield*, I, p. 242; *Metropolis Churches Fund Report*, pp. 82–3.
12 *Metropolis Churches Fund Report*, appendix IV.
13 See for examples, John Allan, *Berthold Lubetkin*, London, 1992, pp. 317–21; Colin Ward, 'Bethnal Green: a museum of housing' in *Housing: An Anarchist Approach*, London, 1976; Michael Young and Peter Willmott, *Family and Kinship in East London*, London, 1957; Susan Beattie, *A Revolution in London Housing: LCC Housing Architects and their Work 1893–1914*, London, 1980.
14 Quoted by Basil F. L. Clarke, *The Parish Churches of London*, London, 1966, p. 160.
15 Blomfield, *Blomfield*, I, p. 243.
16 A copy of this letter is pasted in the back of the copy of the *Metropolis Churches Fund Report* at the Tower Hamlets Local History Library, Bancroft Road, London.
17 William Sinclair (ed.), *Thirty-Two Years of the Church of England 1842–1874: the Charges of Archdeacon Sinclair*, London, 1876, p.v.
18 *Survey of London*, XLI, London, 1983, pp. 112–17.
19 The following account is based on the author's analysis of the individual Kensington churches in *Survey of London*, XLII, 1986, chapter 23.
20 *The Free and Open Church Movement: An Appeal to Members of the Church of England*, London, n.d., p. 21.
21 *The London Free and Open Church Association*, Tenth Annual Report, 1875–76.
22 *Survey of London*, XLI, pp. 235–6.
23 *Church Bells*, 11 October 1879, p. 530; Greater London Record Office, P84/CUT/84.
24 Lambeth Palace Library, Church Commissioners file 62750.
25 Lee, *St Pancras*, chapter 9.
26 Lee, *St Pancras*, pp. 57–8.
27 GLRO, P78/PAU1/22 and 24.
28 St Jude's, Mildmay Grove, *Church Repair Minute Book*, GLRO P83/JUD/66/1, on which this whole paragraph is based.
29 The Union of City Benefices Act of 1860 cleared the way for a policy of demolishing unwanted City churches. The following suburban London churches designed by Ewan Christian were subsidised with money from their sites: St Anthony, Nunhead (1877–78); Holy Trinity, Dalston (1878–79); St Dionis, Parsons Green (1884–85); St Thomas, Finsbury Park (1888–89); St Olave, Woodberry Down (1893–94). There may have been others.
30 T. F. Bumpus, *London Churches Ancient and Modern*, first edition, London, 1883, p. 51; the text was extensively rewritten for the two-volume second edition.
31 *Free and Open Church Movement … Appeal*, p. 21.

Chapter 2 · Chris Brooks

Building the rural church: money, power and the country parish

At the end of the Napoleonic War, the United Kingdom was primarily a rural nation, with only some 20 per cent of its people living in urban concentrations. The great bulk of the country's wealth was in agriculture; the agrarian sector of the economy was by far the largest single employer; the landed aristocracy held a virtual monopoly of political power; and, in England, the national Church was essentially a rural Church. A century later, when Kitchener was thinking of the population from which he would enlist his new armies, nearly 80 per cent of it was in cities. Industry and commerce drove the national economy, and agriculture was frozen in the aftermath of the great winter of depression that had set in in the 1870s. The landed interest, which had been long, if luxuriously, on the wane, had entered suddenly into the bitterness of eclipse; the years between 1910 and 1921 saw the breakup of the great estates and the largest transfer of land ownership in England since the dissolution of the monasteries.[1]

In the early twentieth-century cities the presence of Anglicanism — its many hundreds of new churches, its slum missions, its additional curates, its coal and blanket charities — witnessed to the sustained effort of the Anglican revival of the previous seventy years. At the same time, however, the Church of England retained essentially intact all its country churches and with them the ancient patchwork of rural parishes that still spread across all that England that was not yet under bricks and mortar. Moreover, throughout Victoria's reign, those country churches had been transformed — repaired, embellished, refitted, restored and rebuilt in their thousands. Yet this transformation, unlike that effected for the urban Church, had taken place in a context of overall decline. By 1901, Mingay has concluded, 'the old cohesion of the countryside was breaking up'.[2]

For the first forty years of the nineteenth century rural populations had everywhere increased; not as much as those in cities, but steeply enough. In the census of 1851, Wiltshire, without any large urban settlement, became the first county to report a decline in its population. Ten years later decline was evident in all the southern counties; by the 1870s it was affecting every rural area in England.[3] In the last thirty years of the century, to the grim accompaniment of the great agrarian depression, the depopulation of rural England turned into something that at times seemed like headlong evacuation.[4] Alongside this process, the rural parish was steadily losing political power. In 1830 the parish was the primary unit of local government in the countryside, its vestry empowered to raise a variety of monies through local rates and responsible for the maintenance of the parish church, poor law relief, a substantial part of elementary education, policing, the repair of public bridges and highways, and even sanitation. By the end of the century, successive legislative changes had removed all these responsibilities apart from that of looking after the parish church, and that had become a voluntary undertaking for which no general rate on the parish could be levied.

In such a context, what was the nature and purpose of the process of cultural production — here taking 'cultural' to include religious expression and practice — that created, or recreated, the country church? What did all the physical changes to the parish church mean? Who paid for them, and why? And how far was physical change a token of a more profound social and cultural transformation? One of the reasons such questions are difficult to answer is that every parish and its church was different — as sociologists of nineteenth-century religion have recognised.[5] As a result, enquiry can only be pursued satisfactorily when the details of vestry minutes, churchwardens' accounts, parish correspondence, family papers and local newspaper reports are set against the assertions and generalisations of national sources.

I am going to look in detail at what happened to rural parish churches in south-east Devon, one of the counties that J. H. Clapham considered as exhibiting 'maximum rusticity', with over 60 per cent of its male population engaged in agriculture in 1851.[6] I make no claim that this area is in some way representative of Victorian rural England as a whole; rather it is illustrative, and I will be using comparative material from elsewhere to contextualise such conclusions as I reach. My illustrative area [**7**] stretches from Exeter and the estuary of the Exe eastward to the borders of Dorset and north-eastward to Somerset. The region is one of considerable geographical variety, bounded to the north by the Blackdown Hills — described somewhat theatrically in White's county directory as 'a dreary mountainous ridge'[7] — and to the south by the sea coast, where 'the climate … in the months of July and August', according to C. G. Harper in 1907, 'resembles the moist and enervating heat of the great Palm House in Kew Gardens'.[8] Between the savage hills and the sweltering coast is some of the best farmland in the county, particularly over the western half of the area, known in the last century as the Vale of Exeter.

The region's economic development in the nineteenth century was diverse. Exeter grew steadily from a population of something over 17,000 in 1801 to nearly 50,000 in 1914, and its suburbanising impact on surrounding parishes — though by no means uniform — may be

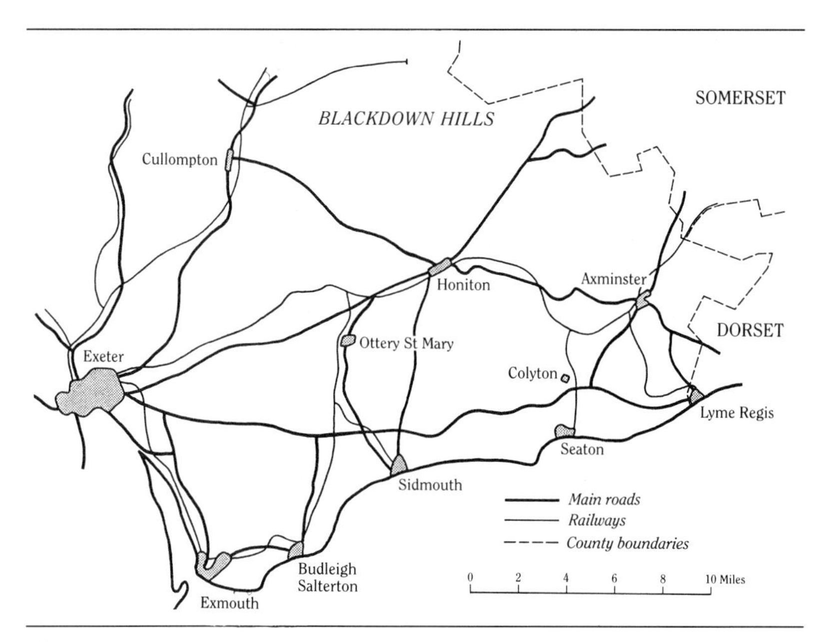

7] South-east Devon in 1900: towns and principal routes

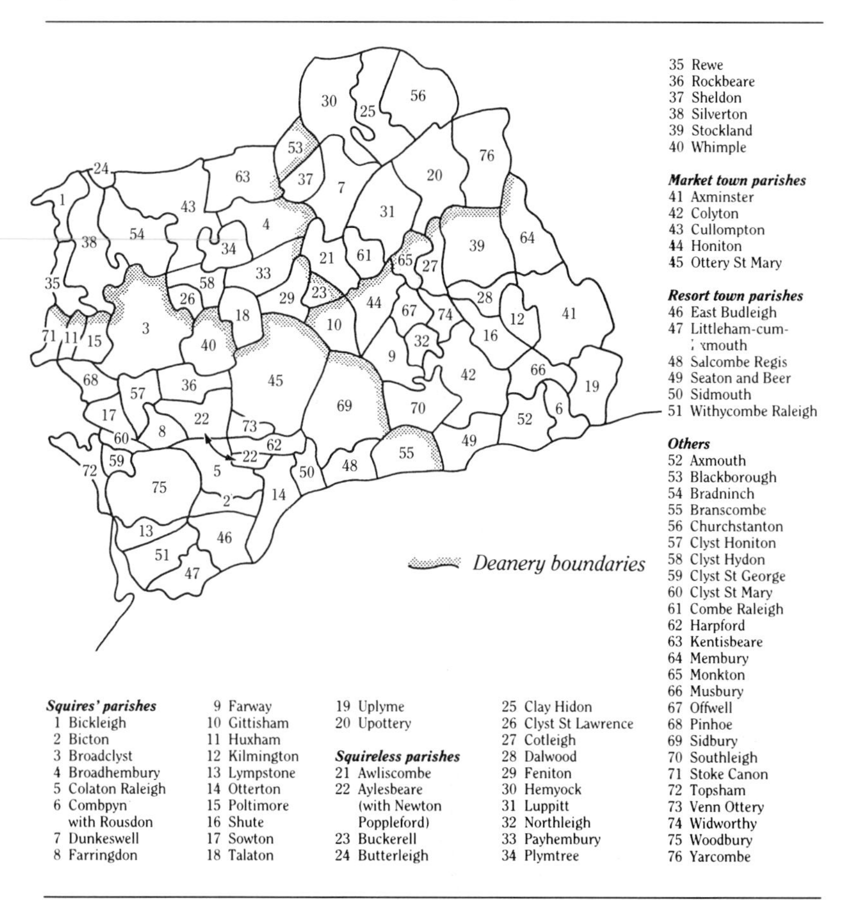

8] Nineteenth-century parishes and deaneries in south-east Devon traced through much of the period, particularly from the 1880s. The five inland market towns — Cullompton, Ottery St Mary, Honiton, Axminster, and the considerably smaller Colyton — experienced population growth throughout the first half of the century, though only Axminster sustained this in the second half. Along the coast the story was very different, with Exmouth, Budleigh Salterton, Sidmouth and Seaton all growing into resort towns. Meanwhile, from the 1850s onwards, virtually every exclusively agricultural parish was depopulated, particularly after the onset of agrarian depression in the 1870s. Rates of loss in excess of 35 per cent over the second half of the century were common, and a large majority of parishes had fewer people living in them in 1901 than they had had in 1801.

The area comprises seventy-six parishes divided between four deaneries[9] [**8**]. Aylesbeare deanery, the largest, covered the south-west of the survey area; Honiton, the next in size, the south-east; Plymtree and Dunkeswell divided up the parishes of the Blackdown Hills between them. The 1851 religious census shows this to have been a region of strong Anglican support, with over 70 per cent of all church attendances in the western part of the area, and between 55 per cent and 70 per cent in the rest.[10] The nineteenth-century history of these south-east Devon parishes and their churches could be told in purely ecclesiastical terms — the view from the clergy desk as it were — or it could be told, for its buildings at least, purely in architectural and stylistic terms. I intend to avoid such purity of approach and put the story together in another way. From my point of view, the pattern, chronological and geographical, of rural church-building — indeed any church-building — was determined neither by the movement of ecclesiastical thought nor by changes in architectural style. Rather, the determining forces lay in the economic relationships of rural England and their place within the dynamics of the Victorian economy as a whole. For those economic relationships shaped the structures of social and political power at the levels of the nation, the region and ultimately the parish, and thus set the terms within which cultural production — for my purpose, the production of the country church and its contents — could happen.

The parish, to risk stating the obvious, is a geographical unit. In the early nineteenth century, as I said earlier, it was also an administrative unit, the principal agent of local government. The administrative effectiveness of the vestry, particularly in the realm of social control, depended on the particular geographical — or, more accurately, socio-geographical — identity of the parish. The Church of England was at its most dominant in relatively small parishes, like those of south and south-east England; an area of much more than 2,500 acres began to pose problems of access and control. The population also had to be of manageable size, so that the parson, helped by the social-visiting of his wife and daughters, might reasonably be expected to know every family. 'An acquaintance with the individual character and circumstances of his flock is of great importance', urged a manual of 1832.[11] Traditionally, a flock of 640 parishioners, say 120 families, was thought about right.[12] The third factor, and the most important managerially, was the pattern of land ownership. It was the Victorians themselves, discussing the operation of the Poor Law, who first made the distinction between 'close' or 'closed' parishes and 'open' parishes: closed parishes were those in which the land was largely or entirely owned by an individual, or, in moderated form, by a small number of landowners who could act in concert; open parishes were characterised by a fragmented pattern of landholding, with no dominant owner.[13] The Anglican establishment like closed parishes. Here the vestry system made possible a monopoly of social power in the hands of the parish's secular and spiritual proprietors. In 'the vast majority of country parishes', wrote a liberally inclined west-country cleric in the 1890s, 'the squire, the parson, and the large farmers form a "ring" which controls all parochial affairs ... This ring practically *is* the vestry ... And the parson is *ex officio* chairman.'[14] Crucial to the effectiveness of such a system, as the Church itself recognised, was the residence or otherwise of the squire — be he the lord of the manor or simply the principal landowner. It was not enough that he should merely possess the land; in order to lead, influence, and if necessary coerce, he needed to live either in the parish itself or near at hand in a neighbouring parish. His absence, from the Anglican point of view, 'was bad for the parish, bad for the rural church, bad for the parson'.[15] If the residence of the landed interest was essential so also, of course, was the residence of the clergyman himself. In 1810 an astonishing 47 per cent of Anglican clergy did not reside or do duty in their parishes; that this figure had been cut to less than 10 per cent by 1850 is a measure of the organisational effort that went into the early Victorian Anglican revival.[16] The social and political object of it all was the creation of the dependent parish, structured on the reciprocal basis of hierarchy and deference, paternalistically ruled by the alliance of squire and parson with, as its twin centres, the big house and the church.

From the sample area of south-east Devon [**9**], I have selected twenty parishes where, through all or much of the nineteenth century, there was a squire who was either resident or who lived sufficiently near at hand — usually in an adjacent parish — to retain his social ascendancy. In most cases the squire was also lord of the manor; in all cases land ownership was concentrated either individually, normally in the hands of the squire himself, or in the hands of a few substantial proprietors. Against this group I have selected twenty other parishes where there was no resident squire; where the lordship was lapsed, fragmented, or owned institutionally; and where landownership was divided. The parishes in each group are deliberately varied in size and in geographical position, though squireless parishes form the majority on and around the Blackdown Hills to the north, while squires' parishes predominate in the south-west of the region. Parishes that do no fall clearly into either category have been excluded, as also have the five market-town parishes and those that saw significant growth as coastal resorts. All forty of the selected parishes were overwhelmingly agricultural, examples of 'maximum rusticity'.

Between 1800 and 1914 the pattern of demographic change in the two categories of parish is markedly similar [**10**]. The total population of the squireless parishes peaked at nearly 12,000 in the early 1840s, that of the

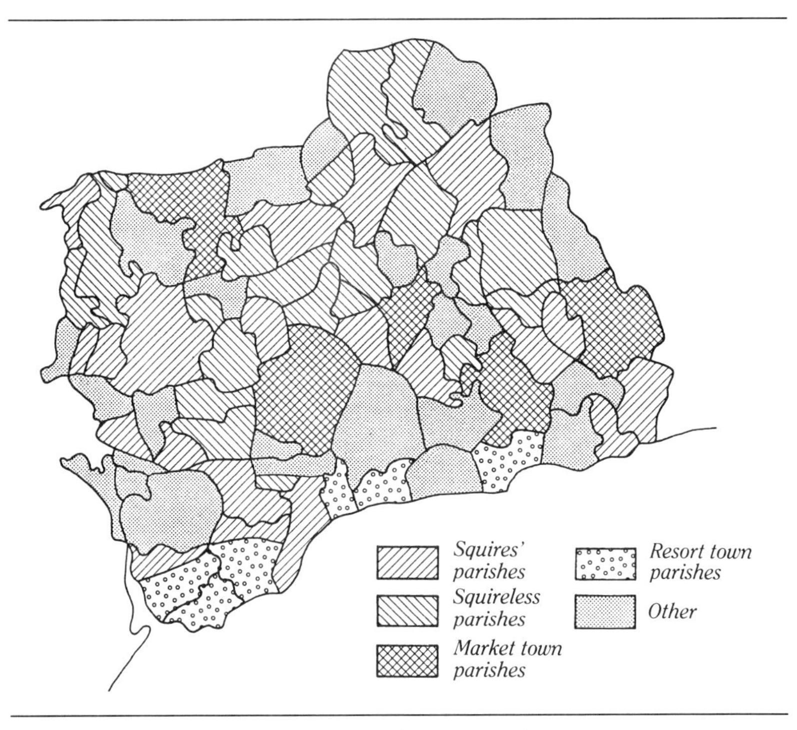

9] Parish types in south-east Devon in the nineteenth century

squires' parishes peaking at 13,000 around 1851. Depopulation followed at somewhat different rates down to 1880, after which there was steep decline in both groups. Against this demographic pattern we can set the decennial rates of church-building, restoration and repair in the two categories [**11**].[17] It is immediately clear that more church-building and restoration were undertaken, and sustained more consistently over a longer period, in parishes where the squire was resident than in squireless parishes; between 1800 and 1880 there were 45 per cent more programmes of work in the former group than in the latter. In both types of parish, however, there are marked discrepancies between church-building activity and demographic changes. Two features stand out. Firstly, the response to the rapidly increasing populations of the first half of the century was slow in coming. Secondly, most church-building and restoration took place in the second half of the century, particularly in the 1860s and 1870s, by which time parish populations were everywhere in steep decline. Clearly then, factors other than demographic change were in play, and these emerge when we look more closely at the different stages of the building effort in the two categories of parish, and at the sources of funding.

Three phases are discernible, their basis both demographic and economic: phase 1 is 1801–50, the period of population growth; phase 2 is 1851–80, the Golden Age of the Victorian High Farming, terminated by the advent of the agrarian slump in the last years of the 1870s; phase 3 is 1881–1911, the years of the agrarian depression and its immediate aftermath, and of sharpest depopulation. Figures 12–17 plot the three phases

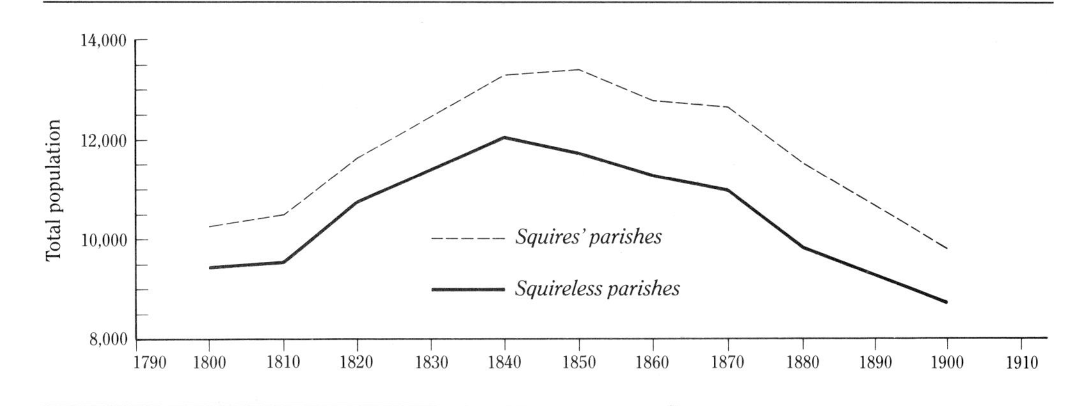

10] Demographic change in sample parishes, 1800–1900

for the two categories, with rates of population change in the individual parishes shown in descending order and set against church-building activity in each. The source of funding, where it is known, is indicated by hatching and falls into three categories: funding by the parish; by a local oligarchy; and by an individual or family. These were the principal sources throughout rural England in the nineteenth century, though to them must be added institutional funding from patrons such as the Ecclesiastical Commissioners or the Oxbridge colleges — though this was of little significance in the parishes examined here.[18]

Traditionally, repairs to the body of the parish church were the responsibility of the parishioners, while the chancel was maintained by the tithe-holder — either the incumbent himself or the patron of the living. The parish raised money through the church rate, levied at so much in the pound on all occupiers of property. Because the rate was compulsory and payable by everybody, whether Anglican, Roman Catholic, nonconformist or straight indifferent, it was a target of protest at a national level, and refusal to levy a rate was increasingly common in urban areas. It seems to have aroused little active opposition in this part of rural Devon,[19] though it was used sparingly and the desire to keep the rate low and repairs to a

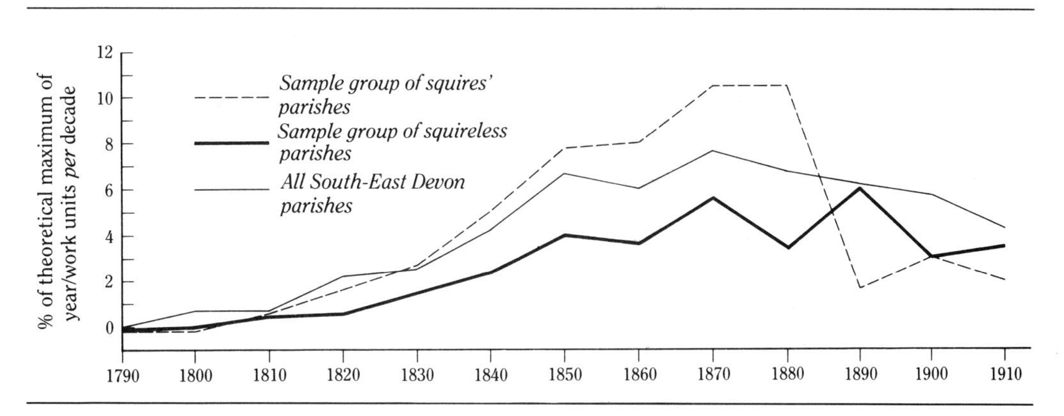

11] Decennnial rates of church-building and restoration in south-east Devon, 1790–1910

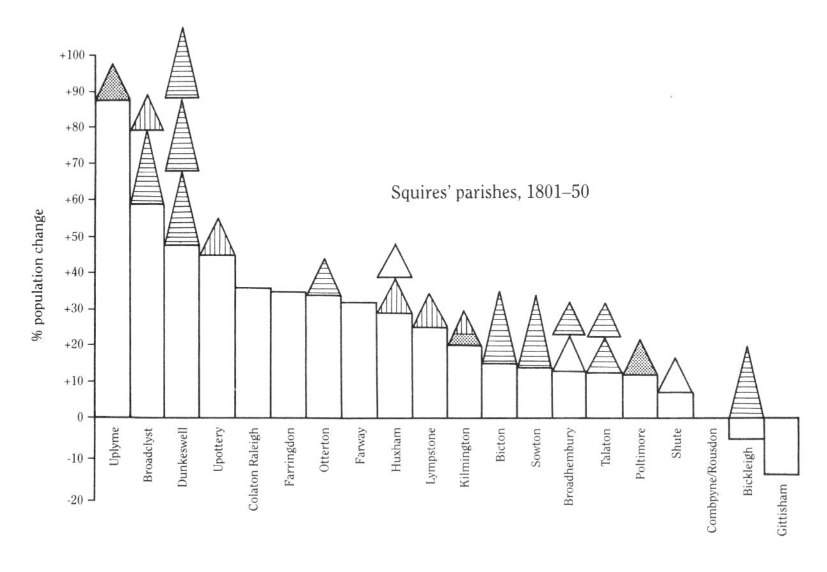
Squires' parishes, 1801–50
% population change
+100
+90
+80
+70
+60
+50
+40
+30
+20
+10
0
-10
-20
Uplyme
Broadclyst
Dunkeswell
Upottery
Colaton Raleigh
Farringdon
Otterton
Farway
Huxham
Lympstone
Kilmington
Bicton
Sowton
Broadhembury
Talaton
Poltimore
Shute
Combpyne/Rousdon
Bickleigh
Gittisham

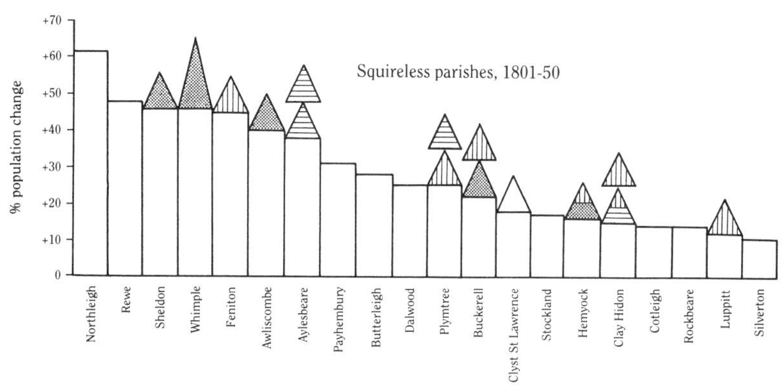
Squireless parishes, 1801-50
% population change
+70
+60
+50
+40
+30
+20
+10
0
Northleigh
Rewe
Sheldon
Whimple
Feniton
Awliscombe
Aylesbeare
Payhembury
Butterleigh
Dalwood
Plymtree
Buckerell
Clyst St Lawrence
Stockland
Hemyock
Clay Hidon
Cotleigh
Rockbeare
Luppitt
Silverton

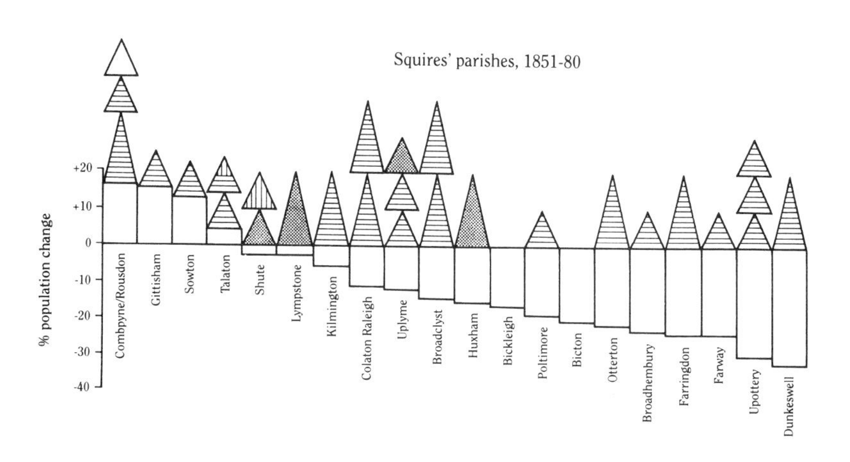
Squires' parishes, 1851-80
% population change
+20
+10
0
-10
-20
-30
-40
Combpyne/Rousdon
Gittisham
Sowton
Talaton
Shute
Lympstone
Kilmington
Colaton Raleigh
Uplyme
Broadclyst
Huxham
Bickleigh
Poltimore
Bicton
Otterton
Broadhembury
Farringdon
Farway
Upottery
Dunkeswell

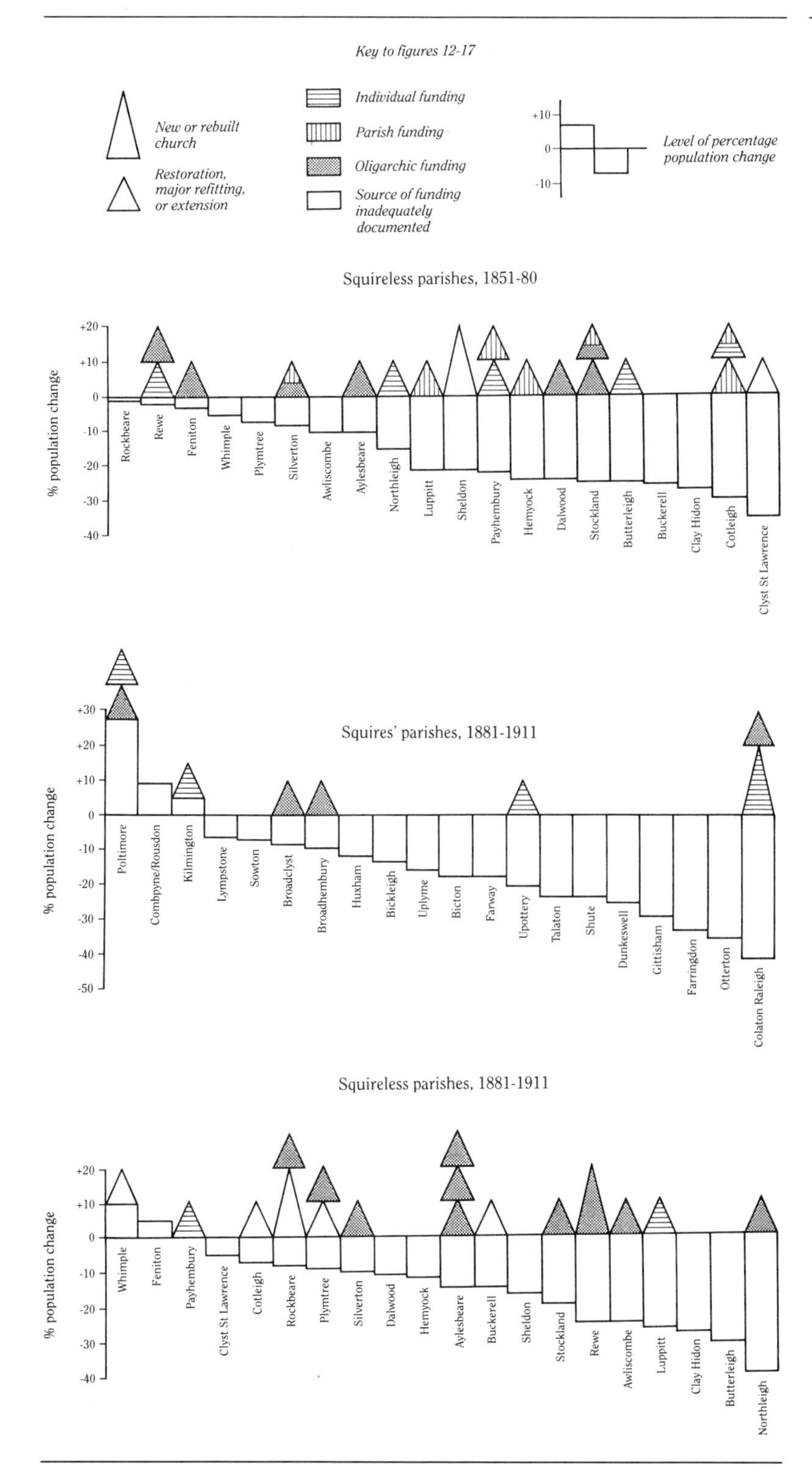

12–17] Church-building and restoration, and demographic change, in sample group of squires' and squireless parishes, 1801–1911

minimum is evident throughout parish records. In 1868 the compulsory church rate was abolished and replaced by a so-called voluntary rate; while in existence, though, the rate was a genuinely distributive source of funding. The most common mechanism for oligarchic funding was the subscription list, often cited in newspaper accounts as an example of voluntary donation by a pious parish, but almost always dominated by a handful of local owners. Individual funding came principally from the squire or the incumbent, often assisted by their immediate families. Significantly, if unsurprisingly, this category was dominated by those squires who were both lords of the manor and patrons of the living.

Basic changes in how church-building and restoration were paid for during the century are apparent when the three phases are compared. In the 1801–50 phase [**12**, **13**], the sources of funding are mixed in both types of parish, and include programmes financed through the church rate. Nevertheless, in the squires' group individual funding accounted for 63 per cent of those schemes for which the source of finance is known, while oligarchic funding played a significant role in the squireless parishes, paying for 32 per cent of the work undertaken. In phase 2, between 1851 and 1880, building and restoration in the squires' parishes reached a peak [**14**]: 80 per cent of the schemes were individually funded, 65 per cent of that total by the squires themselves. Moreover, in the case of the 1862–65 rebuilding of Lympstone to Edward Ashworth's designs, the oligarchic funding was dominated by the lord of the manor, Sir Trayton Drake;[20] and at the little church of Huxham, rebuilt in two stages in 1865 and 1871–72, Lord Poltimore was a major contributor to the subscription list.[21] In this context, parish-derived funding virtually ceased: the sole example was Talaton, where a rate was levied to help offset Ashworth's extension and partial rebuilding of the church in 1859–60.[22] Meanwhile, in the squireless parishes [**15**], though the sources of finance continued to be mixed, oligarchic funding increased in importance, accounting for some 40 per cent of those programmes for which details are known. With the abolition of the church rate in 1868, distributively-sourced funding in the parish ceased and there were no schemes financed by a voluntary rate. In the final phase, in the recession-hit years after the late 1870s, the rate of church-building and restoration in the squires' parishes fell dramatically [**16**]. What is more, 50 per cent of the little work that was done was oligarchically funded, sometimes without the squire even having a major role. In 1894–96, for example, George Fellowes-Prynne restored the tower of Broadhembury church at a cost of nearly £600, several donations coming from the family of a former vicar, £50 from the Ecclesiastical Commissioners and £100 from a Mrs Locke, who does not seem even to have lived in the parish. The Drewe family, lords of the manor for generations and largely responsible for the restoration of the body of the church in the 1850s, made only minor contributions.[23] In the squireless parishes [**17**], by contrast, work continued more successfully, albeit at a somewhat reduced rate, and funding was now virtually monopolised by the subscription list: ten of the twelve schemes — nearly 85 per cent — where details of financing are known were oligarchically funded.

The relationship between these different funding patterns and demographic change can now be looked at in greater detail. Among the squires' parishes growing most quickly in the 1801–50 period, Uplyme was extended and provided with a new gallery by subscription,[24] and Upottery was reseated by parish rate,[25] both in 1826–27. In Dunkeswell parish a comprehensive building campaign was financed by the Simcoe family, who had acquired the Wolford estate, the lordship of the manor, and the patronage of the living around 1784.[26] An estate chapel was erected in 1802, the parish church in Dunkeswell village was rebuilt in 1816–17,[27] and a new church, All Saints' [**18**] designed by Ferrey[28] was built in 1842 for a hamlet clustered around the medieval ruins of Dunkeswell Abbey, near the northern boundary of the parish. Similarly responsive to demography was the church-extension prompted by the Acland family, whose Killerton estate dominated Broadclyst parish; the parish church was extensively refitted in the 1830s[29] and Sir Thomas Dyke Acland provided the sole funding for the ambitious estate chapel of All Saints, modelled on the Lady Chapel at Glastonbury and built in 1839–41 to the designs of Cockerell.[30] Among the squireless parishes with the fastest-growing populations, oligarchic funding produced galleries at Awliscombe in 1818,[31] a new aisle at Sheldon in 1835,[32] and John Hayward's rebuilding of Whimple church in 1845;[33] and an extension to Newton Poppleford, an extra-parochial chapel annexed to Aylesbeare, was individually financed in 1821.[34] Across both categories of parish, however, it is clear that the match between building work and population growth was far from consistent. Taking both groups together, half of the building schemes took place in parishes where populations increased by less than 25 per cent between 1801 and 1851, while half of the sixteen parishes where increases were in excess of 30 per cent saw no substantial work at all.

18] Benjamin Ferrey, All Saints', Dunkeswell, Devon, 1842

In the second and third phases depopulation dominated. Between 1851 and 1880 the four squires' parishes where the number of inhabitants actually increased all had programmes of work. What is far more striking, however, is the high level of church-building and restoration in parishes with declining populations. In Broadclyst (-15 per cent) the little medieval chapel of Columbjohn was restored in 1851 and a new chapel of ease built at Westwood in 1874, both being financed by members of the Troyte family, relatives of the Aclands.[35] In Otterton (-21 per cent) Louisa, Lady Rolle paid for Ferrey's rebuilding of the parish church in 1870–71 at a total cost of £12,000.[36] In the same year, John Garratt funded the rebuilding of Farringdon (-24 per cent) to the designs of William White,[37] whom he had employed between 1860 and 1864 in re-creating the house and chapel of Bishops Court on his estate in the neighbouring parish of Sowton.[38] And at Dunkeswell (-32 per cent) the last of the Simcoes, one of six sisters, left money towards the 1865 rebuilding of the parish church which her family had first rebuilt fifty years earlier.[39] Among the squireless parishes, all of which were depopulating in phase two, the disjunction between demographic change and work on churches is even more apparent: over 65 per cent of the programmes carried out were in parishes which lost more than 20 per cent of their population in the thirty years. After 1881 work in the squires' parishes, sporadic and dramatically curtailed, shows no overall pattern. At Poltimore, where the suburban expansion of Exeter brought about a population increase of nearly 30 per cent, a new aisle was added in 1883–84, funded by donations of which the largest was that of Lord Poltimore, who was peoples' warden as well as lord of the manor; in 1907 he defrayed all but £20 of the cost of restoring and underpinning the tower.[40] At the other extreme demographically, Colaton Raleigh parish, registering a 42 per cent decline in population on top of the 12 per cent of the previous three decades, received a new chapel of ease at Hawkerland in 1889, paid for by the Rolles,[41] and the church, largely rebuilt by Robert Medley Fulford in 1873–75, received a new vestry.[42] Although work in the squireless parishes held up in phase three, the funding provided by local oligarchies seems equally unrelated to demography. Churches that underwent major restoration for the first time in the century include Rockbeare (-8 per cent) in 1887–88,[43] Aylesbeare (-15 per cent) in 1896–97,[44] Stockland (-20 per cent) in 1888,[45] and Awliscombe (-25 per cent) in 1886–87.[46] There were even new chapels of ease; one at Marsh Green in Rockbeare parish built in 1896,[47] and another of 1887–88 in the hamlet of Upexe in Rewe parish, reconstructed by Fulford from the fragmentary remains of a medieval chapel at the expense of the incumbent and his friends.[48]

The key to negotiating the complex relationships between parish types, funding sources, demographic change, and the physical character of the churches themselves, seems to me to lie in the different ideologies that informed the different phases of church-building and restoration — ideologies that were themselves generated by the dynamics of economic and social change.

In phase one, the relatively large number of churches rebuilt and newly built in the squires' parishes is impressive: seven churches in only twenty parishes. Significantly, five of these seven — All Saints' Broadclyst, All Saints' Dunkeswell, and the parish churches of Bickleigh, Bicton and Sowton — date between 1838 and 1850, the early years of Anglican revival and the heroic age of the Cambridge Camden Society. That this did not happen merely spontaneously is demonstrated by a comparison with the development of church-building and restoration in the squire-dominated parishes of east and south-east Leicestershire.[49] As figure **19** shows, the sharp upward movement of building activity in the Devon parishes from the 1830s simply was not matched in the squires' area of Leicestershire. Instead there was a gradual rise to a sudden burst of activity in the 1860s and early 1870s, followed by an equally sudden fall. Remarkably little substantial work was initiated in the earlier phase: Cranoe was rebuilt 1847–49; Little Dalby was largely rebuilt at the very end of the period, in 1851; Horninghold was given a new suite of fittings in 1844, but otherwise left largely untouched. The aspirations of the Oxford Movement and ecclesiology, one might conclude, simply did not filter into the rectories and gun-rooms of east Leicestershire. A crucial factor in explaining this low level of activity was the extent to which the squires were absentees: according to David M. Thompson, 'only 10 per cent of Leicestershire villages had a resident squire'.[50] Morover, even where aspirations towards Anglican church-building existed in this area of rural Leicestershire, they did so without any co-ordinating social or cultural context. In south-east Devon, by contrast, that co-ordination existed.

The Exeter Diocesan Architectural Society had been founded in 1841, a sister society to the Cambridge Camden, and the first such organisation at diocesan level. Under its first secretary, John Medley, the Society's membership included not only clergy but also an impressive number of influential laymen whose wealth and status could be mobilised in support of the High Church cause in the diocese. The Society's architect was John Hayward, rapidly picking up patronage along with Puginian principles — with an importance for the success of his practice that is discussed in Martin Cherry's chapter on church-building and the local architect. It was Hayward who rebuilt Sowton in 1844–45, funded by John Garratt of Bishop's Court, an ex-Lord Mayor of London and relatively newly arrived as a Devon squire.[51] Hayward was almost certainly the architect of the rebuilding of Bickleigh in 1847–48,[52] largely financed by the Carew family, lords of the manor, patrons, and incumbents all at once. And he designed the lavish church of St Mary's, Bicton [**20**], rebuilt on a new site for Louisa, Lady Rolle in 1849–50.[53] All three families involved in these rebuildings included members of the Diocesan Architectural Society. What the Society was able to organise in south-east Devon was something like a programme of church-building and restoration aimed at restating clerical leadership in alliance with the secular authority of the resident gentry and aristocracy. Effectively this was the eighteenth-century partnership of the parson and the squire re-created — and reinvigorated — in the High Church mode of the early Victorian Anglican revival. The initial impact that this had upon the physical appearance of parish churches in

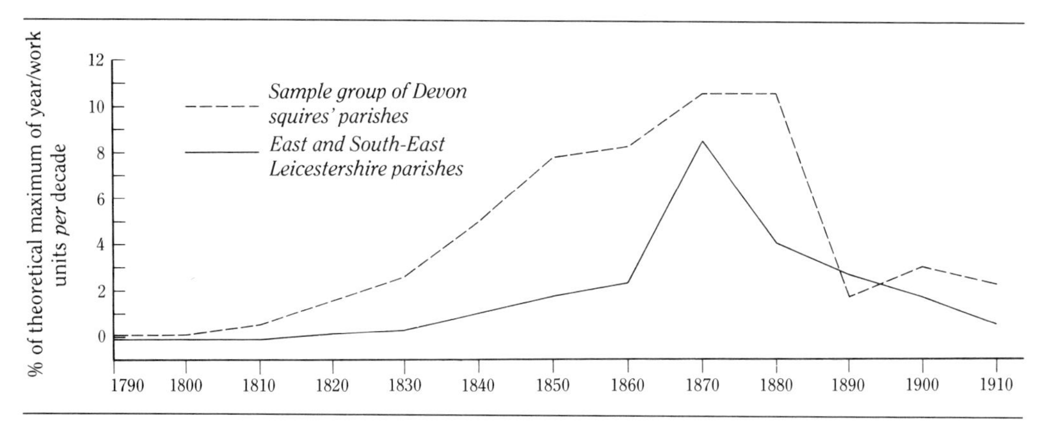

19] Decennial rates of church-building and restoration in squires' parishes in south-east Devon and in east and south-east Leicestershire, 1790–1910

the area is particularly evident when one charts the dates of chancel restorations, that key element of a High Church programme [**21**]. The precise theological complexion of these restorations varied, as did the membership of the Society itself: Bickleigh was conservative in its liturgical arrangements, for example, whereas Sowton was thoroughly Camdenian [**22**]. Nevertheless, all clearly belong within the High Church band of the Anglican spectrum. Pre-1850 chancel restorations, either within an existing fabric or as part of a rebuilding, are strikingly concentrated in the western half of the region, with a northern spur through the Blackdowns into the Simcoes' area of control. In these western parishes the Diocesan Architectural Society was at its most effective. Here there was easy access to the cathedral city, with its strong clerical establishment, its architects and its craftsmen. Here also were the estates, holdings and manorial lordships of many of the landed families whose members supported the Society: the Carews at Bickleigh, the Drewes at Broadhembury, the Bullers at Whimple, the Aclands at Broadclyst, the Garratts at Sowton, the Rolles at Bicton and in the surrounding parishes. As well as reanimating the traditional support of the landed interest, the Society could also bring the power of the new professional élite into its secular-clerical alliance. The Coleridge family,[54] in particular, led church-building and restoration in the large market town parish of Ottery St Mary, prompting the erection of new churches at Tipton in 1839–40,[55] West Hill in 1846,[56] and Alfington in 1849,[57] and largely funding the great restoration of the parish church by William Butterfield in 1849–50.[58]

The alliance forged between clergy and powerful laity in the diocese of Exeter, and the building campaign it initiated, co-ordinated and funded, were precisely what the Cambridge Camden Society was urging on Anglicanism nationally. Its model can be found in that most famous of early Victorian rural parish churches, Kilndown, in Kent. This was the pocket church of Alexander James Beresford Hope, lord of the manor, patron, landed magnate, and, from the late 1840s, the dominant force within the ecclesiological movement. Between 1840 and 1845 Hope transformed Kilndown, a recently-built but pre-Camdenian church, by means of a chancel refitting of intense, if crowded, sumptuousness, with woodwork by Carpenter, metalwork by Butterfield, and decorations by Willement.[59] What significance did Kilndown and its various Devon kindred have for contetemporaries? Firstly, they represented the resurgent mood of High Anglicanism made manifest; Oxford Movement and Camdenian thinking alike protested against secularisation and Erastianism by restating and emphasising all

20] John Hayward, St Mary's, Bicton, Devon, 1850–51

that was catholic, sacerdotal, and sacramental in Anglicanism. Nationally, as Gilbert has shown,[60] this resurgence was also a response to the encroachment of nonconformity, and Obelkevich has demonstrated the central importance of the confrontation at a local level in the Lincolnshire parishes he has studied.[61] In rural south-east Devon, however, inter-denominational rivalry does not seem to have been a major element in the Anglican building campaign. The expansionist strength of nonconformity lay with the militant evangelicalism that had followed in the train of Methodism, and this had relatively little impact in the country parishes of south-east Devon. Doubtless the hostility of some squires was a factor here; Lord Rolle, the largest of the Devon landowners, 'was particularly active against nonconformity'.[62] But the real determinant was economic. In the seventeenth century dissent had thrived in the small textile towns of east Devon; with the decline of the textile trade, 'the region's industrial centre of gravity moved westwards ... towards the mining areas of west Devon and Cornwall'.[63] It was in these parts of south-west England that nineteenth-century noncon-

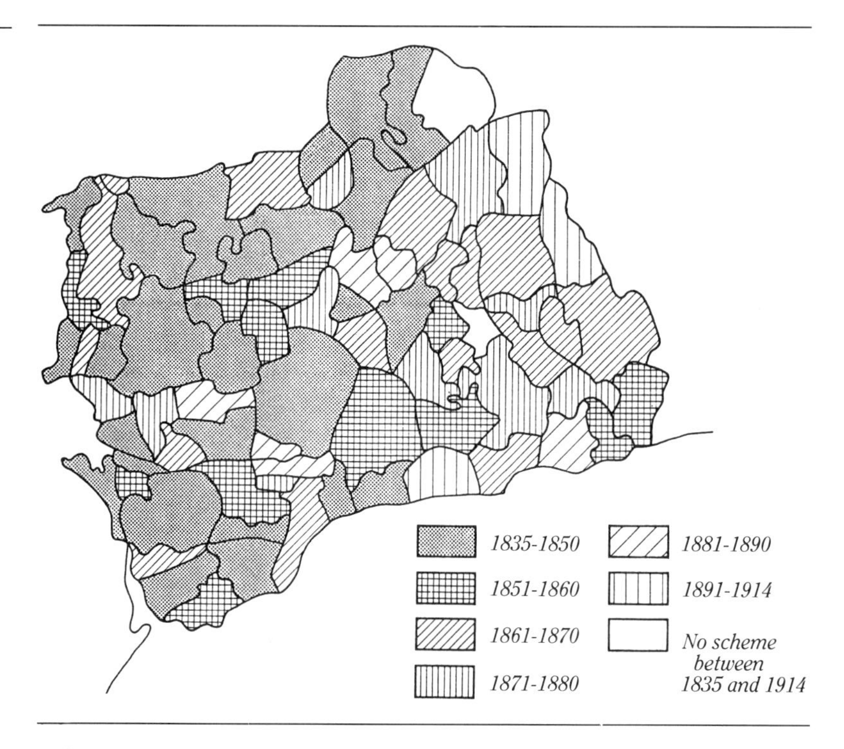

21] Dates of chancel restorations and rebuildings in south-east Devon

formity found sympathetic soil. The Old Dissent of east Devon suvived in and around towns like Axminster, Colyton and Honiton — but it was largely quiescent. The parsons and the squires were not, then, building against a vigorous nonconformist threat in the area. Nor, as has already been made clear, were they building simply to provide accommodation for an expanding rural population. Yet that expansion — or rather, its social and economic consequences — may well have spurred the building programme, for reasons that were ideological rather than straightforwardly practical. Squires' churches like Bicton and Sowton — or, indeed, Kilndown — were expensive, and their single-source funding was a direct assertion of wealth and local paramountcy. And, from the national viewpoint of the landed interest, these churches made their socio-political statement in the face of a restless and often unhappy countryside. Agricultural capitalism and demographic pressure had produced widespread distress and, intermittently, violence.[64] Although south-east Devon was generally quiet, Captain Swing's fiery fingers had touched southern districts of the county in 1830,[65] Tolpuddle was only a few miles over the Dorset border, and in 1847 bread riots brought yeomanry onto the streets of Exeter.[66] Because the parish church and the big house were the architectural embodiments of rural power, the restoration of churches was instinct with political meaning; it was a reaffirmation of the traditional means of social control in the countryside.

Such a meaning was inscribed on the church as part of the ideological transaction between the parish's empowered classes and their social infe-

22] John Hayward, St Michael's, Sowton, Devon, 1844–45. The sanctuary riors and dependents. But rural churches were also acquiring a new audience — a new cultural constituency as it were — whose powers of inscription were outside the immediate determination of parson or squire. Since the middle of the eighteenth century rural Britain in general, and highland Britain in particular, had increasingly been sought by lovers of the picturesque and sublime.[67] Imaginatively, the picturesque tourist was remaking the sequestered village and the rustic church as key items in the landscape of sensibility. 'These tourists, heaven preserve us!' exclaims Wordsworth's 'homely priest of Ennerdale' as early as 1800,[68] already exasperated by their leisured intrusions on the rural parish. In the first decades of the nineteenth century the growth of resort towns along the whole south Devon coast from Torbay to Lyme Bay, the development of suburban Exeter as a place of genteel and professional retirement, and the attempt to realise Dartmoor as a sublime asset like Snowdonia or the Lakes, were beginning to generate a new identity for the Devon countryside and the churches in it. That identity was created by and for people who were essentially outsiders, strangers to the rural scene they surveyed. For them the primary meanings of the parish church were aesthetic, anecdotal and antiquarian. And it was for and by them that the first generally accessible descriptions of the country churches were being written, no longer in the learned volumes of county histories, but in the popular guidebooks that began to pile up for every area of tourist Britain. Among the many that Davidson's *Bibliotheca Devoniensis*[69] lists for south and south-east Devon, there were six for Sidmouth and its neighbourhood alone published between 1810 and 1846. In the audience for such works was the new audience for the rural church, a constituency that was outside the historical orbit of the parochial establishment, but that would come to play a major part in the cultural shaping of the country church itself.

In the meantime, within the rural parishes themselves, the ascendancy of the squire and parson alliance, reaffirmed through the Anglican building programme of the late 1830s and 1840s, was consolidated and extended in the quarter-century or so after 1850. Class relations in the countryside generally improved in a context of sustained agricultural prosperity. Instead of the catastrophe predicted after the repeal of the Corn Laws, came the Golden Age of Victorian High Farming, the apparently triumphant vindication of capitalist agriculture, with its attendant deities of progress and improvement. Although, as we have seen, rural depopulation was growing in almost every parish, the landed interest appeared to have emerged into the second half of the century with undiminished status and economic power — at least at a local level. On the strong foundations of continuing agricultural profits, the squires could rebuild and restore their parish churches. In the squires' parishes of south-east Devon the intensity of the building campaign has already been noted. Between 1851 and 1880, in summary: seven out of the remaining seventeen medieval churches in the twenty parishes were rebuilt, and one earlier nineteenth-century rebuilding was done again; nine out of the other ten underwent at least one programme of restoration; three chapels of ease and one family chapel were built. In other parts of the country, the gentry stirred to similar activity. In north Devon, at the heart of his Stevenstone estate, Mark Rolle funded the rebuilding of St Giles in the Wood in 1862–63;[70] on his Taw Valley lands in mid-Devon the Earl of Portsmouth employed his regular estate architects, Clark and Holland, to enlarge and substantially rebuild the little church of Eggesford in 1867;[71] in the South Hams, on the Earl of Devon's manor of South Huish, the new church of Galmpton was built in 1868;[72] in the early 1870s, in north-east Devon, the eighteenth-century estate church of Filleigh was enlarged and the interior decorated by Lord Fortescue and his family.[73] As we saw earlier, it was the 1860s that brought the great surge of building activity in the parishes of the east Leicestershire squires. A difference from the ecclesiastical climate of south-east Devon is still evident, however, for the great bulk of the Leicestershire work was restoration, and rebuildings or new churches were, in comparison, rare. Major aristocratic estates, by contrast, could acquire a whole crop of rebuilt churches. In south-east Wiltshire, on the Trafalgar estate of Lord Nelson, T. H. Wyatt built Charlton church in 1851 as a substitute for the medieval church of Standlynch, which the Nelsons appropriated to their own use. Standlynch itself was extensively restored around 1860 by Butterfield, who also designed two other new churches for the estate, Landford in 1857–58 and Whiteparish in 1869.[74] The use of a single architect for work on a whole estate was not unusual; in Yorkshire Sir Tatton Sykes employed John Loughborough Pearson to build Hilston in 1862, and restore Kirkburn and Garton-on-the-Wolds, both in 1856–57, and Bishop Wilton in 1858–59.[75]

Sykes, as Jill Allibone has commented, 'considered the restoration and rebuilding of parish churches part of the general matter of estate improvement'.[76] The remark is a revealing one. Discussing developments in rural society in South Lindsey, Obelkevich has noted that traditional village feasts and festivals, largely suppressed as anarchic in the earlier decades of the century, reappeared in the 1850s and 1860s, paternalistically managed by local landowners and clergy. Adapting Tönnies' classic distinction between *Gemeinschaft* — traditionary, pre-capitalist community — and *Gesellschaft* — capitalism's wage-based class society — Obelkevich interprets these reintroductions as instances of pseudo-*Gemeinschaft*: the assumption of fellow feeling and identity of interest as a way of facilitating social control.[77] The rebuilding of parish churches as part of estate management and the revival of parish customs as part of man management came together, I would suggest, in the Anglican introduction of Harvest Festival. Invented by the eccentric Parson Hawker in Cornwall in the 1840s, Harvest Thanksgiving was speedily adopted in rural parishes to replace the traditional Harvest Home, and was given an official form of service by Convocation in 1862 — nicely in the middle of the landowners' Golden Age. Harvest Festival gave devotional form to the economic success of a rural order that now seemed settled,[78] and that was effecting the restoration and rebuilding of country churches at an unprecedented rate. The churches that resulted both articulated the apparent stability of the agrarian status quo, and functioned as components in the machinery of social management designed to keep that status quo in being. That the particular expressiveness, the social meaning, of these churches could become authoritarian is more than apparent, I think, in the parish church of Kingston in the Isle of Purbeck [**23**]. Built to the designs of G. E. Street, it bosses the surrounding countryside from the top of its ridge — doubtless the effect intended by the man who paid for it, the third Earl of Eldon, who, as Pevsner commented acidly, 'regarded it as a Christian duty to provide a new church, not to commensurate with congregations but with his own means and his own dignity'.[79] Architecturally it is magnificent, but its magnificence is overbearing.

Yet the ascendancy Kingston embodied was to prove short-lived, and was in some ways illusory. At Westminster the landed interest was well started on the road of its long decline; in the countryside, population levels continued to slide; and the socio-political power of the parish itself had been whittled away over forty years of legislation. With ironic hindsight one can almost view Kingston's chilly grandeur as valedictory. Indeed, we have already seen that, among the squires' parishes of south-east Devon, the second rebuilding of Dunkeswell was essentially an architectural memorial to the last of the Simcoes. Farway offers an even more striking example of church-building by way of farewell. The restoration of 1875–76 — exactly contemporary with Kingston — was largely funded by Louisa, Lady Prideaux, who held the manor, and work included the rebuilding of the north aisle as a Prideaux family chapel.[80] Yet the Prideaux baronetcy, the oldest in Devon, had become extinct with the death of Sir Edmund Prideaux in 1875 — the year work began — and there were no heirs. Here then was church restoration as elegy, a dynastic chapel that could only function retrospectively. For which audience, for what posterity, was it intended? Increasingly, it would not be the static and habituated congregation of the rustic church. The old, enclosed world of rural England was passing away, opened up by the railways and the urbanised culture that came with newspapers, daily postal services and the electric telegraph. As country people left the land — Farway lost nearly a quarter of its population in the thirty years after 1850 — railways imported the tourist audience that we saw emerging in the first half of the century.[81] The Great Western Railway had reached Exeter, from Taunton via Cullompton, in 1844. In 1860 the London and South Western Railway bisected south-east Devon with a line from Yeovil to Exeter. Edward Ashworth, struck latinate by the occasion, quickly pointed out the possibilities to his fellow-members of the Diocesan Architectural Society: 'a new Railway has been opened, and its swift train, *ponderibus librata suis*, glides past many a hitherto unfrequented village Church which may now claim a notice'.[82] Branches from the main line reached Exmouth in 1861, Seaton in 1868 and Sidmouth in 1874. Two years later, back on the GWR, a spur from Tiverton Junction probed the fastnesses of the Blackdown Hills as far as Hemyock. Murray's first *Hand-Book* for Devon, published in 1850, gave two routes through the south-east of the county and took nine pages to describe what was worth seeing; by the ninth edition of 1879 there were five routes, occupying thirty pages.[83] And where the first edition had had a few picturesque evocations of

23] G. E. Street, St James's, Kingston, Dorset, 1873–80

rustic churches, the ninth recited the antiquarian details of building after building, in a litany of invitation to the church-tourist: Axminster, 'a handsome stone structure ... in part, unquestionably of early date'; Uplyme, 'beautifully situated in a land-locked valley ... has Dec. portions'; Shute, 'an E. Eng. and Perp. building rest. in 1869 ... overshadowed by an enormous yew-tree'; Honiton 'screen is late Perp. ... probably the work of Bishop Courtenay'.[84]

The final stage in the transformation of the Victorian countryside came with the onset of the Great Agrarian Depression — the economic factor that determined the pattern of church-building in phase three. By 1900 a quarter of a century of sliding grain prices, collapsing rent rolls and untenanted farms had permanently weakened landed wealth. Though the breakup of the great estates would not begin for another decade, the rural gentry, the small squires without the margins of the aristocracy, suffered particularly badly. Eastern England, heavily dependent on arable farming, was especially hard hit; by the 1890s in southern Essex rural parish churches, half-emptied of their congregations, stood amid land of which an eighth had reverted to coarse, weed-infested pasture.[85] Because its agriculture was pastoral as well as arable, Devon was saved the worst of the depression, though its impact was real enough — as the sudden curtailment of church-building work in the squires' parishes shows. Nevertheless, as early as the 1870s the shape of funds to come was apparent. Sir Henry Peek purchased the great part of the parish of Rousdon in the late 1860s, along with the lordship of the manor, and set about creating a model paternalist estate, its buildings designed by Ernest George, firstly in partnership with Thomas Vaughan, then with Harold Peto.[86] The derelict medieval church, which had not seen a service for decades, was torn down and replaced by a carefully contrived estate church[87] strategically placed at the end of the walk from the big house [**24**]. Extending his influence to the associated parish of Combpyne, Peek funded the restoration of the parish church there in 1878.[88] The key point in all this is that Peek's money was not dependent upon land, however much he wanted to buy into it; he was the Peek of Peek Frean biscuits.

Peek's annexation of his own corner of south-east Devon was merely the most obvious example of the importance of new money in the last decades of the century. With it, the long processes of change in the socio-cultural complexion of the countryside and rural church crystallised and set into a permanent alteration. As we have seen, oligarchic funding assumed a new significance in the squires' parishes; in the squireless parishes, where far more work was done, it dominated. Here there were no resident squires to insist on a residual social pre-eminence and, since the abolition of the church rate, no distributively-sourced funding from the parish as a whole. Such oligarchies were variously composed and variously led, perhaps most often by the incumbent. It seems clear, however, that they increasingly comprised members of professional and entrepreneurial groups. Their emergence can be traced back earlier in the century. In Ottery St Mary, the central role of the Coleridges — a whole family of attorneys, lawyers and judges — has already been mentioned, as has the importance of the Sanders family's banking fortune in the rebuilding of Whimple in 1845. In 1846 at Uffculme, just north of the sample area, a new aisle, west end and steeple were funded by a combination of Richard Marker, a member of a landowning family but also an attorney who was recorder of Bradninch, John New, a retired doctor whose practice had been in Bristol, and George Smith, the incumbent, who had inherited money of his own.[89] In other words, a professional alliance of the Church with law and medicine — a very differently-based union than that which tied the parson to the squire.

Such large-scale schemes were products of the early Victorian ecclesiological crusade. The oligarchic funding of the end of the century was committed to other objects: to relatively small additions such as vestries and organ-chambers, to improved furnishings, or to restorations which were beginning to show a new reverence for the existing historic fabric of the church. The first repair programme in south-east Devon to be conducted according to the principles of the Society for the Protection of Ancient Buildings was that carried out at Plymtree in 1910.[90] The most representative products of this oligarchic funding were the sets of fittings that began to accumulate in rural churches in the last years of Victoria's reign. Particularly telling was the conversion of such fittings into commemorative objects; lecterns, clergy desks and choir-stalls, pulpits, reredoses and, most of all perhaps, stained-glass windows — each object carefully accompanied by its memorial label, its tag of date and donor. Such a plethora of personal signs, each in effect appropriating a bit of the church fabric to an individual or a family, connotes the appropriation of the church as a whole by the funding oligarchy. The rural church had found its new possessors, and their wealth, of course, came increasingly from professional fees, from commerce, from trade — from the occupations, that is, of the successful middle classes. In areas like south-east Devon, moreover, the people who arrived with the new funding would increasingly be retired, now settling not just in the resort parishes along the coast but in the rural parishes inland. Their backgrounds would most likely be urban, and their retirement to the country would frequently be paralleled by that of the incumbent himself: 'the village began to look like a harbour of rest for a man who gave his best years to the town'.[91] Their arrival, their appropriation of the church fabric, the funding they provided — precisely because it was not based upon income from land — effected a final dislo-

24] Ernest George and Thomas Vaughan, St Pancras', Rousdon, Devon, 1872–74

cation in the reciprocal relationship that had always existed between the rural parish church and the rural parish in which it stood.

That dislocation had been long in coming. The parish church lost the last vestiges of power as an administrative centre with the establishment of Parish and District Councils under the Local Government Act of 1894. It no longer expressed the alliance of squire and parson, for that alliance and the wealth that cemented it would not recover from the Great Depression. It no longer announced the power of the landed interest because that interest had been politically eclipsed, and the enfranchisement of the agricultural labourer in 1884–85 spelt the beginning of the end for deference and the dependent parish. Even though the church still functioned as a place of Christian worship, it did so within parishes that had been half-emptied of their populations; from the 1890s, rural incumbents, recog-

25] Rural Hayes: the church and village of Hayes, Middlesex nising that their congregations were becoming more adventitious, began to post the times of the services.[92] Yet the emergence of middle-class funding saved the rural parish church, and did so not *despite* its loss of power and significance, but precisely *because* of that loss. Severed from its inherited economic, political, and social role — severed, that is, from the reality of power — the rural church could be re-invented as a cultural icon. Here was the fulfilment of the semiotic process that had begun with the discovery of the country church as an object of sensibility. The meanings cumulatively attached to it by seekers after the picturesque, by antiquarian enthusiasts, by initiates of E. E. and Dec. and Perp., now superseded those of the parson and the squire, to be fixed in and by the guardianship of the church's new possessors. The middle-class oligarchies preserved and embellished the rural church not only for themselves, but also for the audience that would be provided by mass tourism. That audience would be broader in its class composition, discovering the countryside by bicycle as well as by train, arriving on day-trips, or as part of an annual holiday. New guidebooks began to be published, aimed at a mass market: with the turn of the century, the *Little Guides* began to appear county by county;[93] at the same time, the Homeland Association, established in 1897, began to produce popular regional guides to rural and coastal Britain;[94] for the real enthusiast, the volumes of the *County Churches* series came out in the years before the Great War.[95] By then, guides to individual churches were becoming increasingly common, even in quite remote parishes. The first picture postcards of churches seem to date from the 1890s, the earliest of them, predictably, in the seaside resorts. And the growing popularity of photography meant that visitors could create and carry away their own

26] Benjamin Williams Leader, *At Evening Time it shall be Light*, oil on canvas, 1897

images of historic churches. In 1894–95 *Amateur Photographer* ran a series of articles on Gothic architecture, later published as a book; without basic architectural knowledge, the Introduction warned tyros, photographers miss 'really important features' or 'do not choose the best positions for placing their cameras'.[96]

The rural church, like the countryside around it, was being remade as part of the national patrimony. The Church of England perhaps did not mind too much, despite public hand-wringing over the decline of the village and its church. However it busied itself in the city, nineteenth-century Anglicanism had never lost the feeling that its true home was the rural parish. When the Church Building Society began to publish a regular journal in 1863, *The Church Builder*, its title-page showed not the great urban missions of the East End and the industrial cities, but a little rustic church before and during restoration.[97] When *The Church Monthly* wanted first-line vignettes for its poems and stories, it chose idyllic views of the country church.[98] However urban and urgent its offical purpose, the Church of England was hankering after its old rural self, and in that longing it joined one of the central cultural and imaginative fantasies of the later nineteenth century. Craving an escape from the city, utopian spirits fostered communities of country craftsmen or helped establish rustic settlements for the urban unemployed.[99] The less practically-minded turned to Helen Allingham's cottages drowned in flowers,[100] or Sydney Jones's villages,[101] the towers and spires of their parish churches presiding untroubled over a lost world of English pastoralism. Even the Great Wen could be ruralised. In his two-volume compilation of 1883, *Greater London*,[102] Edward Walford imagined the metropolis lovingly hedged round by villages and country churches: sheep and misty spires in an evening view of Harrow; the houses of Hendon clustered about the church tower; and the village street of Hayes picturesquely tumbling away from the lich-gate, with no sense that what lay at the bottom of the road — almost literally — were the brick fields from which west London was built [**25**].

No artist played on such sensibilities more successfully than Benjamin Williams Leader, whose *February Fill Dyke* of 1881 came close to definitiveness; church and cottage huddle darkly under ancient elms, as flooded fields mirror a calm, cold twilight.[103] But it is another Leader painting, considered his best by his biographer,[104] that unlocks the ideology of this rural longing and the place of the church within it. In 1882 he painted *In the Evening there shall be Light*, producing a replica of it in 1897, with the slightly emended title *At Evening Time it shall be Light* [**26**].[105] The corrected title ties the picture more closely to its biblical source, the book of Zechariah. Zechariah is in two parts, written at different dates; chapters 1–7 prophesy the rebuilding of the temple of Jerusalem and chapters 8–14 prophesy that, after great iniquities, God will deliver Jerusalem from its enemies. The moment of light 'at evening time' signals the final battle when all foes will be cast down and 'living waters shall go out from Jerusalem'. The standard gloss to the final chapters in the Authorised Version begins 'God defendeth his church'. In Leader's picture the image of the little rural church, standing amid empty countryside in the watery light of the setting sun, is metamorphosed into the apocalyptic, for it is through the defence of the Temple that Jerusalem will be delivered. The bourgeois rural fantasy, the imagination's counter to the intolerable knowledge of urban reality, becomes an enactment of salvation; it is the rural church that will redeem the city. In appropriating the country church, in preserving and embellishing it, the middle-class oligarchies of late Victorian and Edwardian England created and took into their keeping what Benjamin Leader was painting — a cultural myth.

Notes

1 See F. M. L. Thompson, *English Landed Society in the Nineteenth Century*, London, 1963, pp. 332–3.
2 G. E. Mingay, 'Rural England in the Industrial Age', in G. E. Mingay (ed.) *The Victorian Countryside*, 2 vols., London, 1981, I, p. 16.
3 See Hugh Prince, 'Victorian Rural Landscapes', in Mingay, *Victorian Countryside*, I, pp. 17ff.
4 I am conscious that modern economic historians have questioned the nature and extent of the late Victorian depression in the economy as a whole. The fortunes of the agrarian sector certainly varied: corn-producing areas were hit hardest of all, while livestock production remained relatively prosperous. Even so, agriculture's share in net national income fell from 20 per cent in 1855–59 to 6 per cent in 1895–99, and nobody has denied that rural populations declined sharply, or that contemporaries perceived agriculture as being in crisis. See the concluding chapter to J. D. Chambers and G. E. Mingay, *The Agricultural Revolution 1750–1880*, London, 1966 and for the wider economic debate, S. B. Saul, *The Myth of the Great Depression 1873–1896*, London, 1969, reprinted 1981.
5 Among them, Alan Gilbert in his pioneering work, *Religion and Society in Industrial England: Church, Chapel and Social Change 1740–1914*, London, 1976, and James Obelkevich in *Religion and Rural Society: South Lindsey 1825–1875*, Oxford, 1976. This chapter is indebted to both studies at many points.
6 Prince, 'Victorian Rural Landscapes', p. 18.
7 William Whie, *History, Gazetteer and Directory of Devonshire*, Sheffield, 1850; reprinted New York, 1968, p. 37.
8 Charles G. Harper, *The South Devon Coast*, London, 1907, p. 3.
9 Names and boundaries changed somewhat after diocesan reorganisation in the 1870s; I have chosen to retain the pre-1870s arrangement, which had been passed down from the medieval diocese.
10 The complete census figures for Devon have been published by Michael J. L. Wickes, *Devon in the Religious Census of 1851*, privately printed, 1990. For an analysis and discussion of the returns for Devon, and comparison with other southern counties, see Bruce Coleman, 'Southern England in the Census of Religious Worship, 1851', *Southern History*, V, 1983, pp. 154–88.
11 [Anonymous], *Hints to a Clergyman's Wife; or Female Parochial Duties Practically Illustrated*, London, 1832; extracted in Gerald Parsons and James R. Moore, *Religion in Victorian Britain*, 4 vols, Manchester, 1988, III, *Sources*, pp. 245–7.
12 See Gilbert, *Religion and Society*, p. 117.
13 For detailed discussion of the social and political operation of closed and open parishes see Dennis R. Mills, *Lord and Peasant in Nineteenth-Century Britain*, London, 1980.
14 Arnold D. Taylor, 'Hodge and his Parson', *The Nineteenth Century*, XXXI, 1892, p. 360. Taylor was rector of Churchstanton, a Somerset parish on the northern edge of the Blackdown Hills.
15 Owen Chadwick, *The Victiorian Church*, 2 vols, London, 1966–70, II, p. 160.
16 The figures are provided by Gilbert, *Religion and Society*, pp. 130–1.
17 Decennial rates have been worked out by allowing one unit for each year in which work was carried out on each church in the sample group, then representing the cumulative total as a percentage of the theoretical maximum of year/work units for each ten-year period. Thus for a sample group of twenty churches over a decade there would be a theoretical maximum of 10 years x 20 churches = 200 year/work units. Representing decen-

nial totals as a percentage of a theoretical maximum makes it possible to compare church-building rates across differently-sized sample groups. The types of work included comprise new buildings such as chapels of ease, rebuildings of existing churches, substantial restoration or repair programmes and major refittings or reseatings. Smaller works — a stained-glass window or a new reredos, for example — have been excluded if they were not part of a larger programme. Inevitably there is an element of subjective judgement in what is or is not included. In this context, total expenditure, though an important element in deciding what constituted a major scheme of work, is far from providing an objective criterion. Differences in labour and material costs meant that a large structural programme that had a major impact on the fabric of a church — for example, the rebuilding of a chancel employing local labour and largely reusing original materials — could cost less than buying a memorial stained-glass window from a national maker.

18 Of the sample parishes, the patronage of Plymtree was held by Oriel College and the lordship of Clyst St Lawrence by the trustees of Elize Hele's Charity; neither made any subsantial contribution to work done on the churches.

19 In Devon as a whole the average population of parishes in which there was opposition to the setting of a rate was 4,570, considerably larger than any in my sample group; see Gilbert, *Church and Society*, pp. 118–20.

20 Drake provided £1,000 of the £2,160 total; Lympstone parish records, Devon Record Office, *Vestry Book 1808–1958*, 527A/PV2.

21 Benjamin Ferrey's rebuilding of the nave in 1871–72 cost some £450, of which Poltimore, patron and lord of the manor, contributed £100; he had also jointly financed the rebuilding of the chancel in 1865. Huxham Parish Records, DRO, *Restoration Papers 1870–71*, 2811A/PW5.

22 Talaton Parish Records, DRO, *Churchwardens' Account Book 1822–1902*, 4421A/PW3.

23 Broadhembury Parish Records, DRO, *Tower Restoration Accounts 1893–1898*, 1324A/PW61 and PW62.

24 Uplyme Parish Records, DRO, *Churchwardens' Accounts 1779–1830* and *Churchwardens' Book 1830–1965*, 3030A/PW6 and PW7.

25 Upottery Parish Records, DRO, *Churchwardens' Accounts 1769–1830*, 1231A/PW1.

26 Daniel and Samuel Lysons, *Magna Britannia, Devon*, 2 vols, London, 1822, II, pp. 170–1.

27 James Davidson, *Church Notes*, 5 vols, MS, 1828–49, West Country Studies Library, Exeter, s726.5 DEV/DAV, *East Devon*, pp. 349ff.

28 Briefly reviewed in *Ecclesiologist*, II, 1842–43, p. 58; Ferrey's design, signed by him, is displayed in the church.

29 Broadclyst Parish Records, DRO, *Papers relating to restoration*, PW23. The total cost was £2,056; Sir Thomas Dyke Acland was 'a liberal subscriber' and, to save the burden of a formal rate, other monies were lent at 4 per cent by Emmanuel Boutcher as 'an accommodation to his fellow parishers', *Exeter Flying Post*, 7 March 1833.

30 See David Watkin, *The Life and Work of C. R. Cockerell*, London, 1974, pp. 178–81.

31 Awliscombe Parish Records, DRO *Memorandum Book 1708–1847*, PV1.

32 *Exeter Flying Post*, 29 January 1835.

33 Whimple Parish Records, DRO, *Churchwardens' Accounts 1791–1859*, 1418Aadd/PW1, and notes in *Burial Register 1813–1886*, 1418A/PR6, which include the jotting 'Census **AD** 1836 — 731 **AD** 1841–810'. The rebuilding cost £1,500, a substantial part of which was defrayed by the rector, the Revd Lloyd Sanders, the younger brother of the head of one of Exeter's leading banking families; other members of the family also contributed.

34 Davidson, *East Devon*, p. 241.

35 R. Whitaker, *Notes on the History of the Church of St John the Baptist, Broadclyst*, Exeter, 1919, p. 19.

36 William White, *History, Gazetteer and Directory of the County of Devon*, second edition, Sheffield, 1878–79, p. 584; *Building News*, 24 August 1906.

37 Farringdon Faculty Petitions, DRO.

38 See Chris Brooks, 'Bishops Court, Devon', *Country Life*, 15 February 1990, pp. 54–8.

39 The church was designed by C. F. Edwards of Axminster; a commemorative inscription in the church records that it was planned by the incumbent and the last Miss Simcoe as a memorial to the labours of the six sisters, all of whom are represented on corbels in the nave.

40 Poltimore Parish Records, DRO, *Dean Rural's Book 1823–1966* and *Vestry Minutes 1868–1922*, 2810A/PW2 and PV1.

41 William White, *History, Gazetteer and Directory of the County of Devonshire*, third edition, Sheffield, 1890, p. 241.

42 Colaton Raleigh Parish Records, DRO, *Vestry Minutes 1851–1965*, 2973Aadd/PV1.
43 Rockbeare Faculty Petitions, DRO.
44 Aylesbeare Faculty Petitions and Parish Records, DRO, *Dean Rural's Book 1841–1957*, 3155A/PW1.
45 Stockland Faculty Petitions, DRO.
46 Awliscombe Faculty Petitions, DRO; *Exeter Evening Post*, 6 June 1887.
47 *Kelly's Directory of Devonshire*, London, 1935, p. 661.
48 Rewe Faculty Petitions, DRO; *Transactions of the Exeter Diocesan Architectural Society [TEDAS]*, second series, V, 1892, pp. 82–4, 99, 154.
49 My sample comprises an area of sixty-six parishes in that part of Leicestershire identified as squire-dominated in Mills, *Lord and Peasant*, pp. 125–6. Details of the work done on churches are taken from Nikolaus Pevsner, *Buildings of England: Leicestershire and Rutland*, revised by Elizabeth Williamson with Geoffrey K. Brandwood, London, 1984. My conclusions about the pattern of work in these parishes is confirmed by Dr Brandwood in his *Chuch-building and restoration in Leicestershire and Rutland, 1800–1914*, unpublished Ph.d. thesis, Leicester University 1984, and I am particularly grateful to him for his help with this part of the chapter.
50 David M. Thompson, 'The churches and society in nineteenth-century England: a rural perspective', *Studies in Church History*, VIII, *Popular Belief and Practice*, Cambridge, 1972, p. 270.
51 For Garratt see Brooks, 'Bishops Court'. The rebuilding cost Garratt £3,023; his detailed accounts of his expenditure are in Ledger H in the archives privately kept at Bishops Court.
52 Most documentation relating to the church has disappeared; my attribution to Hayward is based upon stylistic grounds.
53 The new church was equally lavishly commemorated in a privately printed volume, *Bicton Church*, by L. A. G., dedicated to Lady Rolle, who presented a copy to the Diocesan Architectural Society; *TEDAS*, IV, 1853, p. 183.
54 For whom see Bernard Coleridge, *The Story of a Devonshire House*, London, 1905, and the entries for various members of the family in *DNB*. The Coleridges numbered Newman and Keble among their personal friends and Sir John Taylor Coleridge wrote *Memoir of the Rev. John Keble*, London, 1869.
55 *Exeter Flying Post*, 7 May 1840.
56 *Ecclesiologist*, new series, V, 1848, p. 320.
57 Paul Thompson, *William Butterfield*, London, 1971, p. 429.
58 The restoration of Ottery St Mary was a particular ambition of the Society, which devoted almost the whole of the first volume of its *Transactions*, 1843, to the church. In 1851 John Duke Coleridge's 'On the Restoration of the Church of S. Mary the Virgin, Ottery S. Mary' reported triumphantly on the completion of the work, *TEDAS*, IV, 1853, pp. 189–217; his paper was reprinted in *Ecclesiologist*, new series, X, 1852, pp. 79–88.
59 *Ecclesiologist*, new series, I, 1845, pp. 91–2.
60 Gilbert, *Church and Society*, particularly pp. 162–72.
61 Obelkevich, *Church and Rural Society*, particularly pp. 168–74.
62 Bruce Coleman, 'The Nineteenth Century: Nonconformity', in Nicholas Orme (ed.), *Unity and Variety: A History of the Church in Devon and Cornwall*, University of Exeter, 1991, p. 132.
63 Coleman, 'The Nineteenth Century: Nonconformity', p. 132.
64 See J. P. D. Dunbabin, *Rural Discontent in Nineteenth-Century Britain*, New York, 1974, pp. 11–61, which includes A. J. Peacock's detailed regional study, 'Village Radicalism in East Anglia 1800–50'.
65 See E. J. Hobsbawm and George Rudé, *Captain Swing*, 1969; Harmondsworth, 1973, p. 102.
66 See Robert Newton, *Victorian Exeter*, Leicester, 1968, pp. 71–3.
67 See Malcolm Andrews, *The Search for the Picturesque: Landscape Aesthetics and Tourism in Britain 1760–1800*, Aldershot, 1989.
68 'The Brothers', *Lyrical Ballads*, second edition, 2 vols, London, 1800.
69 James Davidson, *Bibliotheca Devoniensis: a Catalogue of the Printed Books relating to the County of Devon*, Exeter, 1852.
70 *TEDAS*, Second series I, 1867, pp. 78, 165–6.
71 Eggesford Parish Records, DRO, 161184/box 2b. The Clark and Holland practice was based in Newmarket.
72 White, *Devonshire*, 1878, p. 718.
73 *North Devon Journal*, 16 August 1877.

74 For details of all these see Royal Commission on the Historical Monuments of England, *Churches of South-East Wiltshire*, London, 1987.
75 For details see Anthony Quiney, *John Loughborough Pearson*, New Haven and London, 1979.
76 Jill Allibone, *The Wallpaintings at Garton-on-the-Wolds*, Pevsner Memorial Trust, London, 1991, p. 5.
77 Obelkevich, *Church and Rural Society*, pp. 57–61.
78 Obelkevich sees the new harvest thanksgiving and the revived harvest supper as springing from 'the same desire to express and create a social harmony after the unmediated conflicts of the previous decades' with 'class divisions ... overlaid by a willed appearance of communal solidarity'; *Church and Rural Society*, p. 160.
79 John Newman and Nikolaus Pevsner, *Buildings of England: Dorset*, Harmondsworth, 1972, p. 243. The cost of Kingston was estimated to be a breathtaking £70,000; Eldon is said to have started the church in order to provide employment for his estate workers. Agricultural labourers in Dorset in the 1870s earned around 8*s*. a week; see J. H. Bettey, *Rural Life in Wessex 1500–1900*, Gloucester, 1987, pp. 62–9.
80 *British Architect*, 13 October 1876.
81 The details that follow are taken from David St John Thomas, *A Regional History of the Railways of Great Britain*, I, *The West Country*, revised edition, Newton Abbot, 1981.
82 Edward Ashworth, 'Some account of churches in the Deaneries of Plymtree and Honiton', read 24 January 1861, *TEDAS*, VII, 1863, p. 6.
83 *Murray's Hand-Book for travellers in Devon and Cornwall*, London, 1850; *Murray's Hand-Book for travellers in Devon*, ninth edition, London, 1879.
84 *Murray's Hand-Book*, ninth edition, pp. 35–8.
85 Prince, 'Victorian Rural Landscapes', p. 20. The source of the statistic is the 'Report by Mr R. Hunter Pringle on the Ongar ... Districts of Essex', *Parliamentary Papers*, 1894, 16.
86 See *Building News*, 26 June 1874.
87 *Devon Evening Express*, 29 September 1876; *Exeter Gazette & Daily Telegram*, 30 September 1876.
88 *Exeter & Plymouth Gazette*, 8 February 1878.
89 See Chris Brooks, 'The Victorian restorations of Uffculme church' in *Uffculme: A Culm Valley Parish*, Uffculme Local History Group, Uffculme, 1988, pp. 48–57.
90 The architect was William Weir, and the incumbent at the time had to write to a bemused diocesan Chancellor to explain why Weir's empirically-based repairs did not involve a detailed specification (Plymtree Faculty Petitions, DRO). For a fuller account of the Plymtree work and other restorations in the vicinity, see Chris Brooks, 'Medieval churches and their restoration' in N. H. Cooper (ed.), *The Exeter Area*, supplement to *Archaeological Journal*, CXLVII, 1990, pp. 71–92.
91 Chadwick, *Victorian Church*, II, p. 166.
92 Chadwick, *Victorian Church*, II, p. 171.
93 Published by Methuen & Co., the first volume was F. G. Brabant, *Sussex*, London, 1900.
94 According to the 'Publishers' Address to the Reader', included in many of the early volumes, the guides contained 'everything likely to interest the intelligent visitor concerning the History, Traditions, Worthies, Antiquities, and Literary Associations of the neighbourhoods with which they deal'. The first of the Devon handbooks was Beatrix F. Creswell, *Dartmoor and its Surroundings: What to see and how to find it*, which had reached a third edition by 1903. *Our Homeland Churches and how to study them*, by Sidney Heath, appeared in 1907; of its fifty-two illustrations only one is of a church in a major city — and that is Wren's St Stephen's Walbrook.
95 Published by George Allen & Co.
96 Thomas Perkins, *Handbook to Gothic Architecture Ecclesiastical and Domestic for Photographers and Others*, London, 1897, p. 9.
97 *The Church Builder: A Quarterly Journal of Church Extension in England and Wales*, published by Rivingtons 'in connexion with The Incorporated Church Building Society'.
98 *The Church Monthly: an Illustrated Magazine for Home Reading* began publication in 1888.
99 See Jan Marsh, *Back to the Land: The Pastoral Impulse in England, from 1880 to 1914*, London, 1982.
100 See, for example, Stewart Dick, *The Cottage Homes of England*, illustrated by Helen Allingham, London, 1909.
101 See, for example, P. H. Ditchfield, *The Charm of the English Village*, illustrated by Sydney R. Jones, London, 1910. In the same genre is Ditchfield's *The Cottages and the*

Village Life of Rural England, with water-colour illustrations by A. R. Quinton, London, 1912.

102 Edward Walford, *Greater London: A Narrative of its History its People and its Places*, 2 vols, London, 1883, I, pp. 270, 277, 211.

103 Exhibited at the Royal Academy in 1881, now in Birmingham City Art Gallery. See Rosemary Treble, *Great Victorian Pictures*, Arts Council Exhibition Catalogue, 1978, p. 49.

104 Lewis Lusk, 'The Life and Work of Benjamin Williams Leader, RA', *Art Annual*, 1901, p. 6.

105 According to Rosemary Treble, 'The Victorian Picture of the Country', Mingay, *Victorian Countryside*, I, p. 168fn., the 1882 original is lost; the reduced replica of 1897 is in Manchester City Art Gallery.

Chapter 3 · Christopher Wakeling

The nonconformist traditions: chapels, change and continuity

It is now widely acknowledged that the history of religious architecture in Britain since the sixteenth century cannot be understood if its scope is confined to the buildings of the established church. But architectural historians have lagged some way behind historians of religion in this search for a broad understanding. While writers such as A. D. Gilbert have charted the patterns of Victorian religion, few accounts of Victorian religious architecture have strayed outside the Church of England and the Roman Catholic church.[1]

In recent years the buildings of the protestant nonconformists have been studied more systematically than ever before. There have been several extensive inventories and a number of studies which have gained an urgency by the threat of redundancy and demolition awaiting so many chapels and meeting-houses. Whereas earlier studies were often informed by a preference for Georgian architecture, more recent work has looked with greater interest at the buildings of Victorian Nonconformity.[2]

It is not, I think, merely taste that has led historians to study the early buildings of nonconformity rather than those of the nineteenth century, or to examine Anglican church-building of the Victorian period rather than its nonconformist counterparts. The reason may be equally connected with the less tractable nature of the subject. Protestant nonconformity is a multifarious thing and in nineteenth-century Britain that variety was at its greatest — socially, theologically, politically, organisationally and architecturally. If the Church of England may be likened to a Conservative party in government (albeit a party of factions), the nonconformists should be seen as the assembled parties of opposition — an opposition which might outnumber the ruling party, but lack the ability to overturn it.

Nonconformity, then, is a purely negative label. Like Post-Impressionism, postmodernism or non-figurative art it should not be approached as a coherent movement. We might ask if it is any more sensible to consider nonconformist building as a category than it would be to study Gentile architecture. It may be that when the definitive volumes on Victorian church-building are written there will be no separate treatment of nonconformity. Before assuming this position, however, we should observe that the distinctive treatment of the established and nonconformist churches was a commonplace until well into the twentieth century. Guide books and gazetteers generally employed such a division, as did the architectural press. The *Builder* for instance, had a separate column entitled 'Dissenting Chapels and Churches'. Places of worship often passed from one nonconformist denomination to another as congregations grew or declined, divided or were united. Church of England buildings, on the other hand, very rarely came into nonconformist use, or *vice versa*.

The pair of composite illustrations from J. H. Garett's *Cheltenham: the Garden Town* is a useful example of the separate treatment of nonconformity. Since Cheltenham is largely a nineteenth-century town, and of the buildings shown only the medieval parish church is earlier, a few interesting observations can be made at once about these two categories. We can see immediately that Anglicans and Roman Catholics worshipped mostly in Gothic buildings, usually set in landscaped churchyards; there is one example of a church in the Norman style, and just one that is classical [**27**]. The nonconformists' buildings represent a variety of styles and, with no need for orientation, have a greater opportunity for a display of façades or street frontages [**28**]. All of the Anglicans' Cheltenham churches are illustrated and all are architecturally proficient. Conversely, the nonconformist page shows perhaps half of the town's nonconformist places of worship, and even this selection reveals a range of architectural competence. Finally it may be noted that the Church of England has as its latest building one of 1878–79, St Matthew's, while the nonconformists are represented by no fewer than three of later date: St Andrew's of 1885-86; the Friends' Meeting House of 1902–03; and the Catholic Apostolic Church. From this we may conclude that the nonconformists of the nineteenth century built in more varied ways than the Church of England, and built more often.

The view from Cheltenham in 1910 is important. It is a reminder that the nonconformists were able to thrive not only in industrial communities and among the rural poor. It is, however, a view from a time when, as the author of the guidebook wrote, there was 'a levelling of the differences formerly maintained with some heat between one denomination and another'.[3] I want now to look back over the preceding century, trying to understand something of the variety of nonconformist building without drowning in detail, and looking for broad patterns without simplifying essential differences. It will be convenient for us to keep Cheltenham's example in mind as we examine buildings from different parts of the country. For the sake of clarity I shall divide the period into three, and focus in each on crucial elements of continuity and change.

Before 1850

The Church of England entered the nineteenth century with a system of parishes which in many places had been unchanged since the Reformation. Parliamentary approval was necessary for the creation of new parishes, and church rates (for the upkeep and rebuilding of churches) were often opposed. Although in some places the parochial system had been supplemented or subverted by proprietary chapels and chapels of ease, relatively few new churches were built. In Cheltenham, for instance, the medieval parish church of St Mary was the Anglicans' only place of worship until Holy Trinity was built in 1820–23. Church-building was especially scant in the late eighteenth century and the first two decades of the nineteenth century.

It was in this period that the Methodists made their most dramatic advance, unhampered by the parochial system. They built chapels in almost every town in England, but they were especially successful in the new urban and industrial communities. The burgeoning pottery towns of north Staffordshire provide a good illustration of the process. In Hanley, which had no parish church of its own, the Methodists were much in evidence. Bethesda Chapel was built by the New Connexion Methodists in 1798, enlarged in 1811 and virtually rebuilt in 1819 so as to accommodate 3,000 people.[4] It was not only Hanley's largest place of worship but also a

27] Anglican and Roman Catholic churches in Cheltenham, 1910

sign of the local Methodists' ability to organise their own affairs with confidence. Important pottery manufacturers and civic leaders were the most prominent members and trustees, and a schoolmaster acted as architect. Like contemporary Anglican churches it was of course designed as a preaching box. The interior differed from the Anglicans' perhaps only in its greater openness: the generous encircling gallery and absence of ceiling columns (despite the sixty-nine-feet span) reflect the Methodists' extra emphasis on congregational singing.

In places such as Hanley the Methodists were acting as the establishment party. Their success was hardly welcomed by the Church of England, and the 'Million Pound Act' of 1818 was designed to promote Anglican initiative in the very districts where the Methodists had prospered. The wave of new Anglican churches was as much a response to Methodism as it was a crusade against irreligion. Large numbers of new churches were built as a result of the 1818 Act and its 1824 sequel, and even more were to be built following the simpler procedures for parochial subdivision which were introduced in 1843.[5] Where the Anglicans' building campaign was most effective it seems to have checked the Methodists' progress, at least so far as the building of major chapels was concerned. But during the mid-1830s that progress was resumed with assurance.

The Wesleyans were in some ways best placed to respond to the Anglicans' recent success. As the senior branch of Methodism the Wesleyans

28] Nonconformist churches in Cheltenham, 1910

had a well-established system of regulating and financing their chapel-building and had created a General Chapel Fund in the same year as the 'Million Pound Act'.[6] By the 1830s and 1840s they built with renewed confidence in almost every part of the country. In Cheltenham, for instance, their Regency chapel was superseded by a stately new building in 1839, while in Derby a substantial chapel of 1805 gave way to a yet larger one in 1841, monumental in appearance, designed by James Simpson of Leeds.[7] Such buildings were generally more substantial than their predecessors, but retained essentially the same interior arrangements. At the point where Anglican practice was beginning to be affected by the Oxford Movement, and when Pugin's first churches were taking shape, the Methodists continued to build chapels for which the auditory purpose was paramount.

The Methodists' success in the later eighteenth century and the early nineteenth was paralleled in most of the older dissenting denominations. In the vanguard of this growth were the Independents and the Baptists, both of whom built large numbers of new chapels and retained local autonomy for their congregations.[8] The Independents included some of the most prosperous congregations and were responsible for many outstanding places of worship. At Great George Street in a fashionable quarter of Liverpool, for instance, the Independents built a chapel in 1811-12. When the chapel was burned down in 1840 the congregation set its sights on a more ambitious building. £3,672 were raised within a day of the fire and the sumptuous chapel (designed by Joseph Franklin) which rose on the site in 1841 cost about £14,000 [**29**]. Such confident organisation only emphasised the protracted history of the nearby Anglican church, St Luke's, which was begun in 1811 but not completed until 1831.[9]

Although the particular circumstances of the Great George Street building were not to be found elsewhere, a similar combination of resourcefulness and confidence was widespread. Two examples must suffice. A newly-established Independent congregation at St Michael's Hill, Bristol, included the tobacco manufacturer W. D. Wills among its trustees. The remarkable chapel which it had built in 1842-43 was the work of the young William Butterfield, Wills's nephew.[10] At Bloomsbury Baptist Chapel, London, of 1845-48, one of the leading figures and chief subscribers was the important building contractor, Sir Morton Peto. Peto's contacts with Sir Charles Barry may well have led to the appointment of John Gibson, Barry's recent assistant, as the architect of the Bloomsbury Chapel. Gibson's Romanesque design was significant enough to attract the interest of the *Ecclesiologist*.[11]

Not all of the older dissenting denominations shared in the vigorous building programme of the Independents and Baptists during the early nineteenth century. The Quakers (or Society of Friends) experienced a steady decline in membership during the period, and their building activity was circumscribed. Yet the relatively high socio-economic status of its members meant that where Quakerism was strong, important building work was undertaken. One such example is the 1825 Friends' Meeting House in Norwich, designed by J. T. Patience, where the Quaker banking

29] Joseph Franklin, The Independents' Great George Street Chapel, Liverpool, 1841, from *The Congregational Year Book*, 1847

family, the Gurneys, worshipped.[12] By the end of the early nineteenth century English Presbyterianism was even more of a spent force. However, many of its old congregations had embraced Unitarianism and did so with increasing confidence after its legalisation in 1813.

The Unitarians, with their strong intellectual tradition, were distinguished builders. In some towns their chapels were the expression of a cultured minority. Cheltenham's Unitarian Chapel, designed by H. R. Abraham, and built 1842-44, was a small neo-Norman building, described as 'an elegant structure' by the town's historian, who was a member of the congregation.[13] In other places they were a more vital force. In the Cheshire town of Dukinfield, for instance, Richard Tattersall's Unitarian Chapel of 1840-41 [**30**] upstaged the nearby Commissioners' church of 1838-40.[14] It was a fine design, inventively adapting Gothic construction to the needs of a preaching box and retaining the datestone, funerary monuments and graveyard of the former Presbyterian meeting-house. The building thus emphasised the continuity of the dissenting tradition, and reasserted the nonconformist claim to be the national spiritual focus of the town.

The most dramatic evidence of the nonconformists' success as builders in the first half of the nineteenth century is to be found in the major urban chapels. In our concern for these impressive buildings, however, it must

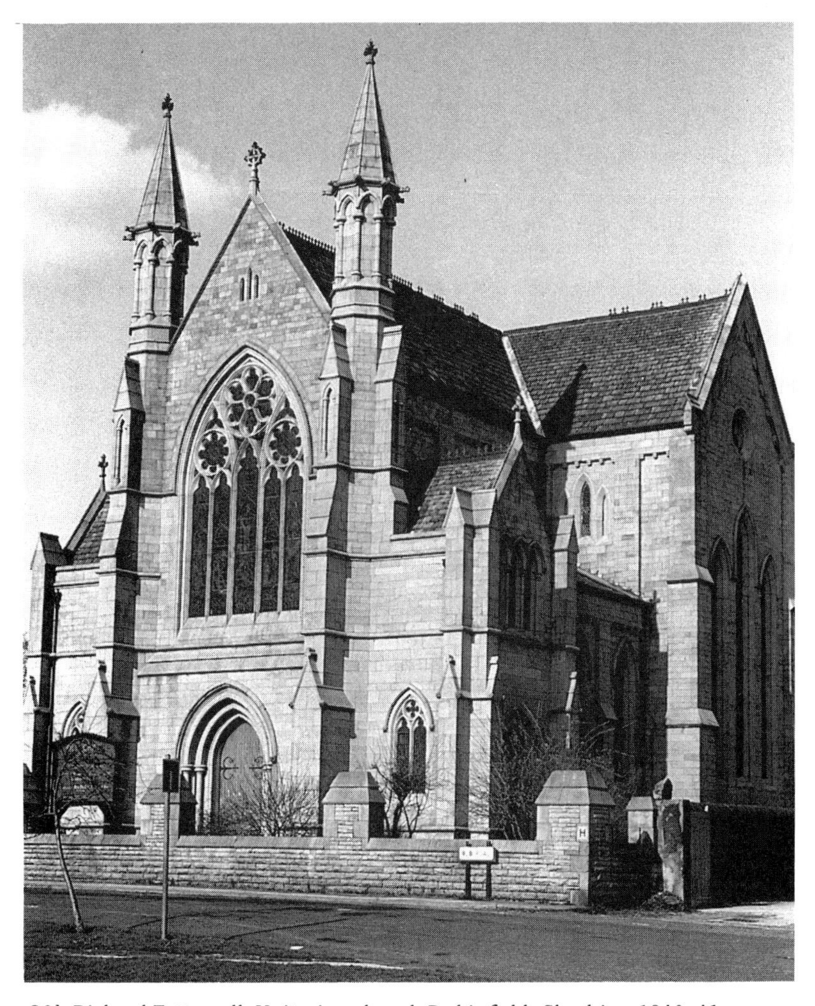

30] Richard Tattersall, Unitarian chapel, Dukinfield, Cheshire, 1840–41

not be forgotten that rural nonconformity had a different tale. In hamlets and villages throughout the country, Methodism was especially active and the Primitive Methodists in particular had many members among the rural poor. For the most part, these rural chapels were small and modest structures, sometimes barely reaching the threshold of polite architecture. The Primitive Methodist Chapel of 1838 at Sutton-on-the-Hill, Derbyshire, is one example (from among many) in which the long-wall type of façade was retained. Such chapels, often built with the aid of labour by the members, are a sign of the Methodists' ability to organise in places where nonconformity had often been weak.

1850–80

During the middle years of Victoria's reign the nonconformists continued to build actively and paid growing attention to architectural matters. Model designs and pattern-books were published for nonconformists' use, as well as treatises of a more analytic character. New chapels were illustrated in the denominational magazines and increasingly also in the architectural press. Chapel-building became a matter of status and interdenominational rivalry was often the spur. In some places different denominations rebuilt their chapels in quick succession. For instance, in Newcastle-under-Lyme the flourishing Methodist New Connexion moved into a new building in 1858.[15] Within a year the long-established Independents (or Congregationalists, as they were coming to be called) began to build a new chapel nearby, Butterfieldian Gothic in contrast to the New Connexion's statelier classical design. At the opening ceremony the minister admitted that a little rivalry had been at work between the two denominations. Furthermore 'he was glad to learn the effect was not likely to stop with them [and] that steps were being taken by the Wesleyan Methodists to build for themselves a place of worship of still ampler dimensions and higher architectural pretensions'.[16] The Wesleyans did indeed build such a chapel close at hand, with French High Gothic features, which opened in 1861.[17]

In Harrogate there was a similar story. Here the Congregationalists built a Decorated Gothic chapel in 1860-62 [**31**], and the Wesleyans erected a new Italianate chapel in 1861-62 [**32**], each employing the architects Lockwood and Mawson despite the Wesleyans' initial anxiety that their design was too expensive.[18] That the same architects were responsible in 1862 for adding a chancel and transepts to the Anglicans' Christ Church, originally built in 1831, illustrates the competitive nature of church- and chapel-building at this time.

The emphasis which nonconformists gave to their distinctive architectural signs is a reflection of the changed context of chapel-building in the mid-Victorian years. Nonconformist membership figures, although continuing to rise after 1850, generally failed to keep pace with the increase in population.[19] Whereas the chapel buildings of the early nineteenth century had been evidence of growth, building activity had since become more often a process of consolidation. One can understand how the need for distinctive architecture became greater as the nonconformist bodies grew closer.

Between about 1850 and 1880 the Church of England's building programme went some way towards reclaiming the ground which it had lost in earlier decades. In Cheltenham, for example, six new churches were built. It is hardly necessary to emphasise here that this generation of new churches was almost always built in a medieval style and was planned for ritual more than for preaching. Nonconformists generally continued to give pride of place to the pulpit in their new chapels and, against the background of Anglican revisionism, reasserted the role of the preacher.

Charles Haddon Spurgeon, the *Wunderkind* of mid-Victorian nonconformity, was the most famous preacher of the age.[20] His was a revival of the eighteenth-century crowd-pulling tradition, and a reassertion of evangelical Calvinism. As a young Baptist preacher he attracted great congregations to the Surrey Gardens Music Hall, and for him was built the colossal Metropolitan Tabernacle (1859-61) near the Elephant and Castle in south

31] Lockwood and Mawson, Congregationalist chapel, Harrogate, 1860–62

London [**33**]. The design, by W. W. Pocock, suggests comparisons not merely with the large Methodist chapels of forty years earlier but also with one of the founding works of protestant architecture, Salomon de Brosse's Protestant Temple at Charenton, of 1623. The interior, with tiers of galleries on slender iron columns, provided thousands of worshippers with an uninterrupted view of the platform from which Spurgeon preached.[21]

Spurgeon's Tabernacle became the most talked-of chapel in the country. It was not merely a preaching place but in a sense a flagship for its denomination. At a time when the Church of England was responding cautiously to its need for new cathedrals, Spurgeon was able to create a bold new building for 5,000 worshippers in the heart of south London. It was paid for by subscription, and its very name was a celebration of the otherness of nonconformity. Its success led to the building of many other Baptist 'tabernacles' in the next twenty years, and prompted the Congregationalists to reassert their tradition of great preaching centres. The rebuilding of the Congregationalists' Westminster Chapel in 1863-65, by W. F. Poulton, followed soon on the opening of Spurgeon's Tabernacle,

32] Lockwood and Mawson, Congregationalist chapel, Harrogate, 1861–62

33] W. W. Pocock, The Metropolitan Tabernacle, Newington, London, 1859–61; from *The Builder*, 1861

and its memorable interior of curving galleries showed an obvious debt.[22] Whitefield's Chapel in Tottenham Court Road was rebuilt on twice its previous scale, and a decade later, in 1873-74, the City Temple, Holborn Viaduct, was built for another popular Congregational preacher.[23]

These metropolitan super-chapels show how nonconformists retained a greater flexibility than their Anglican opponents in the planning and building of places of worship. And the strength of nonconformist building is to be measured as much in its small rural chapels as in its major urban examples. During the mid-Victorian years the building of village chapels seems to have been a matter of growing confidence, and it became increasingly common for rural congregations to have purpose-built premises rather than worshipping in borrowed barns or cottages. The Primitive Methodist chapel of 1868 at Binham in Norfolk may be taken as an example; a simple rectangular building, seating 100, with a neat gable-end façade with a repertoire of classical elements. Its architectural qualities clearly pale beside those of the medieval priory which serves as Binham's parish church. However, it was an expression of the skills and resources of its small congregation, one which would have defined itself not merely in opposition to the parish church, but as an outpost of a connexion which had its major 'temples' in towns like Great Yarmouth and Hull.

After 1880

The late Victorian years were, on the whole, a period of innovation and vitality for the nonconformists' building programme. This is paradoxical, since the challenges were very great. Rural depopulation weakened what were often the most vulnerable congregations, and the drift of the middle classes to the suburbs strained the resources of previously comfortable urban congregations. Similar difficulties faced most religious groups, of course, but the nonconformists proved resourceful in redefining the role of city-centre chapels, and maintained a more pragmatic approach to the planning and financing of their buildings.

An evident response to the migration of the wealthy away from city centres was the appearance of mission halls in the back streets and less fashionable areas of every town. Among the most successful new nonconformist bodies was the Salvation Army. It sprang from the Methodists' tradition of evangelical missions, and brought a distinctly unecclesiastical metaphor to all its work. The Salvation Army Citadel in George Street, Harwich, of 1892, can be taken as an example, a turreted brick fort in the battle against sin [**34**]. All of the major nonconformist denominations engaged in mission work, however, and while some of their buildings were utilitarian sheds it was not at all uncommon for buildings to be part of the mission hall's attraction. The Congregationalists' Mission in Azof Street, Greenwich, designed by W. T. Hollands and opened in 1893, attracted attention with its exotic skyline, and provided accommodation not merely for worship but also for young men's and women's institutes.[24] The Wesleyans' Mission Hall in the Lozells area of Birmingham, of 1894 by Crouch and Butler, emphasised informality in a different way, its broad hall having a large stage on which orchestras and choirs might perform for Pleasant Sunday Afternoons.[25] If this was the golden age of the pub it was also, reciprocally, the golden age of the mission hall.

Funding such missions — indeed funding most urban chapels — was not easy. The Salvation Army financed its buildings with a novel system of shares and subscriptions targeted at the small shareholder.[26] And it became increasingly common for nonconformists to make their buildings visibly the products of their communities. At the Wesleyan Chapel in Long Street, Middleton, Lancashire, built in 1899-1901 to the designs of Edgar Wood, the initials of subscribers were carved elegantly into the stonework facing the street.[27] The United Methodist Church Mission in Corden Street, Derby, of 1910-11 by G. Cash, illustrates the more usual method of recording contributors; two or three courses of initialled bricks are prominently locatd above the commemorative stone slabs which were laid by dignitaries and chapel officials.[28]

At the turn of the century the Methodists built a series of 'central halls' across the country. This was an imaginative campaign to affirm the Methodists' presence in city centres. The Wesleyan Central Hall of 1903 in Birmingham, by E. and J. A. Harper, is an important surviving example, with a long row of shops for rent at street level.[29] These shops not only subsidised the hall and its activities but probably increased the building's appeal to hesitant attenders by diminishing its churchiness. And central halls were far from being merely places for Sunday worship. A full programme of lectures and classes, of clubs and societies, would keep the insititution busy throughout the week. At Birmingham there were club-

34] Salvation Army Citadel, Harwich, Essex, 1882

and classrooms, a library and a ladies' parlour, beside committee rooms and a synod hall in addition to the main hall. In the basement were a ragged school and a kitchen. Success depended not solely on the oratorical power of individual preachers but also, as in early Methodism, on the ability to offer a sustaining organisation which could help transform its members' lives.

There are many reminders of earlier nonconformity in the buildings erected by nonconformists at the end of Victoria's reign. The octagonal type of chapel, admired by Wesley in Norwich and built in some numbers until the Regency, enjoyed a modest revival, although the new octagons were generally larger than before, as steel girders permitted greater spaces to be spanned. T. C. Hope's Grange Congregational Chapel, Bradford, of 1891 is one such example on a prominent site.[30] Nonconformists seem to have gained confidence in their own traditions at this time. The assured Baroque classicism of the Edwardian years which was often adopted by the

Methodists was defended as having been 'very much in vogue at the time of the Wesleys'.[31]

Such an argument was used by the architects Lanchester and Rickards to defend their design of the Wesleyan Central Hall, Westminster [**35**], built 1905-11.[32] Though it was not a central hall in quite the same sense as Birmingham's, the Westminster hall attracted large crowds to its evangelical services and sustained the tradition of the institutional church. It stands beside Westminster Abbey and across from the Palace of Westminster, its architectural confidence a symbol of political as well as spiritual outreach. It can be read as a symbol of the high tide of Methodism, the era of Free Church unity and the rise of the nonconformists as an influence in Parliament.

The building of central halls and urban missions was a powerful indicator of nonconformist resourcefulness at the turn of the century, an adaptation of traditional evangelical principles to the changing circumstances of the late Victorian world. The Church of England was actively engaged in the mission movement of the period, and also began to build two new English cathedrals, but in these endeavours it seems to have been upstaged by the nonconformists and the Roman Catholics. The Anglicans' church-building programme had peaked in the 1860s and 1870s, and although it continued into the early twentieth century, it did so at a diminishing rate. In Cheltenham, to return to our earlier example, the Anglicans built no new places of worship between 1880 and the First World War, while several nonconformist groups built afresh.

Although many nonconformist chapels had been built in anticipation of growth during the mid-Victorian years, many factors caused others to be

35] Lanchester and Rickards, Wesleyan Central Hall, Westminster, London, 1905–11; from *The Builder*, 1905

built in later decades. One was the process of denominational renewal. The regeneration of Presbyterianism and the resurgence of Quaker membership were represented in Cheltenham by St Andrew's Presbyterian Church of 1885-86 and the new Friends' Meeting House of 1902-03. The presence of new religious bodies had its impact, from the distinctive architecture of the Salvation Army to the more sophisticated buildings of Christian Science — such as that in Victoria Park, Manchester, of 1903-08 by Edgar Wood.[33] Village chapels continued to be built in significant numbers, especially by the Methodists, and in fledgling suburbs the nonconformists were happy to build for small congregations. Following the lead of Cadbury, Lever, Howard and others, nonconformist causes were especially well represented in the most progressive new communities.

Despite the difficulties, this was in many ways a golden age for nonconformity. Membership figures continued to grow until and, indeed, beyond 1900, and nonconformists had emerged from the struggles of the earlier years of the century into a position of acknowledged political and cultural strength. Yet, as the Introduction to this book has shown, there were already evidences of decline. Despite the numerical increases in membership, recruitment to the major nonconformist denominations was falling behind the overall rate of population growth, and this was indicative of a more fundamental change in society. Ironically, as nonconformity assumed a more conspicuous position in national affairs. religion generally was of diminishing importance in the lives of most English people.

This account has been necessarily brief, and many important themes have had to be omitted; the development of school facilities in chapels, the role of building funds, the significance of some of the smaller denominations, the phenomenon of nonconformist 'squires' and much else. However, even such a brief survey of the buildings of the various nonconformist bodies — from the centralised Wesleyans to the more independent Congregationalists — indicates the flexibility of their architectural response to the needs of the nineteenth century. On the whole, their buildings were the products of communities rather than expressions of a national identity. Because of this, and because the Free Churches had no corporate orthodoxy, the chapels of Victorian nonconformity come closer to exemplifying the social variety of the nineteenth century than do the churches of the Anglican Establishment.

Notes

1 Alan Gilbert, *Religion and Society in Industrial England: Church, Chapel and Social Change 1740-1914*, London, 1976.

2 Among recent inventories are Christopher Stell's volumes for the Royal Commission on the Historical Monuments of England, *Nonconformist Chapels and Meeting-houses in Central England*, London, 1986, and *Nonconformist Chapels and Meeting-houses in South-West England*, London, 1991, and Philip Temple's *Islington Chapels*, 1992.

3 J. H. Garrett, *Cheltenham: the Garden Town*, sixth edition, Cheltenham and London, 1910, p. 82.

4 H. Smith and A. H. Beard, *Bethesda Chapel, Hanley: A Centenary Record*, 1899; C. Wakeling, 'Methodist Architecture in North Saffordshire: The First Seventy-Five Years' in P. Morgan (ed.), *Staffordshire Studies*, London, 1987, pp. 155–67.

5 Gilbert, *Religion and Society*, p. 130.
6 J. C. Bowmer, *Pastor and People*, London, 1975, p. 195.
7 C. Stell, *Nonconformist Chapels and Meeting-houses in Central England*, p. 77; G. W. Dolbey, *The Architectural Expression of Methodism*, London, 1964, pp. 154-6.
8 Gilbert, *Religion and Society*, pp. 34, 39.
9 J. A. Picton, *Memorials of Old Liverpool*, (second edition, London, 1875), II, pp. 240, 242-3, 288; *Congregational Year Book*, 1847, p. 159; J. Q. Hughes, *Liverpool*, London, 1969, entry 37.
10 P. Thompson, *William Butterfield*, London, 1971, pp. 19, 42; W. F. Ayres, *The Highbury Story*, Bristol, 1963.
11 H. R. Hitchcock, *Early Victorian Architecture in Britain*, 2 vols, New Haven and London, 1954, II, pp. 135-6; *Ecclesiologist*, new series V, 1848, p. 373;
12 H. Colvin, *A Biographical Dictionary of British Architects, 1600-1840*, London, 1978, p. 625.
13 G. Hart, *A History of Cheltenham*, Leicester, 1965, p. 238.
14 H. Colvin, *Biographical Dictionary*, p. 811.
15 *Methodist New Connexion Magazine*, 1857, p. 514; 1858, p. 388.
16 *Staffordshire Times*, 10 September 1859.
17 *Staffordshire Advertiser*, 30 March 1861.
18 *Builder* XVIII, 1860, p. 564; XX, 1862, p. 642; *Building News*, 1861, pp. 429, 511, 828; *Builder*, XX, 1862, p. 825.
19 Gilbert, *Religion and Society*, p. 39.
20 Of the many books on Spurgeon J. C. Carlile's *C. H. Spurgeon, An Interpretative Biography*, London, 1933 may be mentioned.
21 *Builder* XVII, 1859, pp. 105-7, 187, 219-221; XIX, 1861, pp. 302-3; *Illustrated London News*, XXXVIII, 1861, p. 319.
22 *Builder*, XXII, 1864, pp. 722-3.
23 *Congregational Year Book*, 1865; *Builder*, XXXVI, 1878, pp. 986-7.
24 *Congregational Year Book*, 1894.
25 J. Crouch and E. Butler, *Churches, Mission Halls and Schools for Nonconformists*, Birmingham, 1901, pp. 39-42; *Builder*, 16 December 1893, p. 456; *Wesleyan Chapel Committee Report*, 1903.
26 D. R. Blackwell, 'Evolution of Corps Architecture in the United Kingdom' in *Salvation Army Yearbook*, 1959, p. 32; A. R. Wiggins, *History of the Salvation Army 1865-1914*, IV, London, 1964, pp. 232-5.
27 *Builder*, 31 December, 1904, p. 697.
28 *Derby Mercury*, 25 November, 1910.
29 *Builder*, 27 July, 1901, p. 85; 3 October 1903, p. 340.
30 *Congregational Year Book*, 1891.
31 The phrase appears in the *Wesleyan Chapel Committee Report*, for 1901, referring to the chapel in Darlington Street, Wolverhampton.
32 *Builder*, 24 June 1905, pp. 682-3.
33 *Builder*, 3 December 1904, p. 578.

Chapter 4 · Gavin Stamp

The Victorian Kirk: Presbyterian architecture in nineteenth-century Scotland

Religion has been the soul of art from the beginning.

Alexander Thomson, 1874

Scotland presents problems for the ecclesiologist. Most of her medieval buildings are ruins and most surviving churches seem to date from the nineteenth century. Scottish cities present a bewildering variety of these — both Gothic and classical — and the notices next to their (usually firmly locked) doors proclaim them to belong to the Episcopal Church of Scotland, or the Roman Catholics, or to congregations of the Free Church or of the Church of Scotland. And of those owned by this last, the established church of Scotland, many were once the proud and independent symbols of dissent, having been built by the United Presbyterians or by another Free Church congregation. Because of the essentially fissiparous nature of Scottish Presbyterianism, far too many kirks were built in Victorian Scotland, with the result that many have disappeared while a depressingly large residue remain redundant. Nevertheless, because of the architecturally careless and thoroughly confusing nature of Scottish religious history, the Victorian buildings that survive are of great significance; as James Macaulay has written, 'it can truly be claimed that in Scotland the majority of church members worship in buildings belonging to the nineteenth century'.[1]

It may be an advantage to survey Victorian church architecture in Scotland with English eyes, as this can put the achievement into perspective.[2] And, when it comes to the Gothic Revival, that perspective is not necessarily flattering. To anyone brought up in the great academy of Victorian Society tours, familiar with the vital creative achievement of the High Victorian Gothic experiment in England, with the work of such towering figures as Butterfield and Street, Bodley and Pearson, the indigenous Victorian Gothic Revival churches of Scotland are, on the whole, a profound disappointment. Although they owed a greater debt to English precedents than is often recognised, their conventional, ecclesiologically 'correct' exteriors usually enclose mean, starved, unremarkable auditoria on plans which are thoroughly incorrect, or un-medieval.[3]

Nor is this surprising. The moving force behind the great flowering of the English Gothic Revival was the Oxford Movement, the revival of the Catholic tradition within the Church of England, reinforced by the brilliant, blinkered bigotry of the Roman Catholic convert, A. W. N. Pugin. From his theories about the essentially Christian and Catholic nature of Gothic developed the whole 'science' of ecclesiology and the scholarly interest in the revival of authentic medieval traditions and forms. But of what consequence were these in Scotland? The symbols and trappings of medieval religion which so obsessed High Churchmen — naves and aisles and separate chancels, rood-screens and stone altars — should not have been of any interest to a Presbyterian congregation; indeed, such crypto-Popery ought to have been anathema. This was well understood by Scotland's greatest Victorian architect, Alexander Thomson. In his celebrated attack on the Gothic Revival in general and Gilbert Scott's designs for Glasgow University in particular, delivered in 1866, Thomson complained that:

> The Gothic revivalists are fond of catching hold of people by their prejudices. They say that theirs is the national style, and this assertion has come to be admitted almost generally. Yet nobody seems to understand exactly what it means. It certainly had not a national origin, and although it was practised in this country for some centuries, and assumed national and local peculiarities, the same may be said for the Classic styles. But they tell us that it suits the national taste. Now this argument, if it be worth anything at all, can be admitted only after it has been proved that Gothic is the best style, otherwise it is no compliment to the nation. We are next told that we should adopt it because it is the Christian style, and, strange to say, this most impudent assertion has also been accepted as sound doctrine even by earnest and intelligent Protestants; whereas it ought only to have force with those who believe that Christian truth attained its purest and most spiritual development at the period when this style of architecture constituted its corporeal frame.[4]

In other words, Gothic architecture was the style of medieval Catholicism — which was precisely what Pugin had claimed. Logically, therefore, only Roman Catholics should be building in Gothic and adherents of Reformed Christianity should be impervious to the arguments of Pugin and the Cambridge Camden Society. They should certainly not interest devout members of the United Presbyterian Chuch, like Thomson [**36**]. So when, for whatever reason, Gothic was, in fact, adopted for churches it was used merely picturesquely, as a style, without that intellectual and theological basis which underpinned the best work of the English High Victorian Goths.

The Episcopal Church of Scotland was different, however. The legitimate national apostolic upholder of the Catholic tradition, it had been disestablished and severely persecuted in the eighteenth century despite being in communion with the Church of England. By the early nineteenth century it proclaimed its continuing existence in such neo-medieval buildings as

36] Gothic versus classic: the St Vincent Street United Presbyterian church in Glasgow by Alexander Thomson, 1857–59; in the background, St Columba's Gaelic church by William Tennant and Frederick V. Burke, 1902–04

William Burn's St John's church of 1815–18, prominently sited at the end of Princes Street in Edinburgh and Archibald Simpson's St Andrew's (now the cathedral) in Aberdeen of 1816. The Episcopal Church enjoyed a great revival in Victoria's reign and was strongly affected by the Oxford Movement. Many new churches were needed and, as Episcopalians were affected by the same arguments as High Church Anglicans, these were, almost without exception, in ecclesiologically correct Gothic.

Indeed, in architectural terms, the Victorian Episcopal Church seems to have been largely English in character. Until the late nineteenth century, the architects employed were almost always English — Butterfield, Scott, Bodley; perhaps no suitable Scots could be found who understood Gothic so well. The one conspicuous exception to this generalisation, the Episcopal cathedral in Inverness, by the local architect Alexander Ross, merely confirms this hypothesis. The consequence is that such buildings as the Cathedral of the Isles at Millport, St Mary's Cathedral in Edinburgh and St Salvador's, Dundee, must be undertood in an Enlish context and not a Scottish one.[5]

Yet Scottish Presbyterians also built in Gothic. Such is the power of ideas, or the tyranny of fashion, for the correct ecclesiological plan was surely an anachronism. A protestant congregation needed a centralised space, a building housing a large congregation within a short distance from the minister. A long nave, especially with aisles, was an inconvenience; a deep sanctuary an irrelevance. The most convenient plan was that which had been often used in the eighteenth century: a rectangular auditorium with galleries but no aisles. Nor was the orientation necessarily logitudinal, for often the pulpit, on which pews and galleries focused, was placed in the middle of one of the longer walls.[6] And Gothic scarcely lent itself to articulating such a plan — as Pugin rightly argued when he ridiculed wide, aisleless preaching boxes decked out with medieval details. Even so, hundreds of Presbyterian churches were built in Gothic in the nineteenth century in Scotland. Ironically, one of the most conspicuous of these is the Tolbooth Church in the Old Town of Edinburgh, designed in 1839 by Gillespie Graham but assisted by the great Pugin himself.

Victorian protestant architecture is, in British terms, a largely uncharted area. Not only has the architectural history of Scotland been marginalised, but, ever since Eastlake, architectural historians have tended to concentrate on the High Church wing of the Gothic Revival, on the Streets and Butterfields. Although such creative architects clearly represented the British avant-garde, this has resulted in the neglect of the nonconformist experiments in Gothic in England — like those of James Cubitt and Alfred Waterhouse — and of the Presbyterian churches which dominate the picture in Scotland, both in number and in scale. This neglect is all the more unjust as, occasionally, Gothic was adapted to the protestant church requirements in interesting and original ways. It may nevertheless seem initially surprising that, after Pugin, Gothic was ever adopted as a style for the kirk at all — particularly in Glasgow, a city which, like Edinburgh, remained largely loyal to the classical tradition in secular architecture.

In the Second City, by the early nineteenth century, stood three churches dedicated to Scotland's patron saint. St Andrew's Kirk, built for the Church of Scotland in its (original) Georgian square, is a provincial version of Gibbs's St Martin-in-the-Fields (and so, ultimately, of Scottish inspiration); down the road, St Andrew's (former) Episcopal church is a classical box domestic in size and scale. But right by the Clyde, 'placed in an open and favourable situation for displaying its magnificence',[7] St Andrew's Catholic chapel, now cathedral, designed by James Gillespie (Graham) and built in 1814–16, is not only the most prominent pre-emancipation Catholic church in Britain, it is also Gothic in style. The same architect also designed St Mary's Catholic chapel, now cathedral, in Edinburgh in 1813, again in Gothic. Yet despite this anticipation of Pugin's advocacy of Gothic as the true Christian, that is, Catholic style, the established Presbyterian churches in Scotland also adopted medieval styles. Perhaps it is significant that, in marked contrast to all the nearby new Anglican churches, the Scotch Church in Regent Square in London — from which the charismatic Edward Irving would eventually so notoriously be excluded to establish his own church — was a miniature version of York Minster, designed by William Tite.[8] The strange fact is that the revival of Gothic, or medievalism, had deep roots in Scotland which can be traced back well into the eighteenth century.[9]

Gothic was being taken seriously again in Scotland, as in England, because of the new sense of history and antiquity encouraged, in Scotland in particular, by the novels of Walter Scott — appropriately commemorated, in Edinburgh, by Kemp's tall Gothic shrine in Princes Street Gardens. And when visitors came to admire Scott's neo-Gothic-cum-Baronial house at Abbotsford, they could also admire the nearby picturesque ruins of Gothic abbeys at Melrose and Dryburgh. Many books were published on such relics, culminating in the four volumes of R. W. Billings's *Baronial and Ecclesiastical Antiquities of Scotland* of 1845–52. Admiration for medieval architecture was part of a revival of interest in the history and distinctiveness of Scotland itself — a form of cultural nationalism which eventually produced an authentic and convincing expression in the style known as Scottish Baronial.

In 1843 occurred the major event of nineteenth-century Scottish religious history — and one with profound architectural consequences. This was the 'Great Disruption', when, in Edinburgh, after years of controversy about 'Intrusion', or patronage, in the choice of ministers, Dr Thomas Chalmers led nearly four hundred ministers out of the established Church of Scotland to found the Free Church.[10] Soon after, in 1845–50, the New College rose above the Mound to be a theological college and place of worship for the new Free Church. Its architect was W. H. Playfair; but whereas the same architect's two cultural institutions on the Mound below employed the Greek Doric and Ionic, this new building was in Tudor Gothic. Like St Giles's Cathedral, properly the 'High Church', nearby in the High Street, this centre of Presbyterianism was medieval in style.

The eventual result of over a third of the clergy and almost half of its members leaving the Church of Scotland was that every community would have at least two places of worship — a great boon to architects. But if the Gothic stye was to be used with any degree of ecclesiological correctness, a difficulty arose which is best described as the *column problem*. A proper medieval church had a nave and aisles and a separate chancel. For a Presbyterian congregation, a chancel was largely irrelevant, while the arcade between nave and aisles would block the view of the preacher for many members of the congregation. So if columns were to be introduced, they had to be made as thin as possible by exploiting a new building material: cast iron. As that interesting (English) protestant church-planner, James Cubitt, observed in 1870, 'The ordinary Anglican church, with its thick stone columns ... *there* is architecture with imperfect convenience. The average Nonconformist church, with its thin iron ones: *there* is convenience with imperfect architecture.'[11]

A similar problem was presented by galleries, which were loathed by Pugin and the Cambridge Camden Society, and never satisfactory in a 'correct' neo-medieval church. Yet any successful preaching space needed galleries and virtually no Scottish Presbyterian church, of whatever style, did without them. The result was an almost insuperable difficulty; that of successfully combining galleries with a type of architecture which had no place for them. As Cubitt again aptly argued in 1865,

> The difference between a building intended for galleries and one not intended for them is a fundamental one. The whole design, if it be natural and unaffected, will be based on the fact of its having galleries; it will be the aim of all the architect's thoughts, and the test of all his ingenuity, to make these galleries add to, instead of detracting from, the general effect.

And if galleries were desired, 'it may safely be said that, though Gothic *principles*, thoughtfully applied, will solve every difficulty, the mere copying of Gothic *forms* will only lead to shams and absurdities'.[12]

In fact, Gothic churches with no pretentions to archaeological accuracy, which happily exploited the verticality and spaciousness achieved by thin iron columns and which accepted galleries on three sides, could have great charm and character of their own. Good examples in Glasgow — both now demolished — were the Renfield Street Church by James Brown and the Renfield Free Church by Boucher and Cousland. They dated, respectively, from 1849 and 1857 yet were reminiscent of Thomas Rickman's Regency iron Gothic experiments in England. But what was to be done if, in deference to Anglican fashion and a sad search for respectability, architectural 'correctness' was desired (even if galleries were not abandoned) and starved iron columns eschewed?

One solution was offered by the Lansdowne United Presbyterian Church in Glasgow [**37**]. With its tall, thin spire and Early English detail, it was built in the fashionable West End in 1862–63 by Dr Eadie, who chose as his text for the opening sermon, 'I will make the place of my feet glorious'. Not everybody sympathised; at the end of the service the following lines were found pinned to the door: 'This church is not for the poor and needy / But for the rich and Dr Eadie. / The rich step in and take their seat, / But the poor walk down to Cambridge Street' — where stood the

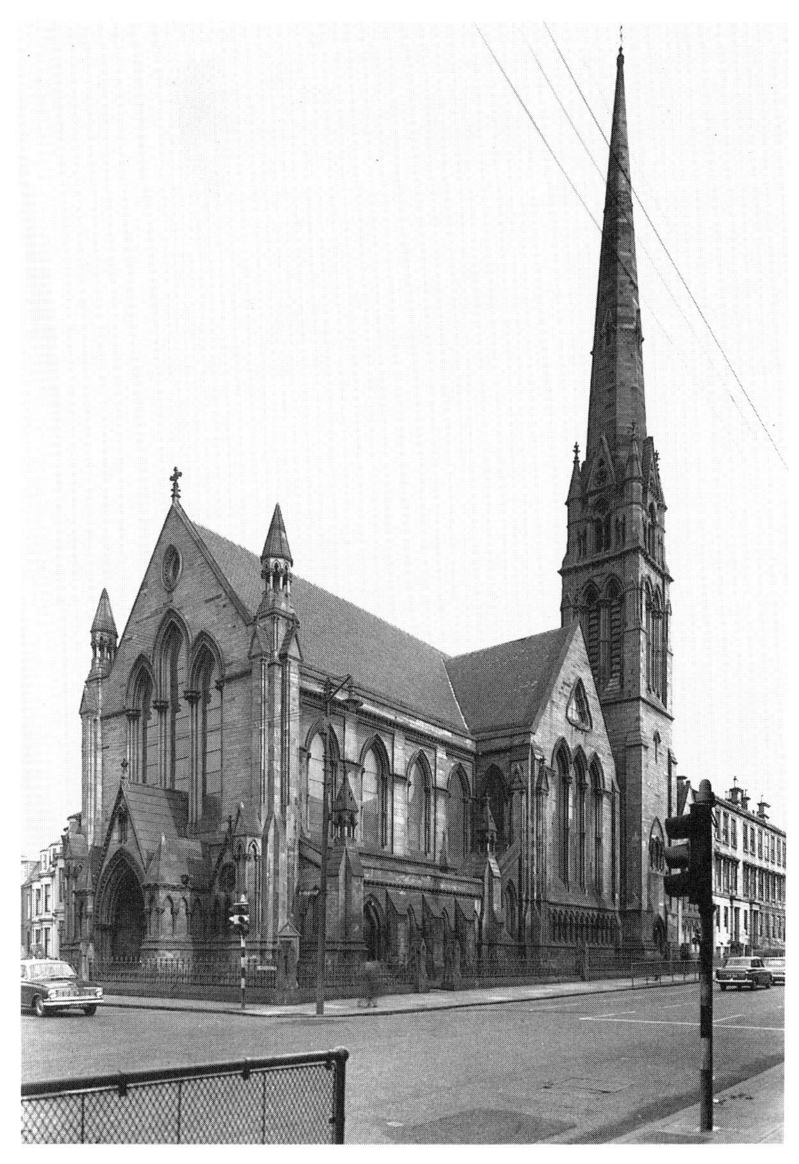

37] John Honeyman, Lansdowne United Presbyterian Church, Glasgow, 1862–63

congregation's old, bare preaching-box.[13] Eadie's architect was John Honeyman, who adopted a neo-medieval cruciform plan. David Walker argues that such a form can be regarded as a development of the traditional 'T' plan for Presbyterian churches, and certainly it was not a simple exercise in ecclesiological correctness. Instead of aisles, Honeyman created passages allowing access to the family pews through doors. Above these were galleries, and there was a gallery at the west end while at the east end a central pulpit stood in a short, narrower apse.

Honeyman, one of Glasgow's most distinguished and versatile Victorian architects, had a deep and serious interest in medieval architecture but, as

Walker has written, he used 'plan forms which not only attempted to bring a more convincing neo-medieval form to Presbyterian church-building but also introduced some new ideas on preaching church planning'.[14] Later, in 1881, Honeyman designed St Michael's parish church in Edinburgh in solid Early English but with the arcades running unbroken to the full-width east wall — so denying a separate chancel — and with the last, taller arch on one side opening into an organ-chamber. The result was a convincing space for Presbyterian worship, but the column problem remained.

Another solution to adapting authentic Gothic precedent for protestant worsip was to choose a model which did without aisles altogether. One such, the celebrated Sainte Chapelle in Paris, was the inspiration for Hillhead parish church [**38**] designed by James Sellars of Campbell Douglas and Sellars. Opened in 1876, this is a most impressive work with its tall, wide interior illuminated by excellent stained glass in the tall windows which march round the generous curved apse. That this is a Presbyterian church is indicated, however, by the west gallery, the raked floor and the substitution of a broad proportion for the verticality of the Parisian thirteenth-century prototype. Nevertheless, this fine building does not have the character of awkward compromise that is typical of so many Presbyterian Gothic churches.

One that does is the Camphill United Presbyterian Church by Queen's Park of 1875–76 by William Leiper (who may well have suggested the idea for the Hillhead church).[15] The exterior looks solid and scholarly and is surmounted by a magnificent thirteenth-century Normandy spire — not for nothing had Leiper worked in Pearson's office in London. But the interior has nothing of the quality of the best French Gothic, or of its distinguished Victorian reinterpreter; instead there is a wide nave separated from wide galleried aisles by miserable thin arcades. There is no chancel; why should there be? Yet without one, such an externally thorough essay in thirteenth-century Gothic seems incomplete. At least this church is superior to Leiper's earlier Dowanhill Church in Glasgow, where a spiky Gothic exterior encloses a wide, barren space filled only by galleries supported on starved iron columns.

Two continental medieval precedents, widely adopted by Anglo-Catholics after the 1860s, also had implications for Scots Presbyterian churches. The first was Albi Cathedral with its internal buttresses pierced by passage aisles, which Bodley used to such effect in St Augustine's Pendlebury: a single vessel from east to west. The other was Gerona Cathedral, where a narrow chancel with passage aisles was combined with a wide nave. Both, of course, achieved an aim which was also shared by protestants: the accommodation of a large congregation without columns impeding the view of the altar. David Walker notes that this plan was first adopted in Scotland in the 1850s for the Episcopal church of St Mary Magdalene in Dundee designed by the (English) architect H. E. Coe,[16] but its most significant and influential expression was in Govan parish church, rebuilt in Early English in 1882–88 by Scotland's 'Premier Architect', Robert Rowand Anderson [**39**].

38] James Sellars, Belmont and Hillhead parish church, Glasgow, 1875–76. Interior

Govan Old is a remarkable building, not least as it was the architectural expression of the 'Scoto-Catholic' ideals of its minister, Dr John Macleod, who wished to bring a degree of dignity and ritual to Presbyterian worship. For this, of course, he looked to Anglo-Catholicism, and it was also to England that Anderson looked for inspiration. The magnificent and sophisticated interior of Govan Old combines a wide nave with passage aisles and the Gerona chancel, but also adds a two-bay transept on the north side. Anderson's biographer, Sam McKinstry, notes that the architect had visited Italy where he observed that the great Franciscan basilicas were laid out so that the arcades did not interfere with the view of the preacher; but, to English eyes, the interior of this church seems above all a reinterpretation of the architecture of J. L. Pearson. It is as if St John's, Red Lion Square, had been transported to the shipyards of the Clyde — except that there are galleries in the transept and at the west end and the roof is timber and not vaulted.[17]

Anderson had become an Episcopalian and had worked in London, in Gilbert Scott's office. Nevertheless, a similar austere lancet style and a similar plan were used by the great J. J. Burnet in the Barony Church in Glasgow, built in 1886 after a competition judged, surely significantly, by Pearson himself. Typical of this supremely accomplished architect, the result is sophisticated and superbly executed, and its wide nave now serves admirably as the Convocation Hall of the University of Strathclyde. Nevertheless, the Barony Church seems like a knowing reworking of the

39] Robert Rowand Anderson, Govan parish church ('Govan Old'), 1883–88. Interior

themes of the High Anglican Gothic Revival rather than a creative adaptation of Gothic to Presbyterian needs.

For that one must turn to that extraordinary English-born architect, Frederick Thomas Pilkington, who seems to have been almost the only Goth to rise to this challenge with both intelligence and true originality. He exploited the theoretical functional flexibility of the Gothic Revival further than anyone — certainly more than Street or even the nonconformist Waterhouse — as he was almost alone in adapting Gothic to unprecedented and thoroughly un-Gothic plans. Pilkington built astonishing churches, surmounted by heavyweight spiky steeples, in Kelso, Irvine and Dundee. His masterpiece, however, is the Barclay Free Church of 1862–64 [**40**] in Edinburgh, where he had established his office. Pilkington had read his Ruskin, for he created a sculptural, organic Gothic, enriched with creeping naturalistic sculpture. Outside, the church is distinguished by projecting curved walls rising to spiky gables supporting roofs with ridges running in all directions. This only makes sense upon seeing the interior, for Pilkington did not attempt to adapt a medieval plan but created a theatre-like auditorium focusing on a central pulpit.

In plan [**41**] the interior is shaped something like a squashed pear. Originally there were three stepped-back tiers of curved galleries facing the pulpit and organ, while the bulging sides of the auditorium are also curved. Coherence is given to this immensely tall and comparatively narrow space by two giant square columns and two dwarf iron columns supporting a central rectangular timber roof structure, while ancillary accommodation is cleverly integrated. It all has to be seen to be believed, but the seriousness and practicality underlying this most original expression of Gothic freedom suggests that Pilkington rose beyond eccentricity to genius. The sadness is that when the wildness of High Victorian Gothic went out of fashion, such buildings were dismissed as eccentric and the valuable lessons Pilkington provided were discarded in favour of pedantic, Anglophile Gothic correctness.[18]

Compared with Pilkington's work, most of the Scottish ecclesiastical Gothic Revival seems tame, particularly in Glasgow. But in the Second City the classical tradition remained strong. In 1856, when the first of Thomson's churches was begun, a local paper noted that although most churches were Gothic, three then in course of erection were Greek.[19] The elder Burnet could build the Elgin Place Congregational Church in pure Greek Ionic as late as 1855–56 and the John Street United Presbyterian Church by J. T. Rochead, opened in 1860, was also classical. As Frank Worsdall remarks, 'Its Italian Renaissance exterior might easily be mistaken for that of a public hall rather than a church, but, of course, that was a United Presbyterian tradition. Under no circumstances must it be mistaken for a Church of Scotland!!'[20] The United Presbyterians seem to have been the wealthiest as well as the most artistically aware of the various Presbyterian sects, and nowhere was this more evident than in the astonishing churches designed by Alexander Thomson which are, or were, Glasgow's glory.

40] F. T. Pilkington, Barclay Memorial Free Church, Edinburgh, 1862–64. Detail of the exterior

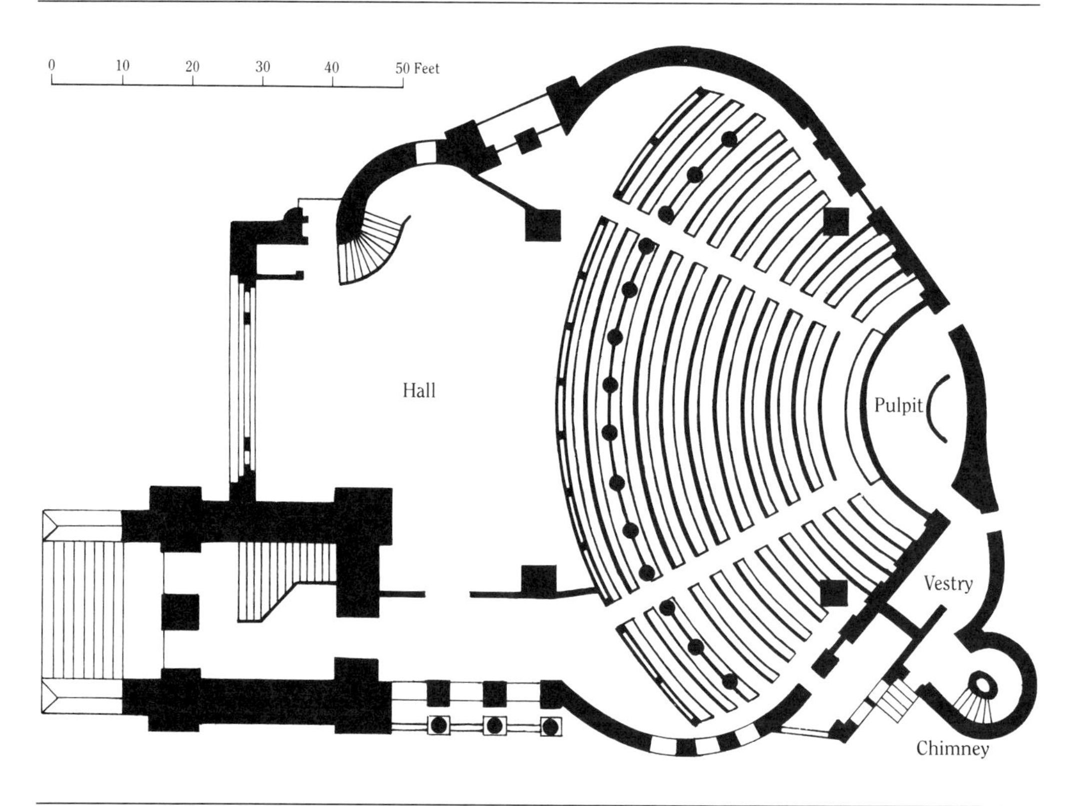

41] F. T. Pilkington. Barclay Memorial Free Church. Ground plan

Henry-Russell Hitchcock wrote that Thomson designed 'three of the finest Romantic Classical churches in the world'.[21] Certainly they were three of the most convincing and sophisticated solutions to the problem of designing urban buildings for Presbyterian congregations. Perhaps this was because Thomson's vision of architecture was profoundly theological: 'Religion has been the soul of art from the beginning', he maintained.[22] He came to dislike Gothic and despised the theological arguments used in justification of its revival. For him, the architecture of Egypt and Greece were all part of the unfolding Divine purpose and so perfectly suitable for modern protestant worship. Mistrusting the arch, Thomson believed in the perennial stability and utility of trabeated architecture and so developed the Greek Revival with conspicuous originality long after it had gone out of fashion in England.

His first church, the Caledonia Road United Presbyterian Church of 1856, shows the influence of Schinkel, with its long clerestories of plate glass between square columns. Internally, this church was rectangular in plan with a west gallery [**42**]. At the St Vincent Street United Presbyterian Church — today the only intact survivor — the auditorium is almost square in plan, but the longitudinal emphasis essential to the idea of a temple was achieved by having wide aisles behind sturdy iron columns with extravagant and exotic capitals. The lower tier of columns supports

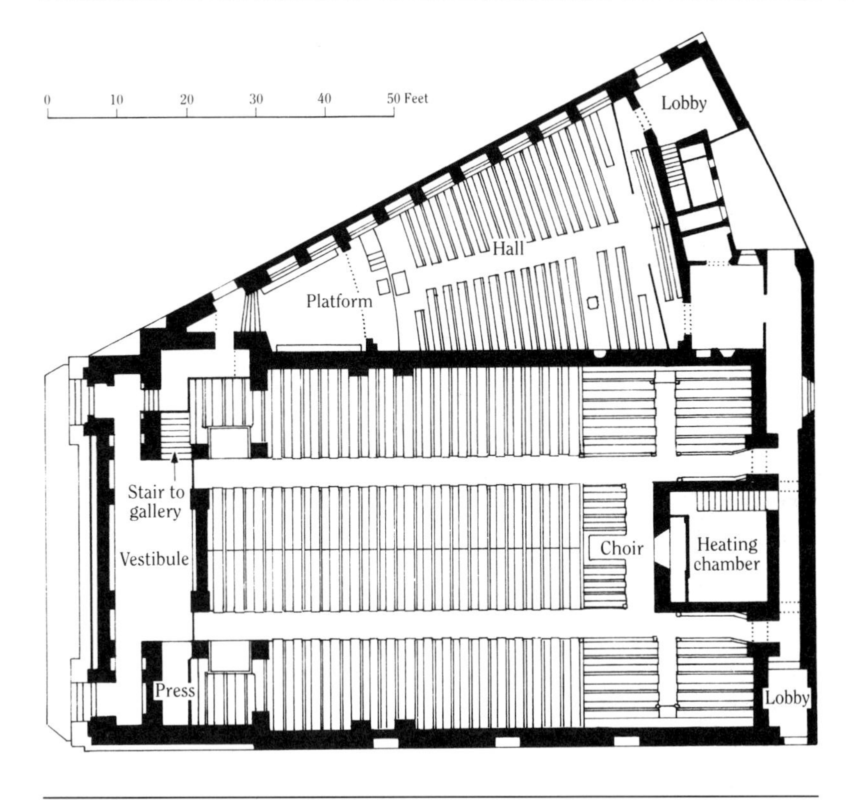

42] Alexander Thomson, Caledonia Road United Presbyterian Church, Glasgow, 1856. Ground plan

galleries on three sides and the seating throughout, executed in superb North American pine, is curved so that those in the aisles all face the raised pulpit. Here is a vision of the Temple of Solomon, made modern with cast iron and plate glass, suitable for non-liturgical congregational worship in the smoky streets of Victorian Glasgow.

Thomson's last great temple, the Queen's Park Church of 1867, was the most exotic of all. Internally, the richly decorated interior focused on the pulpit and raised choir gallery. The floor was raked and galleries were introduced behind iron colonnades on three sides. Surviving photographs make the interior of the Queen's Park Church seem reminiscent of a film set by Cecil B. de Mille, and certainly Thomson's highly romantic vision of the ancient world, of the Near East of the Old Testament, was inspired by the paintings and prints of John Martin. His interiors were richly coloured — that at Queen's Park in collaboration with the artist and decorator Daniel Cottier, which provoked Ford Madox Brown into exclaiming 'Well done Glasgow! I put ... this Thomson-Cottier church above everything I have seen in modern Europe.'[23]

All this may initially seem surprising in Calvinist Scotland, but, as George Hay pointed out, 'It is a common error to represent Scottish post-Reformation kirks as drab repellent structures, but this notion is soon dispelled by serious study of the facts. Calvinist tenets forbade representation of saints or the Deity, but other forms of "decorement" were neither banned nor lacking'.[24] Nor was Thomson alone in using colour in the nineteenth century. For example, Leiper's Dowanhill Church was also brightly, if crudely, decorated by Cottier while the (also Gothic) Anderston parish church of 1864–65 by Marshall Lang was richly painted with stencilled decoration.

Another important point about Thomson's great churches is that they were truly urban. Unlike the best urban work of Anglo-Catholic architects like Brooks or Bodley, most Scottish Gothic Revival churches seem to have been set down on their sites regardless of context and street pattern. Not so the temples Thomson raised in Glasgow. The Caledonia Road Church was not free-standing but lay at the apex of a site formed by two converging streets. To mark this point — a gateway to the city from Caledonian Railway's South Side terminus — Thomson raised a purely symbolic Ionic portico with a tall campanile on one side. And while one side wall of the church followed the street line, he placed a wedge-shaped church hall on the other to run along the converging street. Behind the church, again on each street line, Thomson designed five-bay blocks of tenements further to integrate his monument into the urban grain.

This St Vincent Street Church, similarly, was once flanked by a tenement designed by Thomson, who coped with a steeply sloping site by raising the church up on its own Acropolis: a great plinth of massive stones upon which two more of his purely symbolic porticoes are placed, high above the doors. Finally, to make the church into a landmark, Thomson raised an astonishing tower in which Greek, Egyptian and Indian elements were fused in one distinctive, memorable whole. The Queen's Park Church, in contrast, had no tower but stood out on its flat site surrounded by tenements by having another exotic tapering dome over the pediment. Below this was the tall Egyptianising entrance with a lower pilastraded order threaded through. This order articulated the ancillary accommodation which Thomson cleverly planned fully to occupy the perimeter of the awkward triangular building site. The destruction of this church by incendiary bombs in March 1943 was Glasgow's — Scotland's — worst architectural loss of the Second World War.

One of Thomson's many admirers, writing in 1925, could declare that his churches 'remain the grandest achievement in church architecture since the Middle Ages'.[25] In Scottish terms, perhaps such hyperbole is justified — especially when contemplating that miraculous survivor, the St Vincent Street Church. Nor should the little Chalmers Free Church in Ballater Street in the Gorbals be forgotten. This building, demolished over twenty years ago, was almost square in plan and, with its abstracted classical order and rectilinear massing, bore an uncanny resemblance to Frank Lloyd Wright's Unity Temple. Perhaps the link is that both men derived inspiration from Schinkel.[26]

Thomson had no equals but several followers. James Sellars designed the Finnieston parish church in a Thomsonian Greek manner in 1896 and McKissak and Rowan raised a Thomsonesque steeple above Pollokshields West Church in 1875–79. The classical tradition, indeed, continued unabated in church architecture after Thomson's death in 1875. Hugh and David Barclay built St George-in-the-Fields parish church in Greek Ionic in 1884–85. Thomas L. Watson designed the Wellington Church in 1883 opposite the university, contrasting Gilbert Scott's Gothic with Roman Corinthian, while John Honeyman built two more churches in an Italian classical style; the Westbourne Church off Great Western Road in 1880 and, across the green from Burnet's Gothic Barony, the Barony North Church in 1878. The last classical church to be built in Victorian Glasgow was the Langside Hill Church, erected in 1896 just south of Queen's Park near the site of the final battlefield defeat of Mary Queen of Scots. Designed in the Greek style by Alexander Skirving, it is conspicuously the work of a former assistant of Greek Thomson himself. All these provided rectangular galleried interiors without architectural compromise.

But while classicism gently faded away, at least for Presbyterians, Gothic was taken up with greater enthusiasm and increasing pedantry. The most extreme manifestation of this is not, in fact, Presbyterian but Baptist: the Coats Memorial Church in Paisley of 1885–94, a colossal and expensive pile, superbly executed in unlikely commemoration of the great thread manufacturer and philanthropist. Designed by Hippolyte Blanc of Edinburgh in elaborate English Decorated, it is cruciform in plan; only the width of the nave and the fact that most of the chancel is occupied by a large sunken marble bath for total immersion distinguish this building from a contemporary expensive Anglican Gothic church.[27]

Occasionally Gothic was given a *fin de siècle* flavour. The most celebrated example of this is, of course, the Queen's Cross Church designed in 1897 by C. R. Mackintosh as an assistant in the firm of Honyman and Keppie. Externally, conventional Gothic based on English precedents is given an enjoyable personal mannerism, while the wide rectangular interior, lit by large wide Perpendicular windows, shows intimate knowledge of recent work by Norman Shaw and J. D. Sedding. However, even the charm of Mackintosh's idiosyncratic style, together with the spatial interest of the shallow two-bay transept on one side (a debt to Govan Old), fail to overcome the empty character of the wide space, galleried on one side and at the rear. The problem of Presbyterian design is here emphasised by the vestigial chancel which is crossed by an ornamental beam. Reminiscent of a rood beam, it is essentially an empty gesture included only for artistic effect; the congregation would have had no truck with what they regarded as a remnant of superstitious idolatory. Indeed, the beam was removed and has been replaced only recently.

Mackintosh's church, however, has considerably more integrity than the two in Glasgow by the versatile but facile James Miller: St Andrew's East of 1904 and the Macgregor Memorial Church in Govan of 1902. Each has a showy front, the result of the architect making good use of published illustrations of the latest work by the likes of Sedding, Henry Wilson and Leonard Stokes, but in each case this is attached to an unimaginative Gothic shed behind. These buildings epitomise the essential conflict between Presbyterian needs and the English Gothic Revival tradition at its most refined and experimental.

Considerably more successful — and deserving to be much better known — is the former St George's United Free Church (now St Matthew's) in Paisley of 1905–07. Designed by W. D. McLennan, a local hero, its art nouveau Perpendicular Gothic is obviously indebted to Mackintosh, yet the interior of the building is far more coherent than that of the Queen's Cross Church, and truly original. A wide nave, with raked floor, is covered by an elaborate and expressive timber roof, while rear and side galleries are incorporated behind convincingly purposeful arcades. And the aesthetic treatment of the ceiling extends into the remarkable furnishings. As with many Presbyterian churches, a generous provision of halls and other accommodation wraps around the side and rear of the building, giving constructional integrity to the varied and complex façades which define the street lines. Frank Walker aptly describes all this as 'a Glasgow style idiom both expressionist and constructivist ... Had the massive belfry spire been built it would have outscaled any other piece of *Art Nouveau* architecture in the country.[28]

The pity is that McLennan's triumphant originality was so unusual. Most Presbyterian churches continued to be built in a spare, tasteful, comfortable Gothic that seems American in character and Anglo-Catholic in stylistic derivation; the legacy of Bodley and Garner was surprisingly wide as well as long-lasting. Such buildings as J. Taylor Thomson's St John's Renfield in Glasgow, of 1927, and the Reid Memorial Church in Edinburgh of 1928 by Leslie G. Thomson exemplify this tradition at its best. there were also the churches of Peter Macgregor Chalmers.

> [He] realised that Norman was more adaptable to the Presbyterian service than Gothic, as well as cheaper. His characteristic Scottish churches, with their simple round-headed arches, apses, and stone interiors, are to be seen all over Scotland. They have real merit, but tend to become a type mechanically turned out and lacking in both colour and a sense of adventure.

Such was the opinion of the Scottish author of the wide-ranging and incisive historical study of *The Church Architecture of Protestantism* published in 1934. This was Dr Andrew Landale Drummond, who concluded that,

> in the building of new churches, there is no excuse for traditionalism ... But it cannot be said of either England or Scotland that there is a vital interest in modern Church Architecture, conceived in terms of creative progress. The few people who show any interest tend to be complacent traditionalists who 'canonise the past'; the majority of clergy and church members are indifferent. Church Architecture is therefore an affair of architects. There is little group co-operation between architects and the Churches. Consequently, architects plan in a stereotyped way.[29]

It was not always thus in the vital decades of Victoria's reign.

It was unfortunate that Scotland's greatest Arts and Crafts architect — and a master of Gothic — Robert Lorimer, built so few churches. His Thistle Chapel of 1909–11 was a superbly sophisticated addition to St Giles's Cathedral, while his Scottish National War Memorial in Edinburgh Castle is a glorious and poignant communal shrine. Lorimer was an Episcopalian, and neither of these buildings addressed the problem of Presbyterian worship; both are essentially Bodleian medieval in inspiration. What is intersting, however, is that Lorimer succeeded in giving his Gothic a rugged, Scottish character, notably by adopting the apsidal end supported by massive stepped buttresses which is the dominating feature of the fifteenth-century Church of the Holy Rude in Stirling. This was a feature used earlier by another Scottish Episcopalian (and one who, like Lorimer, had worked for Bodley), Ninian Comper, in his chapel of 1891 at St Margaret's Convent in Aberdeen. But that splendid little building also had little to offer the architects of Scottish Presbyterianism.

Two last Presbyterian churches deserve mention, although they are aberrations. In 1924–26 Kippan Parish Church was 'renovated', that is, rebuilt, in a spare Gothic manner by the Roman Catholic architect Reginald Fairlie. The new church is a wide rectangular space with a west gallery, but what gives it interest is the extraordinary wealth of beautiful furnishings resulting from the residence in the village of that fine artist, D. Y. Cameron. Owing to his influence and munificence there is lovely work by Robert Lorimer and his son Hew and, above all, two exquisite figures in the baptistry by Alfred Gilbert originally made for the tomb of the Duke of Clarence. For once, the ideals of the Arts and Crafts movement were fused with the needs of a Presbyterian parish church — although the result is no more unified artistically than Sedding's Holy Trinity, Sloane Street, London, of three decades earlier. The other is St Conan's Kirk, a weird, tantalising and rambling structure overlooking Loch Awe which was built in stages after 1881 and not completed until 1930. It was designed by an amateur architect, Walter Campbell, who began by reproducing historical styles but who ended by creating a fusion of Romanesque and Scots Gothic which is at once organic, Symbolist, Arts and Crafts and highly personal. St Conan's is a product of eccentricity verging on genius, and its use by the local Church of Scotland congregation seems surprising.

In this essay, the considerable architectural achievements of the Episcopal Church have hardly been mentioned while the Roman Catholic Church has been largely ignored — only in the twentieth century did its churches become significant and adventurous architecturally. My theme has been the churches erected by the various shifting protestant strands — Church of Scotland, Free Church and United Presbyterian — which, despite their divisions, together constituted the dominant religious tradition and culture of Victorian Scotland. A discussion of so wide a subject, from a partial and detached standpoint, in a short essay must inevitably be superficial to a degree. It may also seem contradictory that I should find so many Scottish churches wanting by the high standards of the English Gothic Revival, while arguing that the plan-forms of High Anglicanism were really irrelevant to Presbyterians. 'Incorrect' wide galleried interiors and thin iron columns could surely be regarded as aspects of a Scottish protestant tradition. Unfortunately, after the 1850s so many such buildings seem to lack architectural coherence and integrity, and also appear too Anglophile in their Gothic trappings to be regarded as part of an authentic Scottish tradition. W. D. McLennan's rare triumph in Paisley only serves to emphasise this point.

There may well be many fine churches not discussed here whose qualities might undermine these easy generalisations. Nevertheless, I am convinced that the classical language was usually far more appropriate than the Gothic for Scottish protestant churches — especially when spoken by architects like Honeyman — and that the two giants of Victorian ecclesiastical architecture in Scotland were the only two men who really made a serious attempt creatively to adapt the precedents of the past — whether Gothic or classical — to modern Presbyterian worship: F. T. Pilkington and 'Greek' Thomson. And both, interestingly enough, were among those categorised as 'rogue architects' by that wisest historian of Victorian architectural endeavour and folly, H. S. Goodhart-Rendel.

Notes

1 James Macaulay, *The Gothic Revival, 1745–1845*, Glasgow and London, 1975, p. 263.

2 I approach the subject of Victorian churches in Scotland with considerable diffidence. I am not a Scot (or a Presbyterian) and my knowledge of Scotland is largely confined to the big cities and to Glasgow in particular, which is now my home. Also, as the interest of church architecture is as much to do with interiors as exteriors, it is remarkably difficult to remedy this defect. Except at a few medieval buildings, there seems to be no tradition of church-crawling in Scotland, so that most churches remain resolutely locked all week. Indeed, I feel presumptuous in writing about a subject about which so many know so much more than I. I think of Dr James Macaulay, Dr Sam McKinstry, Mr Ian Gow, the various authors of the *Buildings of Scotland* and of the *Architectural Guides* produced by Charles McKean and the Royal Incorporation of Architects in Scotland and, in particular, of Dr David Walker, who has recently published a survey of Scottish Victorian church architecture entitled 'Govan Old: its place in nineteenth and early twentieth century church design' in the *Third Annual Report* of The Society of Friends of Govan Old, Glasgow, 1993, pp. 4–20; and a study of 'The Honeymans' in *Newsletter* No. 62 of The Charles Rennie Mackintosh Society, Glasgow, Summer 1993.

3 This is not an anti-Scottish prejudice: the nineteenth-century Gothic churches of, say, Germany are equally, if not more disappointing. The fact is that the Victorian Gothic Revival was one of England's supreme artistic achievements.

4 Alexander Thomson, 'An Inquiry as to the Appropriateness of the Gothic Style for the Proposed Buildings for the University of Glasgow, with some Remarks upon Mr. Scott's Design' in *Proceedings of the Glasgow Architectural Society*, 1865–67, p. 46.

5 See Marion Lochhead, *Episcopal Scotland in the Nineteenth Century*, London, 1966.

6 For earlier Scottish protestant plan forms, see George Hay, *The Architecture of Scottish Post-Reformation Churches, 1560–1845*, Oxford, 1957.

7 [Robert Chapman], *The Topographical Picture of Glasgow*, Glasgow, 1820, p. 151. The Edinburgh architect James Gillespie annexed his wife's name, Graham, when he inherited from his father-in-law in 1825. Gillespie Graham was an accomplished medievalist but, like Barry, he later seems often to have employed Pugin; see the chapter in Macaulay, *Gothic Revival*.

8 Dr Sheridan Gilley has pointed out the interesting similarities between Edward Irving and A. W. N. Pugin, brilliant fanatics both. Irving died in 1834, but his secessionists went on to create the Catholic Apostolic Church, whose now-demolished Glasgow building, begun in 1852, was based on a sketch by Pugin. The Catholic Apostolic church in Edinburgh, designed by Rowand Anderson, is Romanesque in style.

9 See James Macaulay, *Gothic Revival*, which has a chapter on Scottish churches and emphasises the often ignored significance of Inveraray Castle, rebuilt — in a medieval style — after 1745.

10 The ramifications of Scottish protestantism are difficult to grasp, especially by outsiders. Essentially, at the beginning of Victoria's reign, there was the established Church of Scotland and the various sects which had split from the state Church since the restoration of Presbyterianism by William III in 1690 as the established religion. Several of these had coalesced as the United Presbyterian Church, as it was called after 1847. In 1843,

after long controvesy over the matter of 'Intrusion', or the English manner of external patronage of ministers in parishes, Dr Thomas Chalmers led the secession of nearly four hundred ministers from the Church of Scotland in the great 'Disruption' to form the Free Church. After great struggles and privations, over 730 places of worship were erected within five years. A further secession, from the Free Church, produced the Free Presbyterians or 'Wee Frees' in 1892. Soon after, in 1900, a majority of the Free Church joined with most of the United Presbyterians to form the United Free Church, and a majority of this alliance joined in the 'Great Reunion' of 1929 with the Church of Scotland, whose independence from state control was then established by Act of Parliament.

11 James Cubitt, *Church Design for Congregations — Its Development and Possibilities*, London, 1870, p. 3, quoted in A. L. Drummond, *The Church Architecture of Protestantism*, Edinburgh, 1934, p. 76.

12 James Cubitt, 'Chapel Architecture in 1864' in *Building News*, 10 March 1865, p. 164.

13 Quoted by Frank Worsdall, *The Victorian City*, Glasgow, 1982, p. 21.

14 David Walker, 'The Honeymans', p. 9.

15 Andor Gomme and David Walker, *Architecture of Glasgow*, London, 1968, whose chapter 'Victorian Gothic' discusses these and other churches. Many of these have been demolished, and more sad losses are illustrated in Frank Worsdall's *The City that Disappeared*, Glasgow, 1981.

16 David Walker, 'Govan Old', p. 9.

17 Sam McKinstry, *Rowand Anderson, 'The Premier Architect of Scotland'*, Edinburgh, 1991, p. 105. See also Dr McKinstry's essay on 'The Architecture of Govan Old Parish Church' in the *Second Annual Report* of The Society of Friends of Govan Old, Glasgow, 1992, pp. 4–15.

18 Drummond, in *Church Architecture of Protestantism*, p. 83, felt obliged to write that 'It is an architect's nightmare, this incongrouous pile', but recognised that 'Pilkington's madness just missed genius' and that 'Had he lived half a century later, when art was less commercialised and ornament less shoddy and mechanised, Pilkington's achievement might have excited less ridicule than today. His originality must be admitted'. Pilkington deserves a full biography. So far, in addition to H. S. Goodhart-Rendel's famous article, 'Rogue Architects of the Victorian Era', *Journal of the Royal Institute of British Architects*, 56, 1949, pp. 251–9, he has only been the subject of a University of Edinburgh dissertation by Hugh Dixon, who published 'The Churches of Frederick Pilkington' in the *Liturgical Review*, the journal of the Christian Service Society, for November 1972. A Newcastle School of Architecture thesis, 'The Life and Work of Frederick Thomas Pilkington' by T. M. Jeffery, 1981 (copy at the National Monuments Record of Scotland), has the merit of including tantalising plans of the Barclay church.

19 Frank Worsdall, *Victorian City*, p. 19.

20 Frank Worsdall, *Victorian City*, p. 20.

21 Henry-Russell Hitchcock, *Architecture: Nineteenth and Twentieth Centuries*, 1963, p. 63.

22 Alexander Thomson, *Art and Architecture: A Course of Four Lectures* read to the Haldane Institute, Glasgow, 1874, no. 2, p. 6. For Thomson's architectural theory, see the essay by Sam McKinstry in Gavin Stamp and Sam McKinstry (eds), *Greek Thomson*, Edinburgh, 1994.

23 *Glasgow Herald*, 9 October 1893, and quoted in, among other works, Ronald McFadzean, *Life and Work of Alexander Thomson*, London, 1979.

24 Hay, *Scottish Post-Reformation Churches*, p. 215.

25 J. Jeffrey Waddell, quoted by Drummond, *Architecture of Protestantism*, from ' "Greek" Thomson' in *Scottish Ecclesiological Society's Transactions*, 1925, reprinted as a pamphlet [Aberdeen], 1925.

26 Stamp and McKinstry (eds), *Greek Thomson*, p. 212, and *The Alexander Thomson Society Newsletter*, no. 7, June 1993.

27 Clyde Binfield, 'A Working Memorial? The Encasing of Paisley's Baptists', in *Crown and Mitre: Religion and Society in Northern Europe since the Reformation*, Woodbridge, 1993.

28 Frank Walker, *The South Clyde Estuary*, Edinburgh, 1986, p. 31.

29 Drummond, *Architecture of Protestantism*, pp. 100–1.

Chapter 5 · Peter Howell

Church and chapel in Wales

When preaching at the consecration of Llanddeiniol new church in 1835, the Reverend John Hughes, Vicar of Llanbadarn Fawr, took as his text Psalm 132, verses 2–5:

> Surely I will not go into the tabernacle of my house, nor go up into my bed; I will not give sleep unto mine eyes or slumber to mine eyelids, until I find out a place for the Lord, a habitation for the mighty God of Jacob.[1]

Such heroic ambition was characteristic of the nineteenth century, but what was different about Wales? In 1886 Bishop Basil Jones of St David's said that Wales was 'but a geographical expression', and in many ways this was true for the nineteenth century, as far as religion was concerned. However, it is difficult to generalise about such a varied country, with its fertile valleys and remote mountain areas, its old market towns and its modern industrial developments.

What about the style of church buildings? The foremost authority on medieval Welsh churches, W. Gwyn Thomas, argues that there is no native Welsh style.[2] Of course there are regional variations, such as the twin-naved churches of Denbighshire, the saddleback towers of Gower, or the towers with projecting top storey of coastal Glamorgan. But the character of the church buildings was dictated largely either by poverty, or the materials used. As regards these, Vernon Hughes has claimed that the only truly indigenous Welsh building material is corrugated iron, which was indeed used for some charming little churches; two examples are the Norwegian Seamen's Church in the Cardiff Docks [**43**] and Abercych in rural Pembrokeshire.

There are striking differences between the first half of the nineteenth century and the second. To start with, there was the general problem in Britain of the lack of churches. This is certainly true of industrial Wales, but elsewhere the problem was often that the churches were in the wrong places; it is important to bear in mind the rarity of nucleated villages in rural Wales. Llanddeiniolen Church in Caernarfonshire was rebuilt in 1843, but it was too remote from the upland slate quarries where most of the parishioners lived.[3] Although the 1851 Religious Census recorded

43] Norwegian Seamen's Church, Cardiff Docks

fourteen places of worship for a population of 4,894, a new church was built up at 'Llandinorwic', near the quarries, in 1857 (Henry Kennedy, architect), and given a spire to make sure that the nonconformists were properly trounced. By contrast, the charming old church of Llandeilo Talybont in Glamorgan was set in a marshy valley, and often cut off by floods, and was in any case too small; eventually in 1900 a new church was built in Pontarddulais (the sad end to this story being that the old church has now been dismantled for re-erection at the Welsh Folk Museum).[4]

The matter of church-building was much affected by nonconformity. In the late nineteenth century this was criticised as a seventeenth-century importation from England, but it was highly successful in Wales; it claimed more than 85 per cent of the population in the 1851 Census.[5] So the problem was often not one of 'church room' in the simple sense. For example, Botwnnog in Lleyn had in 1851 a population of 163, served by a parish church and two chapels. The Calvinistic Methodist one alone could seat three times the population.[6] It is estimated that at this time the Church of England provided 52 per cent of church room in England, but only 30.5 per cent in Wales.

One of the chief problems of the Church of England in Wales [**44**] in the earlier nineteenth century was maladministration and the wrong deployment of resources. Over half the tithes in the Diocese of St David's were alienated. J. B. S. Chichester of Devon received £5,400 per annum in tithes, and paid out about £60 to £70 in stipends. He never contributed to

44] Dioceses, cathedral cities and principal towns in nineteenth-century Wales

any church building fund.[7] Pluralism and nepotism started at the top. Bishop Shipley of St Asaph gave his son William Davies Shipley, within four years of his ordination in 1770, three livings (including Wrexham), the deanery, and the chancellorship, and later on one more living.[8] Bishop Luxmoore, who held the same see from 1815 to 1830, and his family absorbed over £27,000 per annum from church property in St Asaph and Hereford, and after his death his relatives took £7,000 in St Asaph alone.[9]

However, the poverty of the southern sees made some pluralism inevitable. The annual revenues of Llandaff, as reported by the Ecclesiastical Revenues Commission in 1835, were only £924, the smallest in England and Wales, so that the see was held with other offices; Copleston, for example, was also Dean of St Paul's. There was no palace until 1850. The Diocese of St David's covered an area of 2,200,000 acres, but the Bishop received only £1,897 (the third lowest). He did at least have a palace, not at St David's, but at Abergwili (outside Carmarthen). But Burgess was a prebend of Durham, and Jenkinson (1825–40) was Dean of Durham.[10]

In general, the parishes were served, but often by poorly-paid curates. A special Welsh phenomenon was the so-called 'mountain clergy', mostly ill-educated and prone to the bottle.[11] The education of the clergy was a considerable problem. There were some good grammar schools, especially the famous one at Ystrad Meurig in Cardiganshire. In 1827 Bishop

Burgess founded St David's College, Lampeter, with its Oxbridge-type quadrangle designed by C. R. Cockerell. However, it was not a great success, largely because it was too expensive for the humbler students.[12]

More building and rebuilding of churches was undertaken around the second quarter of the nineteenth century than is generally thought, but it was often done cheaply and shoddily. When the Revd Robert Francis Kilvert first visited St Harmon, Radnorshire, in 1876, he described the church, which had been built in 1821 by W. Evans, as follows:

> The church was built in the Dark Ages of fifty years ago and was simply hideous. But ugly as it appeared externally the interior was worse and my heart sank within me like a stone as I entered the door. A bare cold squalid interior and high ugly square boxes for seats, a three-decker pulpit and desk, no stove, a flimsy altar rail, a ragged faded altar cloth, a singing gallery with a broken organ, a dark little box for a vestry, and a roof in bad repair, admitting the rain.[13]

Such churches were often rebuilt later in the century; a brilliant example is John Douglas's clever remodelling in 1896 of the 1814 Gothick box at Maentwrog in Merioneth.

This was a crucial time for the Church of England. In 1832 Thomas Arnold of Rugby wrote that 'the Church of England as it now stands no human power could save'. The political situation was, of course, critical, and Chartism was strong in the south of Wales. Parliament began to make grants to the Church Building Commissioners. In 1835 a rationalising proposal to absorb the Diocese of Llandaff into Bristol and to amalgamate St Asaph and Bangor was successfully fought off in Parliament by the second Earl of Powis.[14] Subsequent bills in the 1830s and 1840s attempted to improve matters of finance and organisation. For example, an 1843 act made it easier to form new parishes, since previously there had been difficulties over lay impropriators, neighbouring parish clergy, and so on. Such difficulties did not disappear; after Miss Clara Thomas built a new church in 1886 at Cwmbach Llechryd in Breconshire, the Rector of Llanelwedd sent a postcard every year to the new incumbent saying 'Cursed be he that removeth his neighbour's landmark'.[15]

Only one Welsh church benefited from the first Parliamentary Church Building Commission's grant, namely St Matthew's, Buckley, Flintshire, built in 1821–22 by John Oates. This was given no less than £4,052 towards an estimate of £4,000. The fact that Lord Kenyon, a Flintshire man, was a Commissioner, must have helped, along with the influence of Sir Stephen Glynne, whose seat at Hawarden was near Buckley.[16]

Out of the second Parliamentary grant thirty-three Welsh churches were helped, from St Michael's, Aberystwyth, in 1830–32, to St Peter's, Swansea, in 1856. The proportion of the grants dropped notably, so that for the latter only £85 was given towards an estimate of £1,495. The intention was that grants should go particularly to industrial areas; Aberystwyth was a strange choice.[17] A far more obvious one was Merthyr Tydfil, which was mentioned (along with twenty-three other towns) in the 1827 Report of the Commission.[18] By 1801 Merthyr was the largest town in Wales, with a population of 7,700; by 1831 its population was larger than those of Newport, Cardiff and Swansea combined; by 1861 its population of 50,000 was still the largest in Wales, although it declined thereafter. However, it received no grant until 1846. A church had meanwhile been built up at Dowlais by the Iron Company in 1827. At its consecration in that year, Bishop Sumner told the incumbent, 'I leave you as a missionary in the heart of Africa.'[19]

The Welsh valleys suffered particularly from the problem of having churches in the wrong places, since the medieval parish churches were usually on the tops of hills. A good example is Eglwysilan, high above the Taff Valley, which has a pub and a few houses for company, although an even more striking one, in the same county of Glamorgan, is the lonely church of Llanwonno. It is extraordinary to think that the vicar of this remote church had responsibility for the Rhondda Valley. Wishing to build a church there in 1850, he wrote: 'Language would fail to describe the very low state of morality that exists in this very populous valley: hundreds are as dark and ignorant respecting the way of salvation as the heathen.'[20] This verdict was reflected by Bishop Ollivant of Llandaff, who claimed that even Dissent had not been able to stem the 'torrent of iniquity and vice' in the coalfield.[21] In fact, at the 1851 Census, out of the population of 250,000 in the coalfield and its ports, only 17,000 attended the Church of England. The dissenters, however, had not been slow to build; in 1800 there were 50 chapels in the diocese, but by 1851 there were 550.[22]

In 1850 the Llandaff Church Extension Society was founded, to carry out what its first secretary H. A. Bruce (later Lord Aberdare) called its 'holy enterprise' of building churches.[23] However, it had an average annual income of only £1,300. It is remarkable that no tradesmen subscribed to it. Despite the new society's efforts, it is significant that between 1827 and 1846 fifteen new parishes were founded in the diocese, whereas between 1850 and 1870 only eleven were added. Most of the new churches were comparatively plain and simple, at least until towards the end of the century. Finer churches were usually due to private patronage. Inevitably, one of several ways in which nonconformist methods were imitated was 'voluntarism'. Occasionally even the church building resembled a nonconformist one; an example was the vast Norman St Mary's, Cardiff, built in 1841–43 by Thomas Foster and Son of Bristol. Its nave and aisles were filled with high pews, there were galleries on three sides, and the pulpit in the centre of the apse eclipsed the square altar-table.[24]

One way of paying for the building or rebuilding of churches was to levy a church rate, but this was little used in Wales even before the 1868 Act which made such rates voluntary, because they were usually so unpopular. A rate was levied at Aberystwyth in 1832, to build a sea wall to protect the new church of St Michael; five nonconformist ministers, who refused to pay it, had their property confiscated, which led to terrible bitterness.[25] On the other hand, when Llanrhystud church, also in Cardiganshire, was rebuilt [**45, 46**], by a heroic effort of the whole community, in 1852–54, there was no opposition to a church rate.[26] The special religious character of rural Cardiganshire has to be taken into account, and particularly that

45] Church of St Rhystud, Llanrhystud, Cardiganshire; the old church, before rebuilding. Engraving

of Llanrhystud itself; in 1904 Archdeacon Evans listed fifty-nine men ordained from the parish in his own lifetime.[27]

The design for the rebuilding of the church was made by Richard Kyrke Penson (1816–86), of Ferryside and Oswestry. Published in the Report of the Incorporated Church Building Society, it was referred for his opinion to the Archdeacon of Salop, John Allen. He replied: 'Why, the proposed

46] Richard Kyrke Penson, St Rhystud, Llanrhystud, Cardiganshire, 1852–54. The new church

restoration appears like the last erection of Turnham Green, or some other suburban school of the revival of Gothic architecture, instead of being fitted for the bluff position of the old weather-beaten and venerable structure.' ('Turnham Green' refers to Christ Church, Turnham Green, Middlesex, a new church built in 1841–43 by G. G. Scott.) As a result the antiquarian architect James Park Harrison was consulted, and agreed with Allen, but Penson refused to budge. However, an aisle was added merely in order to meet the ICBS requirement that at least half the seats should be free.

There was no doubt that many of the old churches of Wales were in a shocking state. The Revd T. Vaughan, Rector of Llandefaelog in Breconshire, wrote to the ICBS in 1831: 'I verily believe that the cold, damp and uncomfortable state of many of the churches in the Principality is not the least cause of dissent from the Established Church.'[28] When the Rector of Aberyscir, also in Breconshire, wrote to the ICBS around 1860, he quoted from Theophilus Jones's *History of the County of Brecknock*, published in 1809.

> It is a miserable little building in which the floor within is of *Earth* ... I cannot help lamenting that those who from laudable motives, no doubt, have visited our prisons did not take the trouble to look over and report, with accuracy, the state of our country churches, most of which are less comfortable than the worst rooms or apartments in a gaol — the dungeons and cells excepted.[29]

Kilvert reported that yet another Breconshire church, at Llanlleonfel, was so little used that a man coming to marry his second wife found a lace handkerchief left behind by his first wife still hanging on the altar-rails.[30]

An interesting example of church restoration is that of Glascwm in the wooded Radnorshire hills. In 1870 Kilvert met the old-fashioned vicar magistrate, Mr Marsden, who announced 'I am bishop here', and, fetching the key, said, 'Come and see the cathedral.' He told his visitor that there was no real dissent in the parish and that all came to church, but he had foreseen the ending of church rates, and so had taken off the roof to force the parish to put on a new one.[31] Nevertheless, in 1891 a major restoration was undertaken by Ewan Christian, architect to the Ecclesiastical Commissioners.[32] It was on the whole well done, though one may regret the insertion of an east window where previously, in accordance with local tradition, there was none. The raising of the money was a tremendous problem; the chancel, costing £480, was paid for by the Commissioners, but £688 was needed for the nave. The ICBS gave a mere £25, the squire gave £250 and the vicar £200, but the parishioners were able to contribute very little.

The generosity of the local aristocrats or landowners was urgently required, though it was not always forthcoming; Mr Chichester has already been mentioned. Some were exceptionally generous, such as Sir Stephen Richard Glynne, who paid for the new church of St John at Pentrobin, Flintshire, in 1843, and contributed to others.[33] His interest in ecclesiology is shown by his important collection of antiquarian notes, now at the National Library of Wales. A more exotic example of aristocratic generosity is the so-called 'Marble Church' at Bodelwyddan in Flintshire, erected at the vast cost of £35,000 by the dowager Lady Willoughby de Broke, so that its Northamptonshire-style spire would form a striking landmark from her family's castle (1856–60, John Gibson).[34]

It was not just churches that were needed. In the early nineteenth century many parsonages were uninhabitable, and the erection of new ones was an essential step towards attracting suitable incumbents.[35] Church schools were also provided in considerable numbers, the cost (despite government grant aid, after 1833, to the National and British School Societies, and later the Catholic Poor Schools Committee) being mostly covered by voluntary contributions.[36]

It was not only the parish churches that required restoration; the state of the four Welsh cathedrals was, in varying degrees, unsatisfactory. Three were restored by Sir Gilbert Scott. The two northern cathedrals are less interesting than the southern ones. It is unfortunate that the fine central spire which Scott designed for Bangor was never executed.[37] The finest feature of his work at St Asaph is the reredos, carved by Thomas Earp. At St David's, Scott's great achievement was to rescue the central tower from the collapse with which it was imminently threatened, although his most visible work there was to replace John Nash's west front with a new one, erected in memory of Bishop Thirlwall.[38] At St David's the eastern chapels had, like the Bishop's Palace, long been unroofed, but the situation at Llandaff was even worse. Not only had one of the western towers collapsed, but the whole cathedral was virtually a ruin, within which John Wood of Bath had formed what was scornfully called the 'Italian temple', although it actually incorporated some Gothic work. A magnificent restoration, begun by T. H. Wyatt, was carried through to completion by the son of a priest-vicar of the Cathedral, John Prichard [**47**].[39] However, not everyone in the diocese applauded the enterprise: the poorer clergy of the hills and valleys, led by the Revd John Griffith, thought that the sumptuous rebuilding used funds which could have been better spent elsewhere.[40]

A problem special to Wales was posed by the need for Welsh-speaking clergy. This varied, of course, from one area to another. On the whole it was the upland and more remote areas whose populations spoke Welsh, and these tended to be served by the 'mountain clergy' referred to above. In 1853 W. J. Conybeare, son of the Dean of Llandaff, wrote in the *Edinburgh Review*, 'Even now, within sight of those cathedrals which we associate with Copleston and Thirlwall, indigenous pastors are to be found who cannot speak English grammatically and who frequent the rural tavern in company with the neighbouring farmers.'[41] It is remarkable that in mid-century the average curate's salary in the Diocese of St David's was a mere £55 per annum.[42] There was no native Welsh-speaking bishop until Joshua Hughes was appointed to St Asaph in 1870.[43] Burgess and Thirlwall both learnt Welsh; the latter was especially proud of his pronunciation, but it was so 'correct' as to be generally unintelligible. He did at least make the effort to hold confirmations in Welsh, unlike other bishops whose English was understood by almost none of their candidates.[44] Not all the bishops were keen to promote the Welsh language. In 1849 Sir Benjamin

Hall (later Lord Llanover) refused to subscribe to the Copleston memorial because of the bishop's opposition to Welsh, and took the opportunity to warn the Archbishop of Canterbury about the need for Welsh-speaking clergy.[45]

Even clergy who tried to speak Welsh often made mistakes, sometimes with comic results. Mr Marsden of Glascwm told Kilvert about a curate who came to him from St David's College, Lampeter; he asked 'why these two backsides may not lawfully be joined together in Holy Matrimony'. Walter Morgan reports that one cleric in the Diocese of St David's, wishing to say 'Hail, King of the Jews', actually said 'an old cow of straw, King of Ireland'.[46] The first consecration of a church in the Welsh language was that of Llangorwen, Cardiganshire, in 1841.[47] This was an altogether exceptional church, for it was built by the local squire, Matthew Davies Williams, whose brother Isaac had been Newman's curate at his new church at Littlemore, outside Oxford. Llangorwen was virtually a copy of Littlemore, and was designed by the same Oxford architect, H. J. Underwood.[48] Naturally it was a bastion of High Churchmanship, which was, on the whole, rare in Wales.[49] An exception was Cardiff, where the third Marquess of Bute, the principal landowner, who had joined the Roman Catholic Church in 1868, used his patronage to install Tractarian clergy, most notably Father Arthur Jones, who employed Edmund and J. D. Sedding to make St Mary's, Cardiff, look properly 'Catholic'.[50]

47] Llandaff Cathedral, the interior, looking east. Restoration by T. H. Wyatt and John Prichard, completed 1869

On the whole, churches in Welsh-speaking areas held services in Welsh. This could lead to the reverse problem — namely, English-speakers deprived of services in their language. It so aggravated the Revd W. E. Jelf, who settled at Caerdeon in Merioneth to coach undergraduates in classics, when the Rector of Llanaber quoted to him the law of Queen Elizabeth's reign which required that services in predominantly Welsh-speaking areas had to be in Welsh, that he built a new church there in 1862.[51] This remarkable building was designed by his father-in-law, a noted writer on Gothic architecture and artist, the Revd John Louis Petit; he sought to express the *genius loci* by means of a plain rectangular structure of rough local stone, with plain rectangular windows and a rough loggia over the entrance, supported on square piers. The critic of the *Ecclesiologist* made merciless fun of Petit's 'great dash of Cymric roughness ... something between a large lodge gate and a lady's rustic dairy', concluding: 'In a word, the effect of the building is something like that of the Swiss chalet on the Barnet road' (i.e. Swiss Cottage).[52] To us, with its sympathetic later additions, it looks delightful. Jelf's real triumph, however, was the English Services in Wales Act of 1863, which provided that services should be held in English if ten or more parishioners requested them.

Later in the century it became the practice in towns to build separate churches for Welsh services; examples are St Mary's, Aberystwyth (W. Butterfield, 1873); St John's, Mold, Flintshire (J. Douglas, 1878–79); St David's, Colwyn Bay, Denbighshire (J. Douglas, 1902–03); and St David's, Cardiff (E. M. Bruce Vaughan, 1890–99 — destroyed in the Second World War).

The great strength of nonconformity in Wales has already been mentioned. Its chief expression in building took place, with growing intensity, in the first half of the nineteenth century.[53] Nonconformists placed little importance on actual structures, and the early chapels were often converted barns; a good surviving example is Capel Newydd at Nanhoron, Lleyn (Caernarfonshire). It was the nonconformists who first established Sunday schools, copied by the Church of England later in the century.[54] Chapels built in the first half of the century were on the whole simple and unpretentious, but they were often rebuilt later — sometimes more than once [**48**].

Needless to say, the funding of chapel-building was entirely voluntary, and every conceivable method of raising money had to be tried, including knitting nights, in the Bala district, and the pawning of family watches. By the 1850s some denominations had Chapel Loan Funds to help needy causes. Much of the work was done by direct labour given freely. This could also apply to the design; some early chapels were designed by the same men who built engine-houses. Sometimes ministers designed their own chapels; the Revd Thomas Thomas (Glandwr) designed many in what became known as 'the Landore style'. Later in the century there were architects who specialised in chapel-building, such as George Morgan of Carmarthen, a versatile stylist, and the Edwardian W. Beddoe Rees of Cardiff, author of a book on *Chapel Building* (1903). In a few cases the chapel might surpass the local church in architectural size and splendour, the outstanding example being Tabernacl Congregational Chapel at Morriston, Glamorgan, built in 1872–73 to the design of John Humphrey, a local man, which cost between £8,000 and £10,000 and can seat 1450. The great nonconformist revivals, of which the last was in 1904–06, naturally helped to boost the various causes.

The attitude of the established church towards nonconformity varied.[55] Bishop Copleston denounced it as 'a sin and an error ... a conspiracy against the state', whereas Sir Thomas Philipps — knighted for the stand he took as Mayor of Newport in 1839 against the Chartists — wrote in 1849 that chapels had been 'reared up by the poor dwellers of their mountain valleys in every corner in which a few Christian men are congregated, and these buildings are thronged by earnest-minded worshippers, assembled for religious services in the only places, it may be, there dedicated to God's glory.'[56] In mid-century a co-operative approach was displayed by such men as Copleston's successor at Llandaff, Ollivant, and the Revd John Griffith of Aberdare.[57] However, the impact of the Liberation Society from the 1860s onwards (see below) militated against this.

Until ten years before the restoration of the Roman Catholic hierarchy in England and Wales in 1850, Wales formed part of the Western District, along with the whole of south-west England.[59] Catholicism had survived in Monmouthshire, which explains why there were a considerable number of Catholic churches in the county, some dating from before the nineteenth century. Newer ones include the large and impressive one at Newport by J. J. Scoles (1838–40); the delightful little Gothic church at Chepstow (1827, now sadly demolished); and the particularly grand and splendid one built by the Benedictines with the aid of John Baker Gabb at Abergavenny (1858–60, Benjamin Bucknall). By contrast, in 1793 there were only three Catholics in Glamorgan,[60] and the 1851 Census recorded not a single Catholic in Montgomeryshire.[61]

When the hierarchy was restored, one of the twelve dioceses was Newport and Menevia. The first bishop was Thomas Brown, a Benedictine, who was Vicar Apostolic of the Welsh District (formed in 1840). His cathedral was E. W. Pugin's Benedictine monastic church at Belmont, near Hereford. In 1895 Wales, apart from Glamorgan, Monmouthshire and Herefordshire (which, even today, counts as part of Wales for the Catholics), was made a separate vicariate, which in 1898 became the Diocese of Menevia; its first bishop was a member of an old Catholic family of north Wales, Francis Mostyn. The new diocese used as its cathedral E. W. Pugin's church of Our Lady of Sorrows, built in 1857 at the expense of a local ironmaster in Wrexham; since 'Menevia' was the medieval name for St David's it was curious that the cathedral should be at the opposite end of the country.

Meanwhile, the Catholics had been building more churches, especially in the industrial south. The conversion (or 'perversion', as *The Times* called it) of the third Marquess of Bute did not result in any public ecclesiastical splendours. St David's Church in Cardiff, built in 1841–42 by Scoles (at the expense of Mrs Eyre of Bath and her son) was replaced in 1884–87 with a much larger one by P. P. Pugin, and this became the co-

48] Pentow Chapel, Fishguard, Pembrokeshire

cathdral with Belmont in 1916, when the Diocese of Newport became the Archdiocese of Cardiff, and sole cathedral in 1920.

A remarkable sequence of events in Flintshire demonstrated the strength of local feeling against the Catholics.[62] The Downing estate was inherited by Louise Pennant, who in 1846 married the Viscount Feilding, heir to the Earldom of Denbigh. In 1849 they began to build a church and rectory, designed by T. H. Wyatt, at Pantasaph. However, in 1850 both Lord and Lady Feilding became Catholics and handed the church over to the Capuchin Franciscans, A. W. N. Pugin being called in to fit the church up in a properly Catholic manner.[63] After an unsuccessful lawsuit, the Anglicans set up a subscription fund to build a replacement church, and it brought in £10,806 — enough to build two, also to the design of Wyatt (Brynford, 1851–53, and Gorsedd, 1852–53).

Almost all the Catholic churches in Wales were designed by architects from outside the country. The only one to attempt something at all 'Welsh' was the Assumption, Rhyl, of 1863, designed by John Hungerford Pollen for his old friend Father John Wynne SJ, a member of a great north Wales family. The altar and reredos incorporated Celtic patterns [**49**]. Only parts of the altar survived the demolition of the church in 1976.

The call for disestablishment was inevitably much stronger in Wales than in England, and it was championed from the 1860s by the Revd John Griffith, by then Rector of Merthyr Tydfil. The 'British Anti-State Church Association for the Liberation of Religion from all State Interference' ('Liberation Society' for short) was fuelled by both nonconformity and radical politics. The movement was encouraged by the achievement of dis-

49] John Hungerford Pollen, altar and reredos, Church of the Assumption, Rhyl, 1863

establishment by Ireland in 1869, and it became part of the Liberal programme after 1885.[65] In 1891 even W. E. Gladstone — whose family were staunch supporters of the Church of England in north-east Wales — came out in favour. The final bill went through Parliament in 1912, but its implementation was delayed by the First World War, and only occurred in 1920. In 1935 it was described by Archbishop Green as a boon to the church.

In Wales the Church of England alone had built at least 827 new churches and chapels between 1831 and 1906.[66] What had been achieved by this great enterprise? Some had no doubts about its benefits. Bishop Samuel Wilberforce of Oxford wrote in the ICBS Report for 1852:

> Not only is the moral and religious character of a neighbourhood altered by the erection of a church, but there is a marked improvement in its social and domestic state, and even in its external appearance. Invariably, as soon as the new church is erected — even, in some instances, before the roof is put on — the houses in the neighbourhood are repaired and whitewashed, the children become more tidy and orderly, and generally a more decent appearance is manifested among the populace.

Even more smugly, in the same report for the previous year, Bishop Vowler Short of St Asaph wrote that 'it was difficult to believe that a Church which had been so active in erecting places of worship as the Church of England had been could have the judgement of the Almighty hanging over it, and he could not help trusting that the providence of God was over the country for good.'

However, later in the century more doubting voices were heard. The Revd John Griffith told the Leeds Church Congress in 1872 'You may build a church on every acre in every field in every parish throughout Wales, and yet if you do not build up men to fill them — men who shall sympathise with the people — men who shall speak to them as soul to soul and mind to mind — your labour will be in vain', and H. T. Edwards, Dean of Bangor, claimed at the Swansea Church Congress of 1879 that one million of the Welsh population spoke Welsh, of whom 800,000 were nonconformists, and complained that new churches were 'doomed to be kept empty by ordained illiterates and mouthers of marvellous Welsh'.[67]

We may at least be grateful for the legacy of church architecture which was left to us by this period, although one can but fear for its survival in a country whose respect for its visual patrimony is notoriously inadequate and where there is still no system for the preservation of redundant churches, of whatever denomination.

Notes

A glance at the references will show that my principal debt is to Ieuan Gwynedd Jones, formerly Professor of Welsh History at the University College of Wales, Aberystwyth. This essay is dedicated to him, as an unworthy tribute of real respect and affection.

1 I. G. Jones, 'Church reconstruction in North Cardiganshire in the nineteenth century', *National Library of Wales Journal*, XX, 1978, p. 352.
2 W. Gwyn Thomas, 'Medieval church building in Wales', in *The Irish Sea Province in Archaeology and History*, ed. D. Moore, Cardiff, 1970, pp. 93–7.
3 I. G. Jones, 'Denominationalism in Caernarfonshire in the 1851 Census', in *Explorations and Explanations*, Llandysul, 1981, pp. 26, 41–2.
4 I. G. Jones, 'Denominationalism in Swansea and district; a study of the ecclesiastical census of 1851', *Morgannwg*, XII, 1968, pp. 83–84.
5 *The Religious Census of 1851: A Calendar of the Returns Relating to Wales*, ed. I. G. Jones and D. Williams, I: *South Wales*, Cardiff, 1976; II: *North Wales*, Cardiff, 1981.
6 Jones, *Explorations*, pp. 24–25.
7 Jones, 'Church reconstruction in North Cardiganshire', p. 356.
8 D. R. Thomas, *The History of the Diocese of St Asaph*, Oswestry, I, 1908, p. 166 fn. 3.
9 Thomas, *St Asaph*, p. 179.
10 W. D. Wills, 'The Established Church in the Diocese of Llandaff', *Welsh History Review*, IV, 1968–69, pp. 235–67; W. T. Morgan, 'The Diocese of St David's in the nineteenth century', *Journal of the Historical Society of the Church of Wales*, XXVI, 1971, pp. 5–49.
11 O. W. Jones, 'The mountain clergyman: his education and training', in *Links with the Past: Swansea and Brecon Historical Essays*, ed. O. W. Jones and D. Walker, Llandybie, 1974, pp. 165–84.
12 W. T. Morgan, 'The Diocese of St David's in the nineteenth century — C', *Journal of the Historical Society of the Church of Wales*, XXVIII, 1973, p. 50.
13 *Kilvert's Diary*, W. Plomer (ed.), London, III, 1940, p. 289.
14 W. D. Wills, 'The clergy and society in mid-Victorian South Wales', *Journal of the Historical Society of the Church of Wales*, XXIV, 1974, pp. 27–43; Thomas, *St Asaph*, pp. 180–4.
15 O. W. Jones and R. W. D. Fenn, 'Church building in the nineteenth century', In *Links with the Past*, p. 227. On Clara Thomas, see also R. Bidgood, *Brycheiniog*, XXI, 1985, pp. 41–3.
16 M. H. Port, *Six Hundred New Churches: A Study of the Church Building Commission and its Church Building Activities*, London, 1961, p. 138.
17 I. G. Jones, 'Religion and politics: the rebuilding of St Michael's Church Aberystwyth and its political consequences', *Ceredigion*, VII, 1973, pp. 119–20.
18 Port, *Six Hundred New Churches*, p. 99.
19 I. G. Jones, 'Church building in Flintshire in the nineteenth century', *Flintshire Historical Society Journal*, XXIX, 1979–80, p. 108.
20 Wills, 'Established Church', p. 244.
21 Wills, 'Established Church', p. 244.
22 Wills, 'Established Church', pp. 235–6.
23 Wills, 'Established Church', pp. 241ff.
24 Illustrated in J. W. W[ard] and H. A. C[oe], *Father Jones of Cardiff*, London, 1908.
25 Jones, 'Religion and Politics' pp. 125–8.
26 I. G. Jones, 'The rebuilding of Llanrhystud Church', *Ceredigion*, VII, 1973, pp. 99–116.

27 Jones, 'Church Reconstruction in North Cardiganshire', p. 353.
28 I. G. Jones, 'Church Reconstruction in Breconshire in the nineteenth century', *Brycheiniog*, XIX, 1980–81, p. 23.
29 A. Saint, 'Charles Buckeridge and his family', *Oxoniensia*, XXXVIII, 1973, p. 361.
30 *Kilvert's Diary*, II, 1939, p. 363.
31 *Kilvert's Diary*, I, 1938, pp. 343ff.
32 Jones and Fenn, 'Church Building', pp. 231–7.
33 Thomas, *St Asaph*, III, 1911, p. 388; Jones, 'Church Building in Flintshire', pp. 104–5.
34 Thomas, *St Asaph*, I, 1908, pp. 389–92.
35 I. G. Jones, 'Ecclesiastical economy: aspects of church building in Victorian Wales', in *Welsh Society and Nationhood: Essays Presented to Glanmor Williams*, ed. R. R. Davies, R. A. Griffiths, I. G. Jones and K. O. Morgan, Cardiff, 1984, p. 218.
36 M. Seaborne, *Schools in Wales 1500–1900: A Social and Architectural History*, Denbigh, 1992, pp. 86–113.
37 Illustrated in Murray's *Handbook to the Cathedrals of Wales*, London, 1873. See also M. L. Clarke, *Bangor Cathedral*, Cardiff, 1969.
38 G. G. Scott, *Personal and Professional Recollections*, London, 1879, pp. 311–16; W. Evans and R. Worsley, *Eglwys Gadeiriol Tyddewi 1181–1981*, St David's, 1981.
39 E. C. M. Willmott, *The Cathedral Church of Llandaff*, London, 1907; D. R. Buttress, 'Llandaff Cathedral in the eighteenth and nineteenth centuries', *Journal of the Historical Society of the Church of Wales*, XVI, 1966, pp. 61–76.
40 I. G. Jones, 'The South Wales collier in mid-nineteenth century', in *Victorian South Wales — Architecture, Industry and Society*, Victorian Society Seventh Conference Report, London, 1969, p. 35. On Griffith, see *The Dictionary of Welsh Biography*, London, 1959.
41 Quoted in Jones, *Links with the Past*, p. 165.
42 Quoted in Morgan, 'The Diocese of St David's', 1971, p. 29.
43 Morgan, 'The Diocese of St David's', 1973, p. 18.
44 R. Brinkley, 'Connop Thirlwall, Bishop of St David's', *Ceredigion*, VII, 1973, pp. 131–49.
45 Wills, 'Established Church', p. 253.
46 Morgan, 'The Diocese of St David's', 1973, p. 42.
47 O. W. Jones, *Isaac Williams and his Circle*, London, 1971, pp. 92ff.
48 P. Howell, 'Newman's church at Littlemore', *Oxford Art Journal*, VI, 1983, pp. 51–6.
49 See, e.g., N. Yates, 'The parochial impact of the Oxford Movement in Southwest Wales', in *Carmarthenshire Studies: Essays Presented to Major Francis Jones*, Carmarthen, 1974, pp. 221–47; A. Quiney, 'Treberfydd and Robert Raikes', *Brycheiniog*, XXIII, 1988–89, pp. 65–74.
50 Ward and Coe, *Father Jones*, pp. 35ff.
51 See William Alexander Greenhill, 'William Edward Jelf', *DNB*.
52 *Ecclesiologist*, new series XXI, 1863, pp. 374–5.
53 A. Jones, *Welsh Chapels*, Cardiff, 1984.
54 Seaborne, *Schools in Wales*, pp. 115–9.
55 Wills, 'Established Church', p. 238.
56 T. Phillips, *Wales: the Language, Social Condition, Moral Character, and Religious Opinions of the People, considered in their Relation to Education*, London, 1849, pp. 239–40, quoted by M. Seaborne, 'The religious census of 1851 and early chapel building in North Wales', *National Library of Wales Journal*, XXVI, 1990, p. 296.
57 Wills, 'Established Church', pp. 238–9, 251–2; I. G. Jones, 'The building of St Elvan's Church, Aberdare', in *Stewart Williams's Glamorgan Historian*, XI, 1975, pp. 71–81.
58 Wills, 'Established Church', p. 266.
59 D. Attwater, *The Catholic Church in Modern Wales*, London, 1935.
60 B. Little, *Catholic Churches since 1623*, London, 1966, pp. 105–6.
61 I. G. Jones, 'Patterns of religious worship in Montgomeryshire in the mid-nineteenth century', *Montgomeryshire Collections*, LXVIII, 1980, p. 108.
62 Jones, 'Church Building in Flintshire', pp. 108–9.
63 Attwater, *Catholic Church*, pp. 189–94; *Centenary Celebrations of the Friary Church of St David, Pantasaph: Souvenir Programme*, 1953.
64 A. Pollen, *John Hungerford Pollen*, London, 1912, p. 287.
65 K. O. Morgan, *Rebirth of a Nation: Wales 1880–1980*, Oxford, 1981, pp. 40ff., 141ff., 183–6.
66 Jones, 'Ecclesiastical Economy', p. 218.
67 Both quoted by Morgan, 'The Diocese of St David's', 1973, p. 52.

Chapter 6 · Jeanne Sheehy

Irish church-building: popery, Puginism and the protestant ascendancy

At the opening of Queen Victoria's reign 81 per cent of the population of Ireland were Catholic, 11 per cent Anglican, 8 per cent Presbyterian and 0.3 per cent other denominations.[1] Both the Church of Ireland and the Catholic Church traced their origins to the fifth century, to St Patrick, who brought Christianity to Ireland in 432.[2] Throughout the nineteenth century each denomination put a great deal of energy into proving its descent from the early Irish Church, in an effort to support its legitimacy as the true Church in Ireland.[3] In the case of the Church of Ireland this claim was supported by its possession of the ancient ecclesiastical sites, which it had retained at the time of the Reformation when it broke with Rome and became the established church. It kept the hierarchical pattern from the pre-Reformation Church, with four archbishops — Armagh, Dublin, Tuam and Cashel — and eighteen bishops. It was a wealthy church, with huge benefices mostly in the hands of a small number of ascendancy families, Beresfords, Trenches, Plunkets — James Godkin, writing in 1867, contended that many of the wealthiest families of landed gentry in Ireland had been founded on episcopal fortunes.[4] Pluralism and absenteeism were rife. Most of the revenue of the Church of Ireland came from land, from tithes, from the rent of agricultural land and from taxes on agricultural produce.

Since the Church of Ireland had taken over the medieval hierarchical structure, its cathedrals were in the ancient ecclesiastical centres, some of which were modern centres of population, such as Dublin, Cork, Waterford and Limerick, but many in places which had long since ceased to have much significance other than ecclesiastical — Killaloe, Clonfert, Ardfert, Ardagh, Kilmore. Its parish churches were often medieval churches restored, or, if new, built on or near ancient sites. By the 1830s the Church of Ireland had its establishment of churches well in place. A vigorous building campaign had been administered, and to a large extent funded, by the Board of First Fruits between 1778 and 1833.[5] The Irish Parliament voted it £6,000 in 1778, and from 1785 until the Union, in 1800, it received a grant of about £5,000 annually. This money was used particularly for building churches and glebe houses, as the residences of the parish clergy were called. After the Union an Act of Parliament in 1808 consolidated the finances of the Board of First Fruits, and allowed it to spend money on repairing old churches, rather than waiting twenty years for them to fall down so that a new one could be built. It continued to get annual government grants, sometimes as high as £60,000, sometimes as little as £10,000, to a total of about £665,000, until it was replaced by the Ecclesiastical Commissioners in the reforms of the 1830s. By 1829 the Board of First Fruits had granted gifts and loans for building 550 glebe houses, building, rebuilding and enlarging 697 churches, and for the purchase of 193 pieces of glebe land.[6] The churches of the Board of First Fruits are easily recognisable, rectangular preaching-boxes with western towers and spiky pinnacled tops. Some of the best are by John Semple [**50**], architect to the Board for the province of Dublin, and James and George Richard Pain, who were the Board's architects for the province of Cashel.[7]

Until the 1820s the Church of Ireland had been getting along quite nicely as a tool of government in Ireland and the ascendancy at prayer. Catholics and protestants rubbed along together more or less amicably, making various kinds of accommodation — Catholics keeping a fairly low profile, the government turning a blind eye to Catholic violation of the penal laws. By the beginning of Queen Victoria's reign this situation had been irrevocably altered by two major events. The first of these was Catholic Emancipation, and the second was the Church Temporalities Act of 1833.

Catholic Emancipation, in 1829, changed the relationship between protestant and Catholic. Antagonism between the denominations hardened — there was increasing resistance on the part of Catholics to paying tithes to support a minority Church, and increasing harshness in gathering them. The Church of Ireland enjoyed government support, evident, for example, in the use of the army and police to help collect tithes and in the grants made for the relief of Church of Ireland clergy who were unable to collect them. On the other hand, the political power of Catholics was rising. Emancipation increased their voice at Westminster, and drew the attention of radical politicians to the anomaly of a wealthy and corrupt Church which represented a small minority of the population. The public inauguration of the Oxford Movement, Keble's first clarion cry in his Assize Sermon in 1833, was sparked off by the Whig government's threat to the Irish Church — a threat that was carried out in the Church Temporalities Act of 1833. The number of high offices was cut, provinces were reduced to two and bishoprics to twelve, including the two archbishoprics of Armagh and Dublin [**51**]. The Act put an end to the Board of First Fruits, and set up a board of Ecclesiastical Commissioners, who took on the job of overseeing church building and repair, and architects were appointed for each of the two provinces.[8]

It is ironic that the Oxford Movement should have leapt to the defence of the Church of Ireland, for the Church of Ireland had very little time for

50] John Semple, Killeshin Church of Ireland church, Graigue-Cullen, Carlow, *c.* 1830. Designed for the Board of First Fruits

51] Dioceses of the Church of Ireland after the reforms of 1833

the Oxford Movement. Since the seventeenth century it had been essentially a protestant Church, partly due to an influx of Calvinist clergy. This tendency was fortified after Emancipation, when the Church of Ireland was anxious to distance itself from any practices that might be construed as popish. The reforms of 1833 were instituted in the teeth of fierce opposition from the Church of Ireland. In order to ease them in, the government appointed Richard Whately, the leading Whig ecclesiastic in England, as Archbishop of Dublin in 1831, an appointment he held until his death in 1863. Though Whately came from Oxford, and was a friend of Keble, he 'abominated the Oxford Movement', so High Anglicanism got little encouragement from him. Whately was not very keen on evangelicalism — he actually disliked enthusiasm of any kind — but he found it very difficult to curb the growing evangelical tendency in the Church of

Ireland, a tendency which continued to widen the gap between it and the Roman Catholic church.[9]

Like the Church of Ireland, the Catholic Church was keen to emphasise its unbroken succession from St Patrick. In 1847 Monsignor Paul Cullen, head of the Irish College in Rome (of whom more later) published an article in *Duffy's Irish Catholic Magazine* intended to refute the assertion of certain recent protestant writers that, until the twelfth century, the Irish Church was independent of the see of Rome. At the Reformation the Catholic hierarchy who did not conform were banished, and so were the religious orders. Secular priests were required to register with the Government. A series of penal laws disabled Catholics from economic prosperity and a place in public life: they were excluded from trades and professions by the requirement to swear an oath abjuring the temporal authority of the Pope and renouncing belief in transubstantiation, and their lands were broken up by forbidding the practice of primogeniture.

Things began to improve with various relief acts in the late eighteenth century, and from then, through the first thirty years of the nineteenth century, the Catholic Church reorganised itself, helped by an increasingly prosperous Catholic middle class, mostly farmers and merchants. It began to consolidate its hierarchical structure and to establish a network of parishes. Though technically it was not supposed to adopt ecclesiastical titles in use by the Church of Ireland, it did, and they became so sanctioned by usage that they survived attempts to extend the Ecclesiastical Titles Bill to Ireland. While by 1836 the Church of Ireland had been reduced to two provinces and twelve sees, the Catholic Church comprised four provinces and twenty-six sees [**52**]. As well as the four archbishops of Armagh, Dublin, Tuam and Cashel, there were 22 bishops, around 970 parish priests, 1,500 curates and 500 regular clergy. In addition, an increasing number of sisterhoods were setting up schools, hospitals, orphanages and so on.[10] Except for the seminary at Maynooth the Catholic Church had no state support, but was funded entirely by its members to provide not only churches and clergy, but a whole system of social services. Some Church income came from dues paid at Christmas and Easter, from offerings at baptisms, weddings and funerals, from saying masses; but most of it came from gifts, subscriptions and special collections.[11]

Contrary to popular mythology, a fair number of Catholic churches were built in the eighteenth century and up to the Catholic Emancipation Act of 1829. These ranged from simple thatched barn-like structures to stone-built slated chapels with some architectural pretension.[12] There were some restrictions — they were not allowed to have spires or bells, and they are generally on inconspicuous sites. Gradually, after Emancipation, Catholic churches became increasingly conspicuous in style and in site, and the number built continued to accelerate. Between 1800 and 1863 the Catholics built 1,805 churches.[13]

By 1837 the Catholic Church had architecturally respectable cathedrals in place at Ballina (Diocese of Killala), Carlow (Diocese of Kildare and Leighlin), Cork (Diocese of Cork), Dublin (Diocese of Dublin), Ennis (Diocese of Killaloe), Mullingar (Diocese of Meath), Newry (Diocese of Dro-

52] Dioceses of the Roman Catholic Church in Ireland from 1831

more), Thurles (Diocese of Cashel and Emly), Tuam (Archdiocese of Tuam), and Waterford (Diocese of Waterford and Lismore).[14] With the exception of Dublin and Waterford, they were all Gothic; the same spiky Perpendicular adopted by the Board of First Fruits for the Church of Ireland. At this early period the two denominations often used the same architects, such as Thomas Cobden of Carlow, for Carlow, or George Richard Pain, for Cork. Sometimes Catholic builders were mocked for their pretension. A clergyman of the Church of Ireland, the Revd Caesar Otway, wrote of Dominic Madden's Tuam Cathedral:

> This temple assumes a florid Gothic, and yet after all it is nothing at all like any of the fine old Cathedrals I have seen in England, France or Germany. It has a pretending, assuming, falsetto look — a Brummegem imitation!! — its immensity of windows, its multitude of little spires, spiking up into the air

put me in mind of a centipede or scorpion thrown on its back and clawing at the sky.[15]

Not long earlier, while on a visit to Cambridge, Otway had seen an architect taking plans and elevations of King's College Chapel with a view to building a similar church in Dundalk. Otway felt that the man's faith in purgatory and Irish pride was strong — the former a reference to the protestant belief that a large part of Catholic income came from the sale of indulgences. The church was St Patrick's, Dundalk, begun in 1835. The architect was Thomas Duff of Newry, one of the leading Catholic architects between Emancipation and the Famine. The building committee included many Catholic merchants of Dundalk: Carroll, whose family founded the tobacco factory; Macardle the brewer; Connick the coal importer; Jennings, the town's leading builders' supplier; and McCann, head of the Dundalk Bakery. The total cost was £25,000, which was raised by weekly collections and by larger donations and bequests, all within Dundalk. As the money became available the work was done by direct labour, supervised by a member of the committee.[16] The use of direct labour, or of labour being donated instead of money, was not uncommon in Catholic church-building.

What is surprising about the first wave of Catholic cathedrals is that they were all Gothic, except for Waterford and Dublin. Dublin, begun in 1816, is in a French neo-classical style. It is tucked away unobtrusively in a side street, and was known at first as the Metropolitan Chapel, and then as the Pro-Cathedral, which is the title it retains. By 1821 it had cost £26,000, raised entirely by public subscription.[17] It was remarked upon at the time that Catholic churches were generally classical, in order to signal their connection with Paris and Rome and to differentiate them from the Church of Ireland [**53**]. In Dublin, certainly, most Catholic churches erected between the 1820s and the 1840s were classical.

Some Catholic cathedrals were built in the old centres, where the Church of Ireland cathedrals were, especially if these were the major cities like Dublin, Cork and Waterford. Most of the rest were built in places that had become important centres of population. There was one place that was of such symbolic importance that Catholics were prepared to go all out to signal their developing power and build an aggressively Gothic cathedral on the most conspicuous site possible, and that was Armagh. Armagh was the ecclesiastical capital, seat of the Archbishop of Armagh, Primate of All Ireland. The town was dominated by the Church of Ireland's cathedral of St Patrick, built on the site of the original stone church said to have been founded by Patrick himself in 445. It was a thirteenth-century building and underwent major restoration by Lewis Nockalls Cottingham in 1834, when Lord John George Beresford was archbishop. Beresford had had to submit to the Church Temporalities Act the previous year, and had his power usurped by an Englishman, Archbishop Whately of Dublin. This major restoration, like so many Church of Ireland projects then and later, was an assertion of confidence in the face of diminishing power. The total cost was £15,000, of which £8,000 was contributed by

53] Kearns Deane, St Mary's Dominican church, Cork, 1832; portico completed 1861

Beresford, £1,000 by the Queen, and most of the rest by members of the nobility — Lord Caledon, Lord Charlemont and various Beresford relations among them.

> Our ancient edifice, thus restored and beautified, will, when completed, highly gratify all lovers of Gothic architecture — and the venerable structure, at first erected by the Irish Apostle, will hold no mean place among the topographical accounts ... of the other sacred temples of Christendom.[18]

As soon as Catholic Emancipation in 1829 lifted restrictions on church-building, thoughts turned to the idea of a Catholic cathedral at Armagh. As commonly with Catholic building projects, the main difficulty was to obtain a suitable site, but Archbishop Crolly, who 'always maintained and cultivated a friendly intercourse with the respectable and educated class of his separated brethren', managed to get one on a hill overlooking the town, opposite the ancient cathedral.[19] On 17 March 1840 he laid the foundation stone of the new cathedral, dedicated, of course, to St Patrick. The design was by Thomas Duff, in the familiar spiky Perpendicular. Progress was slow, and the building had only reached the top of the nave arcade when the Famine put a stop to the work. By the time work resumed in 1854, Duff was dead, and the project was put in the hands of J. J. McCarthy. He redesigned the cathedral in a Decorated style that was more French than English, scrapped Duff's crossing tower, and transformed the west end with towers and spires. Funding was by the usual method of donations, subscriptions, charity sermons and a series of 'Grand Bazaars'. One of these, held in 1865, raised £7,000, and included prizes donated by the Pope, the Emperor of Austria and Napoleon III of France.[20]

Duff's design would have been sufficient challenge to its ancient rival, but by the time McCarthy had finished, the Catholic cathedral, with its white limestone and tall spires, had established a visual dominance over the town which the squatter red sandstone Church of Ireland cathedral could not match [**54**]. Armagh set a pattern of competition in site and style that was repeated in parishes all over Ireland.

The Catholic cathedral at Armagh also exemplifies the change that took place in the use of Gothic for Catholic church architecture, from Duff's English Perpendicular to McCarthy's Puginian, rather French, Decorated. In the interval between the two building campaigns A. W. N. Pugin had come to Ireland and designed cathedrals at Enniscorthy (Diocese of Ferns) in 1839, and Killarney (Diocese of Kerry) in 1842. In 1850 the *Ecclesiologist* said 'We congratulate Mr Pugin on the spread of true principles of Ecclesiology in Ireland', and this was not an exaggeration. Pugin himself had an extensive ecclesiastical practice in Ireland. His fervent disciple J. J. McCarthy began his first church following the 'true principles' in 1846, with St Kevin's, Glendalough, Co. Wicklow. His son E. W. Pugin and son-in-law George C. Ashlin were in partnership in Ireland from 1860 to 1868, and Ashlin carried on the practice after that.[21] Even Patrick Byrne, who had built a substantial number of classical churches in Dublin, is said to have turned to Gothic after reading Pugin in *The Dublin Review*. If Pugin brought 'the true principles of Christian architecture' to Ireland it was J. J. McCarthy who established them as the norm through the Irish Ecclesiological Society which he was instrumental in setting up in 1849. The object of the society was:

> To form a medium whereby Catholics may co-operate with and assist one another in the study and investigation of Catholic antiquities, particularly of the remains existing in this country; to show the exclusive connection between them and our holy religion; and to apply the results of their investigations to the practical wants of the church.[22]

Through the membership of the Society, which included many senior Catholic clergy, ecclesiological Gothic was established for the rest of Victoria's reign as the proper style for Catholic church-building.[23] The adoption of Puginian Gothic coincided with an unprecedented boom in

54] Armagh Church of Ireland cathedral (on the right) and Roman Catholic cathedral

Catholic church-building. The famine which raged in the 1840s devastated the population, which was reduced from nearly eight million to just under six million. Those who had been lost by death or emigration were mostly at the lowest economic level of the Catholic population — so the Catholic Church was left with fewer people to cater for. These were largely the better-off Catholics, whose economic position improved dramatically, and who began buying up land from ruined protestant estates.[24] Some indication of the building boom is to be seen in the enormous output of the offices of McCarthy and of Pugin and Ashlin, and of the practices of men like W. H. Byrne, and William Hague, who soon appeared in answer to a demand for specifically Catholic architects. For by this time religious antipathy had hardened to the point where it was extremely rare for protestant architects to design Catholic churches, or *vice versa*.

As the voice of Irish Catholics grew louder and more confident, Rome began to want to take a hand. Ireland was administered from the Office of the Propaganda Fide in Rome, but the Irish bishops had managed to preserve a great deal of autonomy, and the clergy still more independence of the bishops. Things began to change in 1849, when Rome sent Paul Cullen as Archbishop of Armagh and Apostolic Delegate. He came of a prosperous Catholic family in the Diocese of Kildare and Leighlin, but had spent many years running the Irish College in Rome. He was a convinced ultramontane, whose first allegiance was to Rome. A wily tactician and an able administrator, he put his talents to work imposing order and discipline on the Catholic clergy and people of Ireland. One of his first acts was to convene and preside over the Synod of Thurles in 1850.[25]

This synod tightened up the Church's economic affairs, and measures were taken to ensure that clerical property would revert to the Church, rather than to the priest's relatives.[26] It laid down that parochial houses were to be built, their siting subject to the consent of the bishop. The Irish practice of 'stations', where the priest went round and said mass in one house or another in the parish, was discouraged, and all of the sacraments, except the last rites, were to take place in church.[27] Thus the Catholic parish church as a building became a more important focus for its local community than ever before, and the need to erect churches which would not only hold large numbers of people but would also symbolise their new social centrality became pressing. The need for confessionals and fonts increased, and for altars to be used not just for mass, but also for the exposition of the Blessed Sacrament for the Forty Hours Adoration, a devotion which Cullen introduced from Italy. As Apostolic Delegate, Archbishop of Armagh, then of Dublin and, eventually, as Ireland's first Cardinal, from 1849 until 1878, Paul Cullen presided over the full flowering of Catholic church architecture. That these churches were Gothic is, perhaps, surprising — with his passion for all things Roman one would have expected him to prefer classicism, and there is some evidence that he did. When J. J. McCarthy was given the commission for the chapel of the Dublin diocesan seminary (begun 1873) Cullen insisted that it should be based on Roman classical models, and packed the architect off to Rome to refresh his memory. On the whole, however, Gothic was too well established, and Cullen bowed to the inevitable. Gothic was also regarded as a national style, the style of the churches and abbeys of the Middle Ages, which were either in ruins or in the hands of the rival Church of Ireland. For many Catholics the building of Gothic churches on conspicuous sites was a sign of political as well as religious revival.

> We hope yet to see the day when the zealous piety of the people, guided by educated taste, will once more cover the face of the 'Island of Saints' with structures that shall emulate the sacred splendour of the august fanes that were the boast of 'Cashel of the Kings' and holy Mellifont, and whose ruins remain to attest the ruthless atrocity of our Saxon invaders.[28]

Catholic Emancipation, and particularly the efforts of Daniel O'Connell, had forged a solid link between Catholicism and Nationalism, so that the symbols of the two are often intermixed.

In the meantime the Church of Ireland was trying to recover from the effects of the Church Temporalities Act. In numerical terms it was left slightly better-off by the Famine — it increased its share from 11 per cent of the population in 1834 to 12 per cent in 1861. But the Famine had undermined the protestant landlords who were the Church of Ireland's principal support, so it was financially weakened.[29] Since its churches and cathedrals were in place, it did not need to embark on a wholesale building programme, as the Catholics did. But it did react architecturally to growing Catholic triumphalism. There were several major campaigns of restoration, among them St Patrick's, Dublin, restored 1860–65 at the expense of Sir Benjamin Lee Guinness, the brewer, and Christ Church, Dublin, restored 1871–78 by George Edmund Street at the expense of Henry Roe, a distiller. Two new cathedrals were built: Kilmore, 1858–60, by William Slater; and Cork, 1864–78, by William Burges. New city churches were put up, such as W. H. Lynn's St Andrew's, Dublin, or old ones refaced, like T. N. Deane's St Anne's, Dawson Street, both in the 1860s. There were some country churches as well, often funded by landlords. In general, however, church-building by the Church of Ireland tends to look like a gesture of defiance in the face of inevitable decline towards disestablishment, which came in 1869.

Unlike the Catholic Church, which had taken early to Puginian 'true principles', the Church of Ireland resisted ecclesiological tendencies, associating them with the twin evils of Puseyism and popery. There were one or two attempts to introduce ecclesiology and the Church to each other. The Down, Connor and Dromore Church Architecture Society was set up in Belfast in 1842 — but by February 1843 it had severed its connections with the Cambridge Camden Society, and from then on it devoted itself entirely to antiquarian matters. Attacking it, an unknown clergyman calling himself Clericus Connoriensis spoke of

> the late attempt to introduce amongst us Popish novelties under the guise of antiquity — Ecclesiology, or, as it is now being denominated, Church Architecture ... it would not be difficult to connect historically the rise and progress of Puseyism and the new-fangled rage for Church Architecture.

However, in spite of this resistance, Church of Ireland churches became increasingly ecclesiological, with developed chancels, south porches, baptisteries, honest construction, open timber roofs, even stained glass. This was inevitable as Irish architects shared the development towards the more muscular High Victorian style that was evident in England. Many Anglican architects such as Street, Carpenter, Slater and even Butterfield worked in Ireland, and Irish architects were often articled to English practices. On the whole the Church of Ireland favoured the chunky muscular polychromy of Street, with its Italian influences — such a church, for example, as William Atkins's Leighmoney, Co. Cork, of 1865.[30]

Rivalries between the Church of Ireland and the Catholic Church were played out on a national scale in the cases of Armagh and Cork. The Church of Ireland Cathedral of St Fin Barre, Cork, was begun in 1865, to the design of William Burges, who won the competition. It was ready for worship by 1870, and complete by 1879. The total cost was £40,000, £30,000 of which came from W. H. Crawford the brewer and Francis Wyse the distiller, with a further £8,300 from Crawford to complete the west front.[31] Built at the time of the most ambitious Catholic projects, St Fin Barre's looks, from the outside, more like a Catholic church — it is built of pale grey limestone, is very conspicuously sited, and is decisively French in character, with great western spires and a semi-circular apse and ambulatory. Its local rival is in the neighbouring Diocese of Cloyne, the Cathedral of St Colman at Cobh [**55**]. Begun in 1868 to the design of Pugin and Ashlin, it is a hugely ambitious structure, riding high above the harbour and dominating the town. Building began in the usual way, with funds being raised locally, but it soon became apparent that they would not be enough. By 1877 it had cost £65,000, and would need another £20,000 before mass could be said in it. By 1910 it had cost £150,000, including collections taken up in Australia and America, and the tower and spire were still not built.[32] These rival projects demonstrate that Catholic economic power was not always equal to its ambition, and that the declining, and even disestablished Church of Ireland could still command large sums of money.

55] Cobh, Cathedral of St Colman, by Pugin and Ashlin, begun 1858; detail from a watercolour of 1877 by R. L. Stopford. The cathedral is shown with tower and spire, though these were not completed until 1914; on the right is the Church of Ireland parish church

On a smaller scale such rivalries were played out in practically every parish, especially in the southern part of the country, where the competition between the Church of Ireland and the Catholic Church was uncomplicated by the Presbyterians, who were strongest in the north. The village of Enniskerry, Co. Wicklow, could be taken as a representative example. It was a landlord village, built and presided over by the Wingfields, Viscounts Powerscourt. On the hill to the south of the village, just outside the demesne gates, stands St Patrick's parish church, Powerscourt. Slightly lower down, to the north of the village, is the Church of the Immaculate Heart of Mary, Enniskerry, the Catholic parish church. The dedications themselves declare their denominational allegiances: the Roman doctrine of the Immaculate Conception was made an article of faith in 1854, and its adoption as a dedication for many Catholic churches was part of the 'Cullenisation' of the Irish Church.

From early in the century the parish of Powerscourt had strong evangelical connections through the Revd Robert Daly, who was rector until he was translated to the bishopric of Cashel in 1842, and through intermarriage between the Wingfields and the Jocelyns, Earls of Roden, pillars of the Church of Ireland and determined Orangemen.[33] During the long minority of the seventh Viscount Powerscourt, the third Earl of Roden wielded much power in Enniskerry, as he was one of the trustees of the estate. In 1846 Elizabeth, widow of the sixth Viscount, married the Marquess of Lon-

56] Enniskerry, Co. Wicklow, with John Norton's Church of Ireland parish church of St Patrick, 1857

donderry. As a farewell present to the village she paid for a new parish church [**56**] to replace the old one which was inconspicuously sited beside Powerscourt House, at some distance from the village. The foundation stone was laid by her son on the day he came of age, 13 October 1857. It was a major social occasion, presided over by the Archbishop of Dublin, Richard Whately, and important enough to be reported at length in the *Illustrated London News*. The architect was John Norton, chosen, probably, because he was a safe man who cold build a regulation church without exposing clients or worshippers to architectural or theological extremes.[34] It is a plain but ecclesiologically correct church, with a south porch, a canted apse and a tower and spire to the north-east. The walls are granite, presumably local, in random courses, but all of the dressed stone for windows, doors and so on came from the Nailsworth quarries near Gloucester. The cost, including Norton's fee of £100, was £3,930 12*s* 9*d*, and was totally borne by Lady Londonderry. However, the plan had to be approved by the Archbishop of Dublin, and throughout the building the work was overseen by Welland and Gillespie, the diocesan architects.

For Catholics, Enniskerry was part of the parish of Bray, the nearest largish town, about three miles away. From 1802 until 1860 the Catholics of Enniskerry worshipped in a barn belonging to a family named Dixon, outside the village on the other side of the river. They petitioned the landlord for a site for a new church, but were refused, presumably by Lord Roden, who said he thought *one* Catholic chapel in Ireland one too many. It seems to have been quite often the case at this period that it was more difficult for Catholics to find a suitable site, one which was sufficiently prominent and in keeping with the dignity of a place of worship, than it was to find the money to build a church. As soon as the seventh Viscount came of age in October 1857, the Catholics of Enniskerry petitioned again, and he granted a site for a church, and residence for the parish priest at a rental of one shilling a year. Things then moved so quickly that it seems probable that the project for a new Catholic church had been in hand for some time. By 20 November 1857 the plans had been submitted to Lord Powerscourt, and by the following week he had approved them and suggested a site. It was to Lord Powerscourt's credit that he granted a site so readily, and within the confines of the village. However, the rivalries betwen the churches can be seen in the fact that it is built lower down than St Patrick's, and on the other side of the village, in what was, at that time, a backwater. The designer was Patrick Byrne, long established as the leading Catholic architect in the Dublin diocese. It, too, is Gothic, with nave and chancel, south porch, and a tower and spire on the north-west — though the spire was not completed until later [**57**].

The foundation stone was laid and blessed by Paul Cullen, Archbishop of Dublin, on 4 April 1858, and the ceremony was attended by the Lord Mayor of Dublin and leading clergy of the diocese. The estimated cost of the church was £3,000. Most of this was raised locally — on 12 November 1857 the Catholics of the village had set up a fund-raising committee, which was chaired by Christopher O'Connell Fitzsimons, with Mr Justice Keogh, another prominent local Catholic, also present. These and other well-off co-religionists made substantial contributions — Keogh gave £100, and Archbishop Cullen gave £30. There were also donations from local protestant landlords such as Sir George Hodson of Hollybrook, who gave ten guineas, and Lord Monck of Charleville, who contributed £100.

57] Patrick Byrne, Church of the Immaculate Heart of Mary, Enniskerry, Co. Wicklow, 1857; presbytery, also by Patrick Byrne, 1861

Contributions from protestant landlords to Catholic church-building were not uncommon.

In the meantime the Church of Ireland parish church was progressing, but there were long delays as the architect and the Ecclesiastical Commissioners argued about the spire. In the end Cockburn, the builder, suggested stripping off the slates and covering it with copper, which Norton, reluctantly, agreed to. Eventually the church was consecrated by Archbishop Whately in 1863, though it had been completed in 1859. The interior fitting and decoration were entirely done by English firms: fabric, metal and wooden fittings from Cox and Sons, Ecclesiastical Warehouse, Southampton Street, London; lamps from Thomas Potter of South Molton Street; painting and decoration by John Hardman and Co., and glass by O'Connor. Following Church of Ireland practice it was a very plain interior. Even so there was trouble. The east end had '3 painted glass windows containing the 12 apostles in rich grisaille grounds with foliage canopies rich borders and tracery ope[ning]s' by M. and A. O'Connor of London. In 1863 three of the east windows were smashed, and a card pinned to the churchyard gate which read:

> IF THE PARISH WISHES TO SAVE EXPENSE AND MORE OF TROUBLE THEY WILL KEEP DOWN WHAT IMAGES ARE BROKE AND TAKE DOWN THE REST AS SOON AS CONVENIENT.
>
> NO SURRENDER
>
> [a piece of orange peel] [a daub of blue paint]

This was apparently the work of extreme protestants in the parish, indignant at even the mildest suggestion of popish idolatry. The windows were repaired and replaced, at a cost of £31 5*s* 6*d*.

The Catholic church was dedicated on 12 October 1859, when the sermon was preached by the Archbishop of Cashel. On 17 June 1860 the church, complete but for the spire, was opened with Pontifical High Mass presided over by Cullen. The interior decorations were all of Irish manufacture, the glass by Earley and Powells. Cullen also laid the foundation stone of the presbytery, a modest Italianate villa designed by Patrick Byrne, on 25 August 1861.[35]

Except for some Catholic churches of the 1830s and 1840s both the Catholic church and the Church of Ireland built in medieval styles throughout the nineteenth century. They were mostly Gothic, with some Hiberno-Romanesque towards the end of the century. Both began by using a very similar spiky Perpendicular, and went on to a more Puginian and ecclesiologically correct Middle-Pointed. How, then, is it possible to tell the churches of the two faiths apart? Dedications can often be a clue. Church of Ireland churches are often dedicated to apostles, or to early medieval Irish saints like St Patrick or St Finbar. They never have dedications like 'The Immaculate Conception' or 'The Sacred Heart', which became popular with Catholics after the 1850s. Size can be important — Church of Ireland churches, built to house small congregations, are rarely very large. Site can be another clue — churches in the centres of towns and villages, and on or near ancient sites, will be Church of Ireland, while Catholic churches, however large and imposing, are often to be found on the periphery. Stylistically Catholics favoured French Gothic models with soaring spires, built of pale limestone. The Church of Ireland preferred more compact, muscular forms, Italianate structural polychromy and red sandstone. A notable exception is the Church of Ireland Cathedral of St Fin Barre, Cork, which in site, style and materials is a direct challenge to Catholic triumphalism.

Notes

1 For material on the Church of Ireland I have relied heavily upon James Godkin, *Ireland and her Churches*, London, 1867 and Donald Harman Akenson, *The Church of Ireland*, New Haven, 1981. The figures, from the *First Report of the Commissioners of Public Instruction, Ireland*, 1834, are quoted in Akenson, p. 165, table 34.
2 There was a significant amount of church-building by nonconformists in the north of Ireland, and in towns and cities in the south, but there is not room, in the scope of this essay, to deal with it adequately.
3 Godkin, *Ireland and her Churches*, p. 20.
4 Godkin, *Ireland and her Churches*, pp. 526–33.
5 See Akenson, *Church of Ireland*, pp. 113ff. First fruits were a tax on the first year's revenue of a benefice, dignity or bishopric. They had been levied since the Middle Ages and, until the Reformation, sent to Rome. In 1711 a board was set up to administer the money, which could be spent to aid the building and repairing of parish churches, the purchase of glebes and the building of glebe houses.
6 Akenson, *Church of Ireland*, p. 119.
7 Maurice Craig, *The Architecture of Ireland*, London, 1982.
8 Akenson, *Church of Ireland*, pp. 145–71.
9 For a modern account of Whately see Donald Harman Akenson, *A Protestant in Purgatory*, South Bend, Indiana, 1981.
10 W. J. B[attersby], *A Complete Catholic Registry, Directory and Almanack*, Dublin, 1836, pp. 3ff.
11 Emmet Larkin, 'Economic growth, capital investment and the Roman Catholic Church in nineteenth-century Ireland', *American Historical Review, LXXII*, 1967, p. 858.
12 Kevin Whelan, 'The Catholic Church in Co. Tipperary 1700–1900', in W. Nolan (ed.), *Tipperary History and Society*, Dublin, 1985.
13 Larkin, 'Economic growth', p. 858.
14 For cathedrals of both denominations I have used for reference Peter Galloway, *The Cathedrals of Ireland*, The Institute of Irish Studies, Queen's University, Belfast, 1992.
15 Revd Caesar Otway, *Tour in Connaught*, Dublin, 1831, p. 184.
16 Revd J. F. Stokes, *St Patrick's, Dundalk, Centenary Record*, Dublin, 1947.
17 Godkin, *Ireland and her Churches*, p. 94.
18 *Notices Historical and Topographical Relating to the Cathedral of St Patrick, Armagh*, Armagh, 1835, p. 14.
19 Revd John Gallogly CC, *The History of St Patrick's Cathedral, Armagh*, Dublin, 1880, p. 4.
20 Galloway, *Cathedrals of Ireland*, p. 18.
21 Frederick O'Dwyer, 'A Victorian Partnership — the Architecture of Pugin and Ashlin', in *Royal Institute of the Architects of Ireland, 150th Anniversary*, Dublin, 1989.
22 *The Address of the Irish Ecclesiological Society*, Dublin, 1849, p. 12.
23 Jeanne Sheehy, *J. J. McCarthy and the Gothic Revival in Ireland*, Ulster Architectural Heritage Society, 1977.
24 Larkin, 'Economic growth', p. 862.
25 Desmond Bowen, *Paul Cardinal Cullen and the Shaping of Modern Irish Catholicism*, Dublin, 1983.
26 Larkin, 'Economic growth', p. 863.
27 Terence P. Cunningham, 'Church re-organisation', in Patrick J. Corish (ed.), *A History of Irish Catholicism*, V, 7, Dublin, 1971, pp. 1ff.
28 *Irish Catholic Directory*, 1845.

29 Akenson, *Church of Ireland*, p. 212.
30 Jeremy Williams, 'William Atkins 1812–1887', in Agnes Bernelle (ed.), *Decantations, a Tribute in Honour of Maurice Craig*, Dublin, 1992.
31 Maurice Carey, *St Fin Barre's Cathedral*, Dublin, 1984.
32 Larkin, 'Economic growth', p. 864.
33 Akenson, *Church of Ireland*, p. 133; Godkin, *Ireland and her Churches*, pp. 322–3.
34 A. Gomme, M. Jenner and B. Little, *Bristol; An Architectural History*, London, 1979, p. 439.
35 Jeanne Sheehy, 'Powerscourt and Enniskerry', in Bernelle (ed.), *Decantations*.

Chapter 7 · Chris Miele

'Their interest and habit': professionalism and the restoration of medieval churches, 1837–77

The history of church restoration in the nineteenth century often takes the form of a morality play. Victorian architects deemed to have shown a high regard for the integrity of ancient church fabrics are praised at the expense of those charged with sacrificing ancient fabrics to the reform of the Anglican Church or their own professional advancement. Students of Victorian architecture find it hard to resist this discourse of praise and blame in part because so many are active in the struggle to save Victorian buildings. It is troubling to realise that figures of the stature of Butterfield, Scott or Street apparently showed little regard for the authenticity of ancient fabrics and arrangements. Hitchcock himself, who did so much to insert Victorian architecture into the canon of modern architecture, felt that Scott 'approached buildings for the purpose of reconstructing them with what appears today as a perverse unfaithfulness'.[1]

Yet it is the desire of Gothic Revivalists to sacrifice what we feel are sacred remains to liturgical efficiency and professional interests that is most worthy of study. Church restoration was a contract. Professional architects provided historically purified icons to an Anglican clergy seeking to inspire a revival in religious feeling; in return architects were allowed to monopolise a very lucrative practice. To their credit, the leaders of the architectural profession came to realise that if the practice of restoration were allowed to go unchecked, medieval remains stood very little chance of surviving the century without being so rebuilt, copied or enlarged as to be unrecognisable as ancient buildings. The growth of more careful conservation practices took place within the profession itself, not outside, in the amateur or artistic circles which were home to the opponents of restoration and enemies of professionalism in all its guises. This essay will attempt to put the profession's role in the development of conservation in its proper perspective.

The most articulate and sustained criticism of the profession's handling of restoration was formulated more than a century ago by William Morris, who on 5 March 1877 wrote a scathing letter to the *Athenaeum* attacking Sir George Gilbert Scott's plans to restore Tewkesbury Abbey. Morris used the Abbey project as a pretext for an assault on the entire practice. Restoration was a lie, Morris argued, recalling for his audience Ruskin's celebrated passage in the 'Lamp of Memory'. One could no more restore a building than breathe new life into a corpse. He called for organised opposition to restoration. In April 1877 the Society for the Protection of Ancient Buildings (SPAB) held its first meeting in Morris and Co.'s Oxford Street showrooms. In the now famous letter, Morris expressed his belief that the fight against harsh restoration practices was a direct challenge to the architectural and clerical professions. The 'interest, habit and ignorance' of professional architects and the clergy, as he put it, bound them to the 'destructive' practice of restoration.

For the next two decades whenever Morris or his colleagues in the SPAB took up their pens against restoration, they invoked, sometimes explicitly and sometimes not, an ideal image of a typical restoration in order to ridicule the practice. This literary image corresponds very nearly to the record of Scott's work on the Church of St Mary Stafford between 1841 and 1852 [**58**, **59**]. Scott added an array of features which signal, like flashing lights, the medieval character of the structure at the expense of the literal antiquity of the stones. Parapets, pinnacles, buttresses, copings, all stand out on the rebuilt fabric. Gone are the irregularities produced by age and human use. The church was given an even and machine-like finish. The entire south transept was transformed from a piece of late Gothic architecture to an essay in early thirteenth-century style. It has to be said that the transformation worked on St Mary Stafford was typical of work in the 1840s and 1850s but not of the best work of the 1860s and 1870s. Morris, who had close personal and professional contacts with the most advanced architects of the day including Bodley, Scott and Street, knew that restoration practice had changed since the early days of the Revival, but he simply could not resist the rhetorical potency of the before-and-after view.[2]

The SPAB's first action against the official body of the profession, the Royal Institute of British Architects, was not long in coming. At the May 1877 meeting of the RIBA, J. J. Stevenson, who was one of the Society's most active early committeemen and who had trained under Scott himself, took his former master to task for his role in promoting harsh restoration practice. Stevenson went on to accuse leading church restorers of growing rich from the abuse of the nation's architectural inheritance. Scott was given the chance to defend himself at the June meeting, where he made a huge tactical blunder. He entered a plea of guilty, and lost any chance of a more lenient sentence when he said in mitigation that he had only done what his clients had wanted. If he had refused, then someone with fewer scruples would have done whatever was asked. Scott insisted that it was the clergy, not architects, who over-restored churches. The SPAB had a case, he conceded, but they should have put it to the appropriate RIBA subcommittee, as the Institute was already working to

58] St Mary, Stafford, before restoration

reform the practice of restoration. To critics, Scott's attempt to take cover behind the Anglican clergy showed him to be an unprincipled lackey. Why he never fought back is something of a mystery. If Scott did not know then he could easily have guessed that the financial success of Morris, Marshall, Faulkner and Co. had been assured by commissions for stained glass installed in churches built or restored by Scott, Street, Bodley and Garner. More Morris glass went into ancient churches than into modern ones through the mid-1870s. Morris only began to attack restoration after his firm's domestic product line was well established and profitable.[3]

59] St Mary, Stafford, as restored by Sir George Gilbert Scott, 1841–52

The bitter debate at the RIBA was caricatured in the 27 June 1877 issue of the satirical magazine *Fun* [**60**]. A dour clergyman is shown standing beside a businessman architect, who resembles Scott. The architect works his skill on the fragment of ruined column as a fake medium would invoke the spirit of the dead. He assures the client: 'Not enough evidence to restore? Why I have restored a whole Cathedral from a chip of pavement!' It is merely a matter of knowing the spirit and original intentions of the designer. The architect is a charlatan and has duped the clergy to line his pockets.

The truth about the relationship between architect and clergyman is much more complex than that portrayed in this caricature. Clergy were not sluggish and easy marks led astray by a greedy profession. Morris exaggerated the charges against architects, deliberately ignoring more than four decades of professional attempts to reform the practice of restoration. These reforms were closely tied to the emergence of the architectural profession itself, one of the signal features of the social history of Victorian architecture. Architecture was but one of a host of new professions to emerge in the last century. Surgeon, solicitor, schoolteacher, nonconformist minister, Anglican clergyman, architect and engineer were united in an attempt to give their work the status of a learned, gentlemanly pursuit both more profitable and more independent than a trade. They formed groups to press common interests, to police members, to regulate competition and to set standard fees. The professions sought to replace advancement by patronage with advancement by merit and called for widely recognised qualifications and systems of instruction. They tried to define areas of activity by spreading a body of knowledge codified in a specialist language. The founding of the Institute of British Architects in 1834 contributed to the improvement of the architect's social standing, usually at the expense of the builder. Church restoration satisfied one of the conditions for that profession's development. The specialist knowledge needed to restore an ancient church or to build a new one in a convincing style satisfied the need of any profession for an expertise and vocabulary unintelligible to the lay person.

Before the formation of the RIBA in 1834, the care of ancient fabrics was not as a rule entrusted to architects but rather to local builders or craftsmen, usually instructed by the churchwarden. The 'churchwardenised' interior, as the *Ecclesiologist* referred to typical Georgian furnishings and alterations, was the sign of an amateurism which was rife in the Anglican Church and which, in other spheres of religious activity, had contributed to the rise of nonconformity and secularism.

Work on Oxbridge college chapels, cathedral churches and abbeys, magnets for the antiquarian-architects who would proliferate in the early nineteenth century, often produced results which anticipate the work of Victorian professionals. Take the case of one such antiquarian-architect, Lewis Nockalls Cottingham and his restoration at Rochester Cathedral in 1825. Cottingham solved the fabric's grave structural problems and accentuated the marks signifying the building as medieval [**61**]. The boldness of Cottingham's work at Rochester was measured by the soaring tower which he designed for the crossing and which survives only in nineteenth-century views, having been replaced by C. Hodgson Fowler in the early twentieth century. Although this feature might strike our eyes

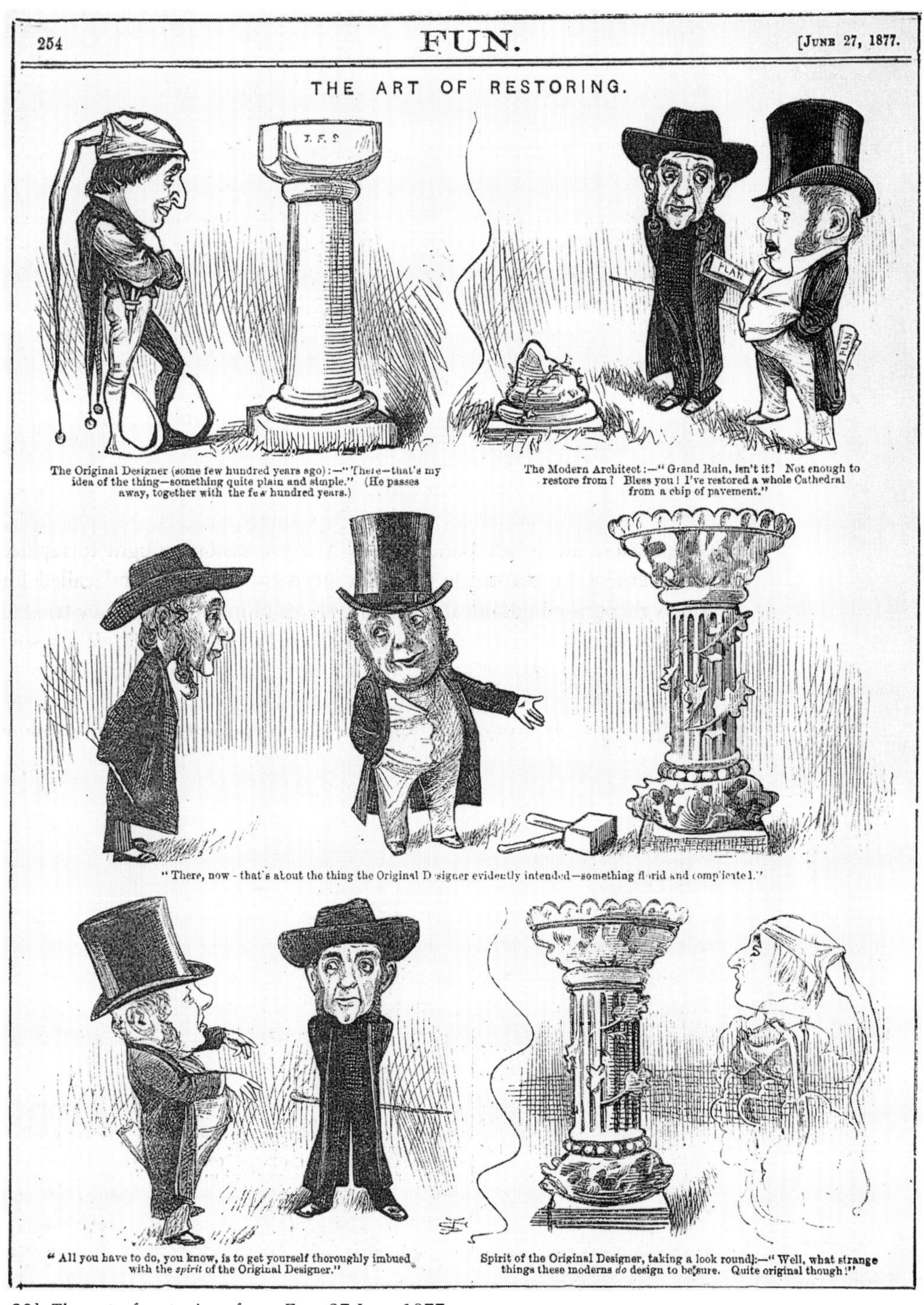
254 FUN. [June 27, 1877.

THE ART OF RESTORING.

The Original Designer (some few hundred years ago):—"There—that's my idea of the thing—something quite plain and simple." (He passes away, together with the few hundred years.)

The Modern Architect:—"Grand Ruin, isn't it? Not enough to restore from? Bless you! I've restored a whole Cathedral from a chip of pavement."

"There, now - that's about the thing the Original Designer evidently intended—something florid and complicated."

"All you have to do, you know, is to get yourself thoroughly imbued with the *spirit* of the Original Designer."

Spirit of the Original Designer, taking a look round]:—"Well, what strange things these moderns *do* design to be sure. Quite original though!"

60] The art of restoring; from *Fun*, 27 June 1877

as un-archaeological, experts called in to review the work praised its accuracy. Cottingham understood that work which relied on the interpretation of ancient remains raised him above the ranks of the builder or estate surveyor. In the frontispiece to his 1825 pamphlet on the restoration, Cottingham chose to portray himself as antiquarian–scholar, gesturing at the tomb of John de Sheppey discovered by workmen in the north wall of the choir [**62**]. The architect lectures the Dean and other prominent people of the district. The workmen are off to one side, assuming a deferential position and the builder is nowhere to be seen. This image reflects the gulf beginning to open up between the work of architects and that of builders and engineers. Here, church restoration is portrayed to be the purest sort of professional activity, because it is scholarly and intellectual.

By the 1840s architects had eventually come to dominate church restoration and church-building. They were the only people associated with building who consistently made it their business to know how to apply architectural history and archaeology, the very stock-in-trade of nineteenth-century architecture. By staking a claim on architectural history, professional architects showed sound business sense, putting themselves in a position to capitalise on a boom in the building market. In the first thirty-five years of Victoria's rule, there would be a huge outpouring of public expenditure on buildings which relied on historical sources of one kind or another. More to the point, between 1840 and 1875 more than 7,000 medieval parish churches were restored, rebuilt or enlarged. This represented nearly 80 per cent of all old parish churches in England and Wales, and is more than double the number of new churches built over the same period. These figures are taken from a document which received wide notice when first published in 1874, but is little studied today, the great parliamentary *Survey of Church Building and Church Restoration*.[4] The *Survey* was ordered by pious Anglican MPs, led by Beresford-Hope, to disprove the charge that large outlays on church fabrics had been paid for by church rates, voluntary since 1868, or pew rents. The *Survey* showed that private donations accounted for the bulk of church-building and restoration.

The cost and dates of works are recorded in only twelve of the dioceses reviewed in the *Survey*; the results of a simple analysis are given in Table 1. In eight dioceses the amount spent on church restoration was equal to or greater than the amount spent on the building of new Anglican churches. The differential in a few cases is startling: in the Diocese of Lincoln roughly £600,000 were spent on restoration versus £230,000 on new church-building; in the Diocese of Norwich £550,000 versus £80,000. In dioceses which were home to large, rapidly expanding industrial cities, Manchester, Winchester, Ripon and York, the number of churches built to serve growing populations was equal to or just greater than those restored or enlarged, as one would expect. The scale of spending on restoration demonstrates just how important this area of practice was to the profession, which rated fees at a percentage, usually 5 per cent, of the total cost of a project.

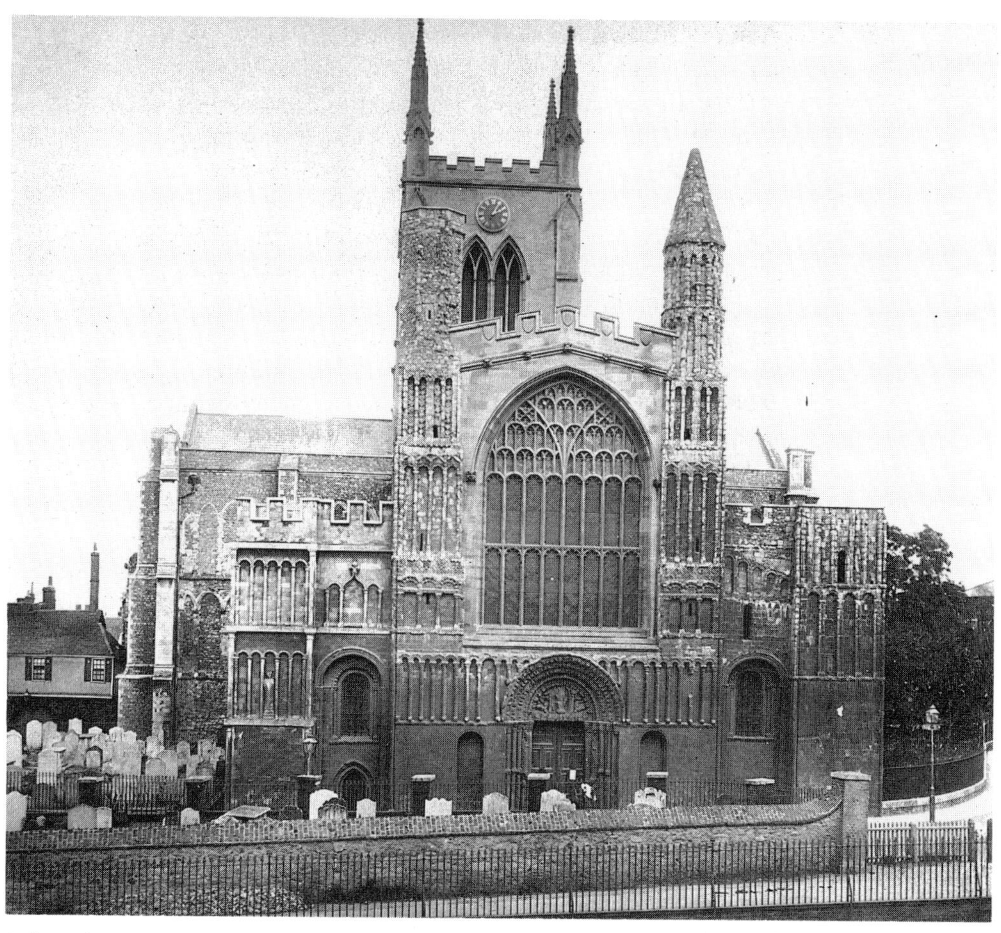

61] Rochester Cathedral in 1853, showing the crossing tower built to the designs of L. N. Cottingham

62] Frontispiece to L. N. Cottingham, *An Account of the Discovery of an Ancient Tomb at Rochester Cathedral*, 1825

Table 1] Expenditures on church-building and restoration between 1840 and 1873–74

Diocese	*Cost of restorations (£)*	*Number of restorations*	*Cost of new churches (£)*	*Number of new churches*
Canterbury	505,008	207	355,032	74
Chichester	329,194	175	353,712	57
Hereford	200,398	117	73,891	20
Lincoln	604,540	117	232,942	20
Llandaff	140,939	104	161,483	50
Manchester	529,384	149	957,650	189
Norwich	552,357	357	82,510	28
Oxford	735,111	292	410,671	138
Ripon	317,222	162	597,400	176
Saint Asaph	205,827	87	173,018	49
Winchester	479,661	152	711,064	155
York	635,290	252	656,045	127
Total	5,234,890	2,449	5,765,045	1,115

Source: *Survey of Church Building and Church Restoration. 1840–1875, Parliamentary Accounts and Papers*, LVIII, 1876.

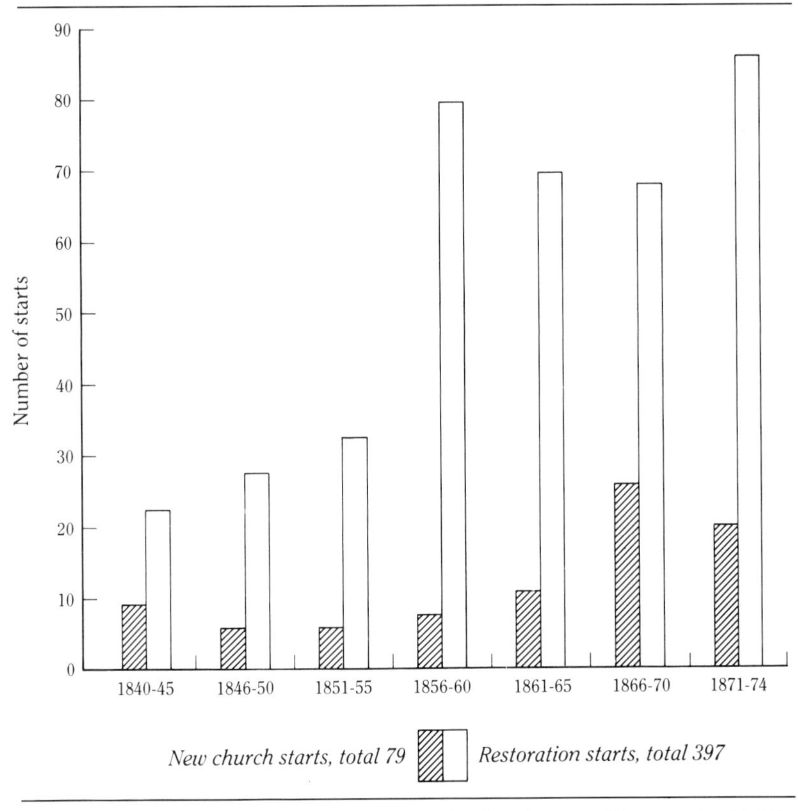

63] Church-building and restoration starts in the Diocese of Lincoln, 1840–74

In seven of the dioceses covered by the *Survey* the start and finish dates of works are provided, allowing the construction of graphs showing the frequency of restoration and new church-building between 1840 and 1874. The rural dioceses such as, for example, Lincoln, follow the same pattern; there was a huge increase in the number of restorations after 1855–60 and in new church-building a few years later, by 1865 [**63**]. Starts of both kinds fluctuated in the second half of the 1860s, but on balance increased, showing that neither the financial troubles of 1865 to 1870 nor the slide of agricultural prices in the 1870s slowed expenditure on church-building, at least up to the middle of the decade. In dioceses which included large cities, such as Manchester, there tended to be a burst of spending on church-building and restoration in the 1840s and again from about 1860 to 1874 [**64**]. Starts seem to have fallen off from about 1850 to 1860 in most of the dioceses analysed.

A national picture is obtained by combining all these results in a single bar chart to show the frequency over five-year intervals of restorations as against starts on new churches [**65**]. While the number of new churches started remained constant between 1840 and 1873–74, the number of churches restored increased by more than a third in the years between 1856 and 1874, the 'boom years' of church restoration. By adjusting for regional variations, this graph gives an accurate picture of the sort of opportunities open to metropolitan architects in the age of railway expansion. It also makes clear that, when compared with the building market as a whole (as measured by the amounts of fixed capital expended on building between 1855 and 1899), church-building and restoration starts were not subject to fluctuations.[5] Through the early 1870s, church work of all kinds was more recession-proof than other forms of civil architecture.

Consider these graphs and statistics alongside some basic demographic information. In the thirty years measured by the censuses of 1851, 1861 and 1871, the number of people who identified themselves as professional architects increased by more than 150 per cent.[6] Church restorations were helping to feed one part of an ever-growing profession. A small restoration was very well suited to learning the business of architecture. Many of the established church architects of the period passed along small jobs for church restorations to those who had just completed their articles.

The RIBA was aware of the problems caused by the boom of church restoration, and tried to regulate the practice. There is evidence for a change in sensibility as early as 1860, after which there is a move away from the speculative reconstruction and large-scale rebuilding of the 1840s to a moderate approach which showed a considerable respect for weathered surfaces and the irregular appearance of medieval fabrics. A few projects signalled the change in practice, most notably William Burges's restoration of Waltham Abbey, which began in 1859. In completing the east wall of the nave and stabilising the clerestory and the aisles, Burges refused to harmonise old and new elements, even though there was ample evidence allowing him to reconstruct the vanished work.[7] George Edmund Street was equally circumspect in his 1860 restoration of Stone Church near Dartford, where many original features and finishes as well

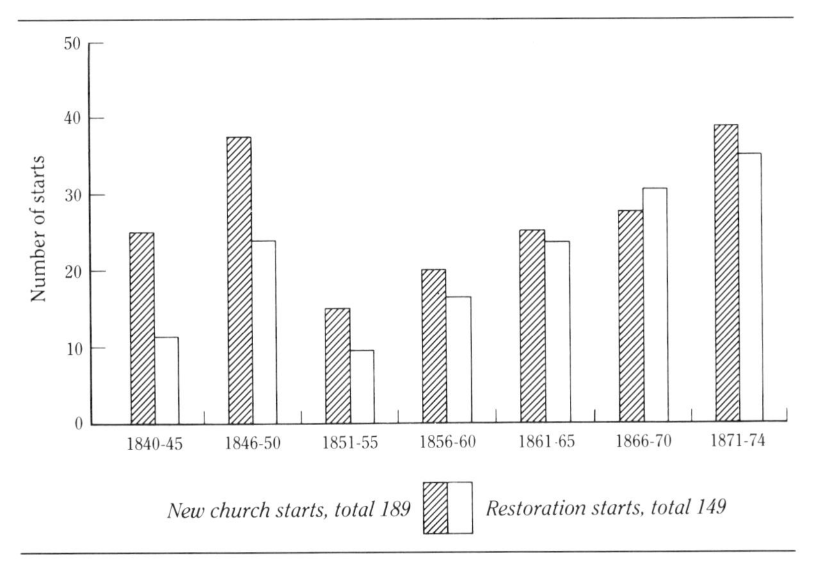

64] Church-building and restoration starts in the Diocese of Manchester, 1840–74

as post-Reformation additions were retained. Street's unvarnished nave roof has all the blunt matter-of-factness of vernacular construction and does not draw attention from the splendid thirteenth-century nave arcades. When it came to the chancel and tower, however, his intervention

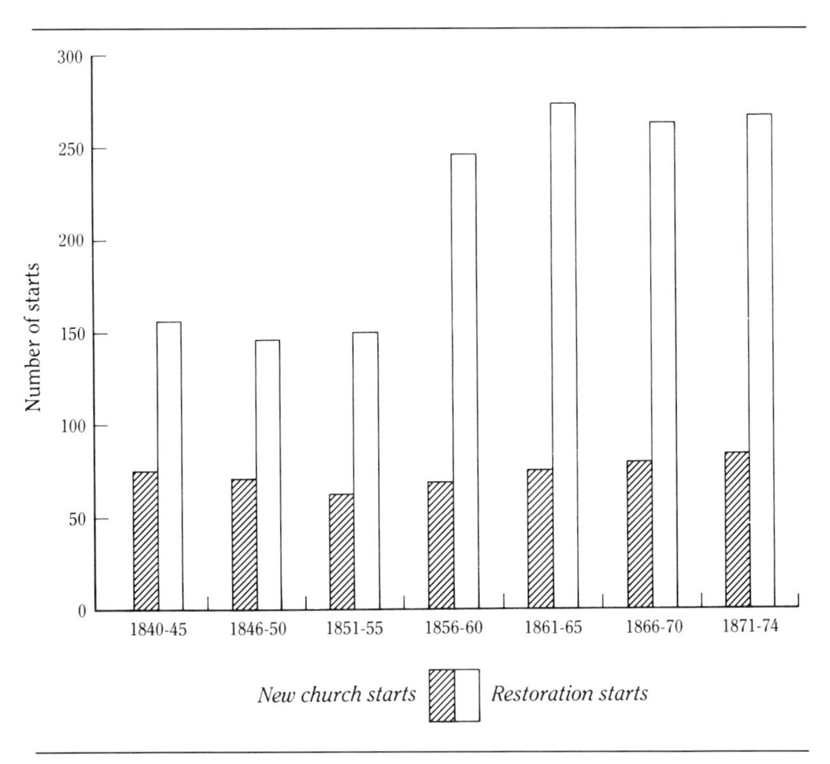

65] Church-building and restoration starts in the dioceses of Hereford, Lincoln, Llandaff, Manchester, Norwich, St Asaph and Winchester, 1840–74

was more aggressive; he provided a new stone rib vault, the outlines of which were taken from ghosts in the chancel walls, and proposed a broach spire for the truncated tower. Since such features were the *sine qua non* of Victorian Anglicanism, one can hardly expect Street to have departed completely from the norms of the day. As far as the interior was concerned, however, he did refuse to introduce strong colour contrasts, in anticipation of the very aesthetic advanced by the SPAB.[8] Finally, one could point to William White's restoration of Newland Church in Gloucestershire in 1861–63, which the architect himself described to the RIBA and the Ecclesiological Society as an illustration of a more careful approach to monuments.[9]

The years 1857 to 1864 also saw a series of debates on restoration sponsored by the RIBA, the Ecclesiological Society and other amateur architectural societies in which the work of restoration architects at home and abroad was severely criticised as insensitive and harsh.[10] In November 1863 a small group of prominent associates and fellows of the RIBA signed a petition asking the Committee of the Institute to set up a formal board of enquiry or permanent subcommittee into the practice of restoration. More than a dozen of the most prominent church restorers signed; at the head of the list were Scott, Street, Burges, White, Pearson, Salvin, Slater, Ferrey and Christian.[11]

In autumn 1864 an advertisement announcing the restoration of Heckington church in Lincolnshire was brought to the attention of the petitioners by a concerned member of the RIBA. In response, the Committee on the Conservation of Ancient Architectural Monuments and Remains (CCAMR) was formed, a permanent RIBA subcommittee meant to oppose harsh or ill-judged restorations. At its inaugural meeting in November 1864 the Secretary of the CCAMR, William White, drafted a letter to the architect of the Heckington restoration, Charles Kirk of Sleaford, asking just what he proposed to do and recommending that only works necessary for the stability of the fabric be contemplated. The CCAMR was concerned that the splendid architectural sculpture at Heckington should not be replaced by neat copies. Kirk's plans were found acceptable and Donaldson wrote a letter of approval which the vicar then published as the frontispiece to his illustrated fund-raising pamphlet, giving the works a kind of RIBA certification.[12]

At the first meeting of the Conservation Subcommittee, White had also been instructed to draft a pamphlet outlining restoration guidelines. This appeared before the close of 1864 under the title *General Advice to the Promoters of the Restoration of Ancient Buildings*. Sent to associates, fellows and all affiliated societies and offered for sale to the public, *General Advice* argued for moderate intervention and a respect for original features and weathering. Large-scale reconstructions and the removal of features in the interest of liturgical expediency were condemned.

No less important were clauses which argued that the professional architect was the only person fit to care for ancient remains. Vicars were enjoined to make no plans before consulting an architect who was specially trained in the care of old buildings and who promised to adhere to the Institute's principles. Architects were told that they had to make more frequent visits to the building in their care to ensure that the builder was following the specifications to the letter. As a further safeguard, the architect was advised to select his own clerk of the works rather than trusting the builder to provide one as was customary. The architect's clerk was to be on site frequently to oversee the safety of original remains. The RIBA also advised architects to add special clauses to specifications giving the architect the right to inspect all old material before it became the property of the builder. Since the 1830s builders had stood accused of replacing all old work with new carving, and then selling the ancient remains to a growing number of collectors. Finally, the RIBA cautioned architects not to assume that common workmen would have any appreciation for the subtle art of ancient buildings, which consisted in the very irregularity of old carving, its handicrafted look. The architect was to present himself not just as someone with archaeological expertise but as a man of taste, a specialist connoisseur of medieval art.

Between 1864 and 1870 the CCAMR intervened in sixteen cases. Most were instances of the Committee bolstering the professional opinion of its own members. In 1866, for example, Benjamin Ferrey asked the subcommittee to persuade the vicar and restoration committee of St Mary Magdalene in Taunton that the west tower should not be completely rebuilt. Scott, who was sent as a representative of the RIBA to address Ferrey's client, managed to strike a compromise after close to two years of wrangling. The vicar and restoration committee agreed to the reuse of the original carved fragments on a completely rebuilt tower carcase able to withstand the strain of bell-ringing better than the ancient fabric.[13] In the same year, Scott helped Richard Norman Shaw persuade the restoration committee of St John's Briggate in Leeds to retain the fine Jacobean chancel screen *in situ*.[14]

After 1874 the CCAMR was granted a new lease on life, perhaps in response to the critics incited by the *Survey of Church Building and Restoration*, who charged architects with over-restoring ancient buildings in order to increase their fees. The accusation that commission fees discouraged architects from containing the cost of public buildings had been made since the 1840s, and was renewed in the 1860s with regard to Street's work on the Law Courts.[15] The early 1870s also brought new personnel to the CCAMR, including George Godwin, who had championed the cause of conservation in the pages of *The Builder*, and J. P. Seddon, who showed a greater willingness to retain old material than many of his contemporaries. The final goad to the RIBA subcommittee was the announcement of the auction of St Etheldreda in Ely Place, the late thirteenth-century chapel which is the only remnant of the Bishop of Ely's London palace. Scott devoted part of his 1874 RIBA Presidential address to a fund-raising appeal to purchase the structure for an Anglican congregation.[16] Another member of the CCAMR, Ewan Christian, petitioned his principal employer, the Ecclesiastical Commission, to buy the building and open it as the centre of a ministry to business people in the city.[17] Ferrey wrote a letter to his great Welsh patron, Sir Watkins Williams

Wynn, to ask whether he would not consider making a gift of the chapel to the Welsh Episcopalians, who had been using the building for Welsh services since the 1850s. The CCAMR eventually collected more than £3,000.[18] The sum was not large enough; the Institute was outbid by Father Lockhart of the Catholic Rosminian Order, which owns the building still. The publicity given to the St Etheldreda campaign marked the start of a period of great activity for the CCAMR. Revised guidelines were sent to Church of England authorities and all diocesan surveyors and architects. From 1874 to 1876 the CCAMR pressed twenty cases.[19]

It is remarkable that Morris and the SPAB refused to work with the CCAMR or even mention its existence in early published statements. Morris preferred to stress the novelty of his enterprise and turned a blind eye to changes which had taken place in professional practice since 1860. He admitted only one precursor, John Ruskin. It is significant, therefore, that in 1874, the very year which marked the start of the RIBA subcommittee's most active period, Ruskin insulted the profession over its handling of restoration. When Ruskin learned of the preliminary returns of the 1874 *Survey of Church Building and Restoration* he was outraged. When Scott wrote to offer Ruskin the RIBA Gold Medal, Ruskin refused as a protest against architects content to draw commission fees for restoration work.[20]

On the sensitive matter of professional fees, the CCAMR deferred to the Institute's Practice and Charges Subcommittee which met for the first time in 1862, publishing guidelines in 1862, 1863 and 1869. Nothing in these circulars suggests that the Institute was trying to reform the practice of restoration by recommending speical fee schedules. In the early 1870s, however, the Practice and Charges Subcommittee did address the matter of church restoration along with other small-scale projects, generally defined as works which cost less than £500. The 1872 professional fees pamphlet recommended that inexpensive projects, projects which demanded 'special skills', or those which required extensive site supervision (all conditions which commonly applied to church restoration) could be rated at more than the widely recognised standard of 5 per cent (as high as 10 per cent), so that professionals would be properly compensated for labour-intensive but inexpensive works.

The 1872 pamphlet tended to confirm practice as it had developed since 1860 rather than to offer any new standards. The matter of fees is difficult to research since the few surviving office ledgers are scattered and do not always note the total expenditure on a project. The casework files of the Incorporated Church Building Society (ICBS), however, record both total expenditures and fees charged. An examination of more than fifty ICBS files relating to restoration makes clear that in cases where costs came to less than £500, a fee of at least 10 per cent of the total cost was charged; for work costing between £500 and £1,500, fees were rated at between 6.5 per cent and 8 per cent. Works above £2,000 were rated in the same way as new works. R. K. Penson's minor works at West Walton Church, Norfolk, in 1859 came to only £405, on which he charged a fee of £45.[21] In 1865 Pearson received 10 per cent on an equally low-paying job, the reseating of Idmiston

Church in Wiltshire.[22] For G. E. Street's extensive work on Clun Church between 1871 and 1873, which cost nearly £7,000, the architect charged a commission of 5 per cent, or £350.[23] The vicar at Clun was not getting off easily in the way of professional fees, however. In addition to paying the architect his 5 per cent he had also to pay £150 for the salary of Street's clerk of the works, who closely supervised every aspect of the restoration.

In the early Victorian period, the clerk of the works was usually in the employ of the builder. The cream of the architectural profession often insisted that a builder or clerk of their own choosing be selected in the interest of obtaining better results. The architect's clerk of the works did not evolve exclusively to press more careful standards of restoration; he was part of a larger movement to give the architect greater control over the execution of designs. Given the increasing number of church restorations, however, it was inevitable that some clerks became specialists. In addition to monitoring the building works, these men inspected archaeological fragments and had the right to stop works when excavation turned up fresh evidence. They were also there to make sure that unusual or rustic features were not recut and removed.

The status of the clerk of the works was not well defined. Some had moved up through the building trades; others were men of more genteel pedigree who, for one reason or another, were content to assist in the business of architecture. Clerks are known to have moved from the employ of a builder to an architect, and even to have set up their own businesses as specialist advisers. The best known of Scott's clerks was James Irvine (1824–1900) who arrived in Scott's office at the age of fourteen. By the mid-1850s Irvine had become an expert on medieval remains with a speciality in the interpretation of pre-Conquest fabrics and foundations. His artistic acumen also came to be highly trusted, and he was soon recognised for his scholarly and archaeological skill. Scott even passed along commissions to him or released him from service temporarily in order that he might pursue projects which exercised his expertise, such as the excavation of the Roman Baths in Bath at the close of the 1850s, or the restoration of the west front of Wells Cathedral in the early 1870s, where he clerked for Benjamin Ferrey. In 1874 Irvine was recommended to the vicar of Bradford-on-Avon as someone who could restore the little stone chapel discovered not one hundred yards from the parish church. Irvine became embroiled in scholarly dispute over the date of this building, which some claimed as seventh-century, but which Irvine insisted was early twelfth-century, despite its pre-Norman character. Irvine went on to oversee Scott's restorations at Peterborough and Rochester, which entailed extensive excavations to underpin the foundations and thus opportunities to document and analyse the pre-Conquest foundations in detail. His notes and drawings remain important documents for medieval archaeologists.[24] Another clerk whom Scott trusted with archaeological and historical research was Frater, who oversaw Scott's works in Wales and Cheshire, in particular the restoration of Chester and Bangor cathedrals.[25] A Mr Bacon, Scott's clerk at Ely, was also consulted as an independent expert from time to time.

The picture which emerges is therefore more complex than the one portrayed in the published statements of the RIBA's CCAMR. Architects did not mistrust builders and craftsmen *per se*, but only those who had not specialised in the care of old fabrics and who had been selected by competitive tendering over the objections of the architect. The common practice of putting restoration contracts out to competitive tender among several builders upset the relationship between the architect and the builder who could be trusted to take special care of old fabric. The 1864 CCAMR pamphlet strenghtened the hand of architects by advising churchmen to select the builder recommended by the architect. Nevertheless, the records of church restorations are filled with accounts of architects trying to press their choice of builder on an unwilling client. In August 1867 J. P. Seddon urged the restoration committee of Llanbadarn Fawr in Wales to accept the tender of Thomas Williams, a builder of Cardiff, with whom Seddon and Prichard had worked on the restoration of Llandaff Cathedral and other projects in Wales. The restoration committee wanted to put the project out to competitive tendering; Seddon was told that Williams's bid would be considered along with three others. The Committee eventually selected a Mr Davies, whose bid was the lowest. Seddon threatened to withdraw unless Williams was appointed; Davies, Seddon wrote 'is perfectly good for new work ... he had not [however] a gram of an idea about old work ... [I have] taught and employed [Williams] for many years'. If the Llanbadarn Fawr committee employed Williams as builder, they would save the salary of a clerk of the works. Williams's special skill was reflected in a higher estimate, some £2,100 versus Davies's £1,600; the salary of an independent clerk (which varied between 6*s* and 12*s* a day) was not large enough to make up the difference. Seddon did better to argue the economy of hiring someone with special skills: 'This is a case in which the skill of the operatives may save hundreds of pounds and I have little doubt that I could with Williams save a large portion of the [original] walling and consequently the cost of the work.' The committee finally agreed to hire a clerk of Williams's to oversee Davies's workmen.[26]

A different sort of specialist clerk also emerged in the second half of the 1850s, a clerk of the works who was in fact a young architect finishing articles and moving from apprentice to salaried employee. Again Scott was among those who pioneered the use of architects just out of their articles for sensitive restorations. In this way the young architect was given an object-lesson in building craft and, at the same time, had the opportunity to make important patronage contacts with the local gentry and clergy. George Edmund Street used men just out of their articles to the same end; in 1861 he wrote: 'No work affords better training for an architect than the study which is involved to become a thoroughly good restorer of ancient buildings.'[27]

Young architects were from the class above men like Williams, from families rich enough to afford articles and aspiring enough to push their child into a gentlemanly profession rather than a trade. Many of Scott's young architect-clerks were Oxbridge graduates. His sons, John Oldrid and George Gilbert Jun., were the paradigms for the new type, paying close attention to novel or difficult works and carrying out purely historical research in literary or archival sources. Charles Buckeridge and Thomas Garner completed their training in this way, with Scott eventually passing along to them small commissions in Oxfordshire and Warwickshire respectively. Thomas Graham Jackson recorded this system in his recollections.[28] Scott was not the only architect to help his former articled clerks establish independent practices. From 1856 Thomas Hardy supervised the restorations of the Dorchester-based architect John Hicks; Hicks eventually gave Hardy complete control of the restoration of the isolated church of St Juliot, in north Cornwall. When Hardy moved to London in 1862 it was as an expert clerk assisting Arthur Blomfield in his vast restoration practice.[29]

The architectural profession was therefore not the grasping monolith portrayed by Morris and the SPAB. Architects were trying to create new professional standards and practices in response to a ground swell of demand raised by the Anglican Revival. It is no secret that church restoration and the Gothic Revival were tools of Anglican reform. The Church of England, by promoting church-building and restoration, brokered a huge transfer of capital from the purses of church patrons to the purses of church architects.

The foundations for this capital transfer were laid after the end of the Napoleonic wars in the Church Building Act of 1818 and the subsequent establishment of the Church Building Commission. The Commission stimulated the building economy at first by direct government grant and then by acting in concert with related bodies which were privately funded. To help raise funds for church-building and restoration, the Commission was assisted by the Incorporated Church Building Society which was also founded in 1818.

The ICBS aimed to increase the number of sittings in each parish which were free of charge by making grants to help fund any programme of church enlargement. More free seats, it was hoped, would encourage poorer parishioners to return to the Church of England, abandoning dissenting sects and secular entertainments. Between 1818 and the late 1830s the ICBS did not have a well-defined design or conservation policy. It was concerned only that grant-aided projects were built to last. From 1826 the ICBS had been advised by Joseph Good, a student of John Soane's who became surveyor to the Church Building Commission. By the start of the Victorian period, Good had begun to insist on more archaeologically accurate restorations; soon afterwards the ICBS was intervening directly in restoration practice, recommending that architects, not builders, were best suited to enlarge old buildings.[30]

The ICBS refused to release any grant money before receipt of a certificate signed by the architect confirming that works had been completed according to his specifications. No amount of financial hardship would persuade the committee to release grant funds before the architect certified that the job had been well done.[31] The Society's preference for professional architects and specialist clerks steadily increased. By 1850 the printed ICBS application contained a blank for the architect's and clerk's fees. Applications which were drawn up by church architects of high repute were grant-aided almost as a matter of course; in 1868 the secretary of the Society assured the vicar of Birstall in Leicestershire that the use of George Gilbert Scott as architect virtually assured the success of his application.[32] This preference is not surprising when one considers that the architectural advisers who succeeded Good were drawn from the ranks of leading church architects and restorers. In the 1840s and 1850s Ferrey was asked to give advice periodically; by 1860 Pearson was a regular adviser; G. E. Street and Ewan Christian were called in when the volume of work was great.

Although the post of architectural adviser to the ICBS was voluntary, it offered opportunities to develop professional contacts; it was one of several new professional ecclesiastical appointments to be had by the aspiring architect. At the very top was the architect to the Ecclesiastical Commission itself. William Railton and Benjamin Ferrey worked for the Commission in the 1840s; by 1851 Ewan Christian was its official architect and in this capacity restored many churches and church chancels in the patronage of the Commission. Another new professional post was that of diocesan architect. Strictly speaking, dioceses had architectural advisers or surveyors before the Victorian reform of the Church; during the 1840s, however, the diocesan architect assumed a new and important role in setting architectural policy and in enforcing the architectural side of the bishop's programmes. The power of bishops in the Victorian period was on the rise, and with it the power and advantage to be had from being the diocesan architect. One of the best known was G. E. Street, appointed Architect for the Diocese of Oxford in 1850 by Bishop Wilberforce. This appointment represented a tremendous professional opportunity for the young Street and helped to establish him as one of the period's leading architects. After the appointment Street left his newly established London office, first for Wantage and then Oxford, in order to be nearer to his duties. When he returned to London in 1856, his career and reputation were firmly established; more than a third of Street's total production is to be found within the Victorian boundaries of the diocese.[33] Through the influence and patronage of a powerful bishop, Street built new churches, parsonages, parish schools, the bishop's Diocesan Training College in Cuddesdon, and, of course, he restored churches. T. H. Wyatt was official architect to the Diocese of Dorset and Sarum, and Joseph Clarke to the Diocese of Canterbury. Both areas are rich in their work.

No less important for the success of an aspiring church architect and restorer were connections with the county archaeological and architectural societies which sprang up all over the country between 1839 and 1850. Some societies had official ties with the Church hierarchy, and those which did not had a high proportion of clerical membership, sometimes as great as 40 per cent or 50 per cent. The earliest and most influential societies were those founded by Oxbridge undergraduates, fellows and clergy; The Oxford Society for Promoting the Appreciation and Study of Gothic Architecture, or Oxford Architectural Society (OAS), was founded in February of 1839, and the better-known Cambridge Camden Society (CCS) in May of the same year. The committees offered to advise anyone contemplating the building of a new church or the restoration of an old one. This offer, however, soon brought requests so far beyond the expertise of the OAS that, before the end of the year, it was forced to engage a professional architect, John Derick, for a nominal sum. Later the Society took the advice of Ferrey, Buckler, Cranstoun, Butterfield and Scott.[34] What attracted these men was not the nominal fee to be had but the opportunity to be put in touch with Oxbridge undergraduates, from whose ranks the great majority of clergy were drawn. Having given free advice on the restoration of Great Haseley church, Derick eventually got the commission to restore the chancel. In 1845 the Oxford Architectural Society took control of the restoration of Dorchester Abbey and appointed one of their official architects, James Cranstoun, to the job. A year later they had replaced Cranstoun with the architect who would prove to be a favourite among Oxford men, William Butterfield.

The Cambridge Camden Society intervened even more directly in the professional lives of architects by the acid reviews in its journal, the *Ecclesiologist*, and by publishing lists of approved and condemned architects. Salvin served the Society as an architectural adviser from 1839; Buckler had a similar arrangement for a short time, restoring the church at Old Shoreham with John Mason Neale, co-founder and chief propagandist for the Society, from 1840.[35] Salvin, however, received most favoured status and a great deal of notoriety when the Society appointed him architect to the restoration of the Church of the Holy Sepulchre in Cambridge, a project which the Society assumed control of in the autumn of 1841 and which was intended as a demonstration of their principles.

Most of the thirty-odd architectural societies founded in the 1840s engaged the services of a specialist church architect and passed along commissions from their membership to these men. E. F. Law, the Northampton-based architect, benefited greatly from his appointment as architect to the Architectural Society for the Archdeaconry of Northampton. In the West Country, the Exeter Diocesan Architectural Society also chose a local light to advise on architectural matters, John Hayward. In their chapters, both Chris Brooks and Marin Cherry stress the importance of the Exeter Society's patronage network in the development of Hayward's career. Such local societies ensured that the professional benefits and prestige to be had from church construction and restoration flowed to provincial as well as London-based architects.

The importance of these societies for establishing professional control over the practice of church restoration cannot be overestimated. Architectural societies were forums where architects could consort with the district's clergymen and its resident landowners and gentry. The easiest way for an architect to tap this potentially deep well of patronage was simply to join a society and adhere to its principles. In marked contrast to the Society of Antiquaries, where one had to be nominated by a Fellow, the new Victorian societies were open to anyone who paid the annual subscription. For 2*s* 6*d* an architect could attend general meetings and annual summer excursions. These events promoted open intercourse among members as equals, corporate identity and singleness of purpose. Nowhere else could an architect meet so many prospective clients on equal terms as a gentleman. Nowhere else could he show off his professional skills to prospective clients. From time to time a society would devote an entire meeting to the work of one architect. As Diocesan Architect of York, Street was the most favoured architect of the Yorkshire Architectural Society. In the summer of 1877 the Society offered its members a full day out with the architect himself, focusing on his works for the estate of Sir Tatton Sykes in the East Riding. The day began with a church service in York Minster; then Street led the group on a tour of the fabric and explained his work on the transepts. Then the party of about forty men and women boarded a reserved railway coach for East Heslerton to see a church just completed to Street's designs, after which carriages whisked them away to visit nine churches that he had built or restored.[36]

However much support and encouragement the Ecclesiastical Commission, the ICBS, the bishop, a local society or even the landowner might give to a church restoration or building, the most important figure in initiating any restoration was the vicar. There is ample anecdotal evidence to suggest that this was so. Statistical evidence proves the point beyond all doubt. In Table 2, the start date of some 225 restorations is correlated with the institution date of the church incumbent as recorded in the *Clergy List*. The results are sorted into four categories defined by the number of years which elapsed between institution and the start of a restoration. Of the restorations in the sample, 45 per cent began within three years of the installation of a new incumbent, and almost exactly two thirds of the restorations in the sample started within the first five years of a new appointment. Conversely, churches which went unimproved tended to be in parishes without a resident incumbent, where the living was very poor, and, frequently, where there was no resident squire or principal landowner.[37] Typically, a church which the Victorians left unrestored was one which had no vicar to promote improvements, or which, in the absence of lay leadership, was so poor that restoration was a luxury that had to be done without.

The official and unofficial institutions of the Church were not simply fodder for a hungry profession. Churchmen charged architects with the task of refabricating the most enduring icons of Anglican worship in the most efficient and persuasive way possible. An exact and certain system of knowledge, such as that provided by archaeology and architectural history, dispensed by a modern and reformed group of professionals, would bring the Church new strength and vigour, or so it was believed. In the process architects used archaeology and architectural history to help establish their profession as a learned and gentlemanly one.

The drawing of a stark moral contrast between evil restorer and noble conservationist was perhaps not the point of the SPAB's attack. The SPAB, or at least the core of its executive committee which consisted of Morris and his cronies, was perhaps challenging both the new-found bourgeois identity of the architect and the Church of England's militant role in English society. A church conserved according to SPAB principles was the very opposite of the icon constructed by early Victorian architects and clergymen. In 1885 the SPAB was given a chance to practice what it preached. Morris's friendship with the Revd Oswald Birchall, the noted Christian Socialist who was rector of Buscot and Inglesham, resulted in the SPAB committee being handed executive control of the repair of Inglesham church [**66**]. The architect was an SPAB favourite, J. T. Micklethwaite. Work went on, with generous donations from Morris, for the next decade. The results are barely perceptible; the church was left nestling in its snug churchyard like an accent in an eighteenth-century watercolour. Set beside the social history of restoration, the act of conservation, which enshrines the very decay of the church fabric, is a commentary on the decline of the institution of the Church. Inglesham's countrified aspect shows no sign of the hand of the ambitious and busy metropolitan professional. The act of letting alone makes a more definite statement than might at first be supposed. Conservation turned Inglesham into a monument to a lapse of faith in the triumph of professionalism, and an acknowledgement that the Church on earth is fallible. More than that even; because the scrupulous preservation of the physical fabric arrests the church at a particular historical moment, it connotes a similar end to the building's spiritual mission. At Inglesham, the church — and perhaps the Church — lies off the beaten path, and the ideology of its conservation implies that that is where it should be left.

Table 2] Correlation between dates of clerical institution and church restoration, 1800–1909

Dates	*0 to 3*	*4 to 6*	*7 to 9*	*10 or more*	
1800–09	1.0				no. of cases
	0.4				% of total
1810–19					no. of cases
					% of total
1820–29			1.0	2.0	no. of cases
			0.4	0.8	% of total
1830–39	8.0	2.0		4.0	no. of cases
	3.2	0.8		1.6	% of total
1840–49	18.0	2.0		4.0	no. of cases
	7.2	0.8		1.6	% of total
1850–59	24.0	1.0	1.0	18.0	no. of cases
	9.6	0.4	0.4	7.2	% of total
1860–69	26.0	16.0	5.0	9.0	no. of cases
	10.4	6.4	2.0	3.6	% of total
1870–79	14.0	15.0	5.0	9.0	no. of cases
	5.6	6.0	2.0	3.6	% of total
1880–89	9.0	1.0	1.0	7.0	no. of cases
	3.6	0.4	0.4	2.8	% of total
1890–99	11.0	4.0	1.0	3.0	no. of cases
	4.4	1.6	0.4	1.2	% of total
1900–09	2.0	1.0		1.0	no. of cases
	0.8	0.4		0.4	% of total
Total %:	45%	21.1%	6.8%	27.8%	254 cases

Source for dates of clerical institutions: *The Clergy List*.

66] Inglesham Church, Wiltshire, conserved by J. T. Micklethwaite with the advice of the SPAB, 1885–1906

Notes

1 Henry Russell-Hitchock, *Modern Architecture: Romanticism and Reintegration*, New York, 1929, p. 68.
2 J. Masfen, *Views of the Church of St Mary Stafford*, London, 1852.
3 C. Harvey and J. Press, *William Morris; Design and Enterprise in Victorian Britain*, Manchester, 1992, pp. 70–93.
4 Parliamentary Accounts and Papers, 1876.
5 Harvey and Press, *William Morris*, p. 76.
6 W. J. Reader, *Professional Men*, London, 1966, appendix.
7 J. Mordaunt Crook, *William Burges and the High Victorian Dream*, London, 1981, pp. 181–5.
8 For Street's account of these works see *Archaeologia Cantiana*, 1860, pp. 97–134.
9 *Sessional Papers of the Royal Institute of British Architects*, 1863–64, pp. 29–42.
10 *Ecclesiologist*, new series XV, 1857, pp. 342–5; new series XIX, 1861, pp. 70–8, 213–15, 311–12. *Transactions of the Royal Institute of British Architects*, 1861–62, pp. 79–80.
11 An account of the foundation of the Committee is to be found in the November 1864 entry in *Minute Books of the Committee on the Conservation of Ancient Monuments and Remains*, British Architectural Library, Royal Institute of British Architects; hereafter CCAMR.
12 Committee in Aid of the Restoration, *Restoration of Heckington Church*, Heckington, 1864.
13 *CCAMR*, 2 March 1868.
14 First noted in *CCAMR*, 25 November 1865.
15 G. Tyack, *Sir James Pennethorne*, Cambridge, 1992, p. 124.
16 *Papers Read at the Royal Institute of British Architects*, 1874–75, pp. 1–14, 3–4.
17 *CCAMR*, 15 January 1874.
18 *CCAMR*, 3 March 1876.
19 See, for example, *CCAMR*, 10 March and 8 December 1875; 6 April 1876.
20 See 'Ruskin and the RIBA Gold Medal', E. T. Cook and A. Wedderburn (eds), *The Complete Works of John Ruskin*, 38 vols, London (1903–09), XXXIV, pp. 513–16.
21 Lambeth Palace Library, Incorporated Church Building Society Records (hereafter ICBS) no. 3644.

22 ICBS no. 6316.
23 ICBS no. 7933.
24 H. M. Taylor, 'J. T. Irvine's work at Bradford-on-Avon', *Archaeological Journal*, CXXIX, 1972, pp. 89–118. The Museum of Antiquities Library in Edinburgh has a collection of Irvine's articles and some personal notes, as well as his voluminous collection of historical notices of the Shetland Islands.
25 Frater's correspondence with Scott, held in the Chester Cathedral Muniments Room, is noted in an article by Virginia Jansen of the University of California at Santa Cruz, scheduled to appear in the British Archaeological Association volume on Chester. I am grateful to Professor Jansen for sending me a draft of her work.
26 O. G. Rees, 'Papers and correspondence about the restoration of Llanbadarn Fawr church, 1862–70', *Journal of the Historical Society of the Church of Wales*, X, 1960, pp. 52–65.
27 'On the restoration of ancient buildings', *Builder*, XIX, 1861, p. 389.
28 Basil, H. Jackson (ed.), Recollections of Thomas Graham Jackson, Oxford, 1950, pp. 54–60, 216–17.
29 *The Architectural Notebooks of Thomas Hardy*, Dorset Natural History and Archaeological Society, Dorchester, 1966, pp. 1, 3–4, 22–3.
30 ICBS no. 3230, St Mary the Virgin, Dover; 6 May and 8 June 1843.
31 Discussed in correspondence held in ICBS no. 4443 for Coggeshall church, Essex; see letters dated 18 February 1852, 14 February 1860, 3 December 1863 and 8 February 1869.
32 ICBS no. 6868, 4 October 1868.
33 J. Hutchinson and P. Joyce, *G. E. Street in East Yorkshire*, University of Hull, 1981, p. 5.
34 See early entries in 'Calendar of correspondence of the Oxford Architectural and Historical Society, 1835–1900', Bodleian Library, MSS Dep.d 538.
35 J. M. Neale, 'An account of the late restoration of St Nicholas, Old Shoreham, Sussex', *Transactions of the Cambridge Camden Society*, 1839–41, pp. 28–40.
36 Associated Architectural Societies, *Reports and Papers*, 1877, p. xxvii.
37 Most of the churches described in Mark Chatfield, *Churches the Victorians Forgot*, Ashbourne, 1979, fall into one of these categories. Using the Clergy Lists for 1853, 1877 and 1891, I determined that a third of the churches in his sample were livings held in plurality, a third had no incumbent, and the rest were exceptionally poor livings. Of these, one carried no stipend at all, and the others had annual stipends under £150 — far below the £360 minimum which the Revd R. S. Hawker of Morwenstow reckoned as necessary to sustain the life of a gentleman.

Chapter 8 · Martin Cherry

Patronage, the Anglican Church and the local architect in Victorian England

This essay grew out of the study of two local Victorian architectural practices — the Haywards of Exeter and the Goddards of Leicester. The design of new churches and the restoration of old formed a major part of their work; indeed, success in church work helped to establish them as leading architects in their localities and provided a substantial proportion of their income. Yet, despite the key role church commissions played in the business of both practices, their experience proved remarkably different. The history of these two firms throws up several instructive insights into the workings of patronage and the role of the professional in the middle years of the nineteenth century.

By the late 1880s John Hayward (1808–91) enjoyed a reputation as 'the senior architect in the west of England'.[1] His fame as a church architect had been established early. In 1843 the Cambridge Camden Society, self-appointed arbiters of liturgical propriety, enthused over Hayward's St Andrew's, Exwick (near Exeter) as they had over no earlier contemporary church: 'we do not hesitate to pronounce this the best specimen of a modern church we have yet seen.'[2] Although he was soon displaced as one of the Society's favoured sons, he retained his position as the doyen of West-Country architects. How was a local architect able to achieve this regional prominence? As will be shown, the process was complex, but the key elements were Hayward's training in a metropolitan office, his early attachment to the dominant network of leading churchmen and local gentry in Devon — effectively a party or interest group whose institutional mouthpiece was the Exeter Diocesan Architectural Society (EDAS) — and his ability to learn this group's aesthetic vocabularly quickly and effectively and use it to good account.

The last point is an important one since it is generally acknowledged, even by historians who wish to play down the role of the high churchmen in the mid-nineteenth century, that the ecclesiologists' views on church ordering had largely prevailed in the Church of England by the late 1860s.

In other words, Camdenian liturgical principles became the norm.[3] Those who had mastered the correct grammar and vocabulary of the Gothic Revival were at a distinct advantage over those who had not.

The experience of Henry Goddard of Leicester (1792–1868) was markedly different from that of Hayward. As we shall see, he lacked both Hayward's skills and his 'connection'. Even so, like Hayward in the south-west, Goddard was considered to have been the leading architect of his day in Leicestershire.[4] Church commissions were no less important to him than they had been to Hayward. But, unlike Hayward, Goddard's work was held in low esteem by those whose judgement on style and architectural propriety came to matter most. As late as 1854 Joseph Clarke, the architect for the Incorporated Church Building Society, criticised his restoration of Barwell church:

> I have largely inspected this church for the Society, and though I cannot say the works have been carried out in the way our committee would desire, very much more has been effected than would otherwise have been the case, but for the very salutory fear of our inspection. A local architect has been employed, and as usual in such circumstances, unless he is of sufficient standing or knowledge, the old churchwarden way of doing things is maintained, and the better things which the present day requires in all church work is never looked for where a local surveyor has interest enough to get himself called a 'church architect'. But happily I have staved off a good deal, and got the work carried out better than I feared would have been the case at first.[5]

The fortunes of the Goddard practice in the 1850s and 1860s illustrate the shortcomings for an architect of the prevailing conventional patterns of local patronage and the absence of a generally accepted form of professional accreditation. Between the late 1830s and the 1850s Henry Goddard had built up a general practice in Leicester and the county that involved many church restorations and the refashioning of many parsonages. For a number of years the strictures of the ecclesiologists made barely any impression in Leicestershire and there was little incentive for Goddard to learn new tricks. But in time his failure to master the approved forms of the ecclesiastical Gothic Revival seriously threatened his business. Commendation by gentlemen and incumbents as a dependable local man who could do a decent job tolerably well and at a moderate price took Henry Goddard only so far. As the aesthetically undemanding requirements of a traditional High Church clientele gave way to the more rigorous and increasingly dominant influence of those who held ecclesiologically sound principles, so the inadequacies of Henry's background and his lack of 'connection' became apparent. His inability to provide 'the better things which the present day requires' meant that patrons threatened to look elsewhere and it needed a radical shift in attitude towards his church work if the situation were to be retrieved. That this change in attitude took place may largely be attributed to the growing involvement of Henry's son Joseph (1840–1900) in the work of the practice.

While there were many contrasts between the professional worlds of John Hayward and Henry Goddard, the similarities were striking enough, and much about them both would have been familiar to a local architect of the eighteenth century. Career prospects were greatly enhanced in the early years of the eighteenth century by an attachment to a party or interest group (important for parish, borough or county surveyors, for instance), or a network of aristocratic, gentry or — as in Hayward's case — ecclesiastical contacts. 'Connection' was doubly important in the absence of any form of professional validation; an architect without local contacts would be judged on the reputation of the architect with whom he served his time. Leading metropolitan architects such as Soane or Barry became significant brokers between patrons and aspiring younger men. This aspect of professional life was not to change radically for many decades, as the careers of those who passed through Scott's office testify. But the development of the professional societies came to provide a major channel through which local architects could more effectively control their lives by distinguishing themselves from less 'competent' men (such as builders), by establishing scales of fees and by reforming the conduct of competitions. All this is well enough understood and I do not wish here to argue a crude development in the nineteenth-century architectural world from classic patterns of patronage in the 1830s and 1840s to professional exclusivism in the 1870s and 1880s. Such a Whig interpretation of architectural history conceals great complexities. Joseph Goddard's career illustrates that these advances in professional status were not enough in themselves. While architects succeeded in defining themselves as a group apart from others, they never managed wholly to control access to their profession. The trend away from political patronage towards competitive examinations that can be observed within the Civil Service, especially in the years following the Northcote–Trevelyan Report of 1854,[6] is hardly relevant to the architectural profession since highly specialised work was more often than not controlled by nomination. This was equally the case with a wide range of activities from schools inspectors and members of agricultural boards to the clergy itself.[7] Control over nominations — and indeed over architectural competitions — was difficult to achieve. It required the architect to operate in a number of areas that in themselves touched on his professional work only in a peripheral way.

The route to success for a local architect in the later decades of the Victorian period was not simply a matter of competence combined with an attachment to a circle of patrons or a single interest group. It required full integration with the dominant provincial élite, and this could happen in a variety of ways and at a variety of levels. Involvement in the establishment of museums, art galleries or philosophical societies was a means of influencing local taste. Contacts with other *cognoscenti* needed to be maintained and strengthened, sometimes by marriage. Relations with other social groups could be influenced by determining the contents of the educational curriculum or by setting up mechanisms for negotiations with trades unions, and there was always the possibility of active engagement in local politics. All these factors provided an essential concomitant to the effective conduct of strictly professional matters.

Let us now look in a little more detail at the careers of our chosen local architects. Until quite recently the Victorian local architect has received a bad or indifferent press from historians. This view is based in part on a largely erroneous interpretation of views held at the time on church architects. Of course, there are numerous cases where local architects were passed over simply because the patron or incumbent was prejudiced against local men. When Wilmot Henry Palk, the aristocratic vicar of Chudleigh in Devon, was considering architects for the restoration of his church in the late 1860s he ruled out Joseph Rowell, who had worked for his brother Sir Lawrence Palk in Torquay, as not being a specialist church architect; he ruled out Edward Ashworth, whose church practice in Devon was second only to Hayward's, because he was a local practitioner; and then ruled out Henry Woodyer as inappropriate by virtue of his being a gentleman.[8] But the choice of church architect was normally a more rational affair. In the absence of formal qualifications, young and untried architects were judged on the quality of their professional pedigree: with whom had they trained? An attachment to one of the major offices gave a young man at the beginning of his career a distinct advantage over those of more humble provenance. This was especially true when — as with the ecclesiologically-minded churchmen who played such a prominent role in Devon in the 1840s — the patrons' requirements were particularly exacting. The prerequisite was excellence in draughtmanship and competence in surveying techniques; liturgical propriety and the correct use of mouldings could easily be acquired if the basic skills were in place.

That John Hayward was a highly accomplished draughtsman is clear from his earliest published work, the measured drawings that illustrate an account of the splendid medieval collegiate church of Ottery St Mary that appeared in the first volume of the *Transactions of the Exeter Diocesan Architectural Society* of 1843 [**67**].[9] Hayward, who was then in his early thirties, had been established in practice in Devon since the mid-1830s, but he was not a Devon man. Born in London, he was related by marriage to Sir Charles Barry, in whose office he served as a pupil.[10] The son of a 'house and ornamental painter', he was exhibiting at the Royal Academy from 1826; where the specific subject of his exhibition pieces is known they are classical.[11] It would be gratifying to think that he learnt his Gothic vocabulary in Barry's office at the time the drawings were being prepared for the Palace of Westminster competition, with Pugin somewhere in the background. In 1831 and 1832 he was temporarily resident in Bath from where he submitted competition designs for King Edward VI's school at Birmingham.[12] Barry won the competition with a Tudor Gothic design, and it is not inconceivable that Hayward was involved in this work. It is not known whether or not he returned for a short time to London, but certainly he had settled in Exeter by 1834. Interestingly, the pictures he exhibited at the Royal Academy in the early 1830s were of Gothic subjects.

Exactly how John Medley, rector of St Thomas, Exeter and a little later a prebendary of Exeter — of whom more later — and the other local leaders of the ecclesiological persuasion in Devon settled on Hayward as their favoured architect is not known, but the Barry connection must have counted for something. Barry was an active champion of his protégés, and past and present members of his office developed a strong *esprit de corps*, as the success of the informal Barry Club testifies.[13] The professional network was further reinforced by familial ties. Furthermore, architects were not reticent in drawing their skills to the attention of potential patrons, as did (for instance) Edmund Sharpe and George Gilbert Scott to the Cambridge Camden Society in the early 1840s. But it can only remain conjectural that it was factors such as these that brought

67] John Hayward, View of the Lady Chapel, Ottery St Mary

Hayward into the vanguard of architectural thinking in the county and –fleetingly — in the country.

Earlier I described the ecclesiological movement in Devon, as expressed through the Exeter Diocesan Architectural Society, as being a party or interest group. These two terms are not synonymous, of course, but together they convey the essence of the phenomenon. EDAS provided a forum where High Church ideals about liturgical propriety — not necessarily Tractarian ones — could be discussed freely by clergy and laity together. Of the society's membes, 43.5 per cent were clergymen when it was established in 1842, a proportion that remained pretty constant throughout the decade; the corresponding figure for 1850 was 47.6 per cent.[14] EDAS flowered in the diocese of Exeter under Henry Phillpotts (bishop from 1830 to 1869), a High Churchman of the old school who, while sceptical about some of the views held by the tractarians, was generally sympathetic to the Oxford Movement and was anxious to raise the standard of public worship in his diocese. He espoused a programme of church-extension and parochial expansion to which members of EDAS contributed actively, and from which local architects benefited enormously: 77 new parishes were founded in the diocese during his episcopacy (44 in Devon, 33 in Cornwall).[15] Other programmes close to Phillpott's heart, for example the setting-up of a diocesan theological college — the buildings for which were designed, significantly, by Hayward — and the reduction of benefices held *in absentia* (reduced from 92 in 1830 to 12 in 1869), were applauded by reforming High Churchmen. None of these policies was, of course, an exclusively High Church one but, taken together with his championship of the revived religious orders, they were seen to be so by Low Church congregations, especially in Plymouth, Torquay and some of the smaller towns like Honiton.[16] Low Church fears were aggravated by Bishop Phillpotts's convening of a diocesan synod in 1851, a remarkable act of consultation and dialogue between a bishop and his clergy. The synod caused widespread concern in some circles and met with a hostile response from the Attorney General who considered it without precedent, if not quite illegal. But it served to strengthen the bonds of the High Church community in Devon and Cornwall.

Such shared interests tied the High Church community together and created a network of like-minded men who would provide commissions for architects who combined skill with sympathy. Although EDAS was established almost a decade before the 1851 synod — in fact a precursor association was founded in 1837 — it is tempting to see the society as an extension of the clerical institutions through which major issues were debated (and which reached their high-water mark at the 1851 synod) into the world of the informed laity. The society was much more than its name implied; like the Cambridge Camden Society it had a mission to combat ignorance and indifference in the parish and exert wherever possible some quality control over church design. Like the Cambridge society it had a conscious programme of reform and a well-thought-out organisational structure — financed by subscriptions — to carry it out. Its members formed a web of informed opinion through which the objectives of the society could be made widely known, the resistance of parish functionaries overcome, and the resolve of architects to act 'with a more devotional and self-denying spirit' underpinned. The rhetoric of the *Ecclesiologist* is familiar enough; similar opinions were similarly expressed by the Exeter society:

> I suspect that our architects, in taming down their designs to the level of vestry notions, have so accustomed themselves to the lowest tone of their noble art, that they no longer feel its degradation. In good truth an architect must often find himself in a very desolate position. He produces a design, the result perhaps of long study, and of refined perceptions, but the farmer cannot disassociate the notion of the Church from tithe and rate. The squire, it may be, hates the rate and longs for the tithe. The rector, redolent of College honours, shrinks from the imputation of architectural skill as low and mechanical. Every shilling is grudged, and the design (curtailed of its fair proportions) is reduced to a meanness which at length is felt by all, and acknowledged, to be scandalous. Then comes the revulsion of compunctious feeling. The parish will not be called shabby. Some desperate attempt at ornament, no matter what, must be made; and frequently, in the end, more is expended to make the church fine than would have sufficed to make it beautiful.[17]

When formally established, EDAS consisted of over two hundred members. Included among their number were leading gentry and noblemen such as Viscount Courtenay, Earl Egremont and Lord Clinton. Hayward was the society's architect from its inception and served also as the diocesan architect. Very early on, and in time to be recorded in the first annual report, the society established an important role in approving designs placed before the Diocesan Church Building Society. Among the church designs that were placed before the society were a number by Hayward himself. It is not possible to tell how many (if any) amendments to his designs were made in the light of members' comments. At some point they were undoubtedly presented as exemplars, but this was not always the case. It was only with St Andrew's church, Exwick (1841–42; [**68**]) that the full rigours of the Camdenian model were imposed, and this was evidently the result of John Medley's direct and personal influence. Some members appear to have been indifferent at first to the notion of a 'correct style'. Two churches built by leading lights in the Exeter society illustrate this; while it is true that they were begun before the society was formally constituted — although its precursor association was in place — they were still in process of construction when the plans for Exwick were being drawn up. One — Killerton chapel (1838–41) by C. R. Cockerell — for Sir Thomas Acland was inspired by the Lady Chapel at Glastonbury Abbey and was recognised at the time as a major example of the Norman revival style. In 1841 Philip Delagarde commended it in a paper he read to EDAS:

> at the fine Chapel consecrated of late at Killerton, a roof has been applied for which I imagine there is no actual authority; such a roof as, possibly, never was placed over a Norman building, but as such, we cannot doubt, a Norman architect would gladly have put on, had he known how to frame it.[18]

Such words could not have passed the lips of an ecclesiological purist. The other church, Tipton St John (1839–40; [**69**]), was designed by Hayward

68] John Hayward, St Andrew's, Exwick, Exeter, 1841–42; pronounced by *The Ecclesiologist* the 'best specimen of a modern church we have yet seen'.

himself for the Coleridges of Ottery, key players in the High Church revival in Devon. It was an unecclesiological job in the lancet style with two features that were entirely unacceptable to Camdenian thinking: a shallow chancel and a west gallery.[19]

The leap from church designs such as these to ecclesiological correctness was made by John Medley. He was the driving force behind the setting-

69] John Hayward, St John's, Tipton St John, Devon 1839–40

up of EDAS, and Exwick church — so enthusiastically received by the Cambridge Camden Society — was largely his achievement. The review in the *Ecclesiologist* (cited above) significantly describes Medley as 'the founder and general designer of this beautiful church' and Hayward as the architect. Medley graduated from Wadham College and became a friend of John Keble; he was a serious student of Gothic architecture and his *Elementary Remarks on Church Architecture* (published by EDAS) was 'most safely' recommended by the Cambridge Camden Society.[20] Medley's zeal and energy helped to convert High Churchmen such as Sir Thomas Acland and the Coleridges to the ecclesiological cause. A further illustration of his impact upon those with whom he came into contact concerns the erection of the tomb of his wife, Christiana. Her father, the sculptor John Bacon junior, came out of retirement to carve her effigy, which forms part of a liturgical scheme in the sanctuary of St Thomas, Exeter, of which Medley had been vicar since 1838. As the *Ecclesiologist* pointed out, the tomb in its architectural setting was remarkable for its 'catholick taste and feeling', and all the more notable as the ecclesiologists were in Bacon 'welcoming a leading Neo-Classicist to the Gothic fold'.[21]

In the absence of private papers or letters, it is not possible to throw direct light on the relationship between Medley and Hayward. Both were members of the Cambridge Camden Society and were zealous in promoting the new ideas through EDAS, of which Medley was the founding secretary and Hayward — as we have seen — architect. It is tempting in the light of the *Ecclesiologist*'s statement that Medley was the 'general designer' of Exwick church to see him in the role of mentor. Numerous examples of such partnerships can be cited: Dr John Craig and the local architect, J. C. Jackson at All Saints, Leamington; W. H. Dilkes and Pearson at Ellerker; Dean Hook and Chantrell at St Peter's, Leeds, come to mind, and comment has recently been made on the deep influence of Beresford-Hope on Salvin at Kilndown.[22]

The speed with which Hayward acquired the relevant vocabulary is suggestive of Medley's influence, especially given the un-ecclesiological character of his first surviving church at Tipton St John. It also shows considerable business acumen on the part of Hayward when the web of contacts focused on Medley and his circle, and the prospect of lucrative commissions resulting from this are taken into account. The leap from pre-ecclesiological Tipton to the ecclesiologically exemplary Exwick between 1839 and 1841 was a remarkable feat. The Puginian early Decorated Exwick was noted by the *Ecclesiologist* for the richness of its decoration and the correctness of the iconography and symbolism displayed in the glass and painting. There were some criticisms — the use of tie-beams (forgiven because they were introduced to meet the Incorporated Society's requirements), the positioning of the porch, the use of iron railings around the churchyard and a chancel that was a shade too short — but overall the Exeter society was heartily congratulated.

Hayward's success at Exwick brought him a great deal of further work. Notable among this was the commission to design the Scottish Episcopalian ecclesiological flagship church at Jedburgh [**70**] for the Camden

70] John Hayward, St John the Evangelist, Jedburgh, 1844–45

Society's co-foundress, the Marchioness of Lothian. The consecration was attended by some of the leaders of the High Church movement including John Keble, Robert Wilberforce and Dean Hook.[23] As with Exwick, the society was full of praise:

> The noble founders have spared neither personal trouble nor money in making this church in some sort worthy of its purpose. We believe that few modern churches can compete with it in the ecclesiological propriety and decorative richness of their internal fittings and enrichments.[24]

It is clear, too, as with Exwick, that some of the society's comments on earlier proposals were taken on board and, given the fact that Butterfield designed the lich-gate, the school, and some of the plate at Jedburgh, it seems likely that his advice would have been sought on the overall design.[25]

More than half of Hayward's major ecclesiastical designs in the 1840s — and about half of all his principal new churches and restorations date from between 1839 and 1850 — were commissioned by members of the Exeter society, although Hayward's position as diocesan architect would have made him the obvious man to turn to, whatever a cleric's views on liturgical correctness. This network of contacts together with the free advertisement provided by the *Ecclesiologist* for Exwick and Jedburgh helped bring him several commissions from further afield. Once established, however, Hayward was no longer tied to the ecclesiological party and began to attract clients from outside that particular interest group. In 1844, for example, Hayward designed Little Milton church near Oxford for Bishop Richard Bagot, who, though respected in the end by the Tractarians, was unsympathetic to their aims and what he saw as their lack of judgement. Even further removed from High Church traditions was the liberal evangelical John Francis Jeune, Master of Penbroke College, Oxford. When he decided to expand the college to accommodate growing numbers of Fellows and undergraduates in 1844, he commissioned Hayward to do the work, and this led to further projects there in 1846–47, including the building of a new hall. Hayward's reputation by the mid-1840s was not based solely on his ability to deliver designs in the best taste; he could do it cheaply, too. When reviewing Exwick, the *Ecclesiologist* began by describing it as 'an admirable example, not only of what a church ought to be, but also of the very moderate sum which is necessary for a really Catholick building'.[26] Jeune may have encountered Hayward at some point previously — perhaps Hayward was involved in Barry's rebuilding of King Edward VI's school at Birmingham where Jeune was then headmaster — for he observed that 'Mr Hayward was the only architect in [his] experience whose estimates were not exceeded by the expenditure.'[27]

By the mid-1840s Hayward's Exeter practice was secured. Church work remained important for the next decade or so — Bicton church for the Rolles (1850), St Luke's College for training teachers for church schools (1852–54) and St Philip and St James, Ilfracombe (1856) are the most important — but after the mid-1850s it became less significant as a proportion of his total output and, presumably, proportionately a less significant source of income to him. From the late 1850s and into the 1860s, his major works were principally secular.

It is interesting that after the heady reviews of Exwick and Jedburgh in the *Ecclesiologist*, Hayward's work ceased either to be noticed there, or, when discussed, was no longer received with high acclaim; by 1850 he was falling behind the times. Of Herodsfoot in Cornwall the journal remarked that the church 'would have been considered creditable to the architect ten years ago, but it is by no means a good example of the present state of ecclesiastical art'.[28] Much about the early designs for St Philip and St James at Ilfracombe proved unsatisfactory also; window tracery was deemed to be commonplace, the tower pinnacles lacked propriety, and the drawing was feeble. It is clear from a communication received by the journal that the unfinished state of the church made an accurate account of it from observation in the field difficult to give. Evidently there were confused signals coming up from the West Country, and in the end the *Ecclesiologist* considered it the 'finest new church in North Devon'.[29] Nevertheless, it is clear that by 1860 the Ecclesiological Society had largely forgotten who Hayward was.

It is no concidence that by this time John Medley, Hayward's patron and doubtless the correspondent responsible for drawing the Camden Society's attention to Exwick, had long ago left the country. Appointed bishop of New Brunswick in 1845, Medley embarked on a mission to build a new cathedral at Fredericton and took Frank Wills, Hayward's chief assistant, with him. Wills designed St Anne's chapel, Fredericton (to serve as temporary accommodation for Bishop Medley's services and later as a parish church) and this shares many similarities with Exwick. Wills designed much of the cathedral — Butterfield produced a scheme for the crossing and east end on behalf of the Ecclesiological Society — and superintended the building operations. He played a major role in the development of the Gothic Revival in the United States, to which he moved from Canada in 1848. Settling in New York, he became one of the three approved architects of the New York Ecclesiological Society. One of the others, Henry Dudley, was Wills's partner and had also served in Hayward's office. Wills's description of Dudley as 'an English gentleman who for twenty years past has been engaged in the erection of many of the best churches in England' was doubtless exaggerated, but it reflects the atmosphere of enthusiasm and hyperbole and the mixture of zeal and self-interest that provided the cohesion of these ecclesiological affinities and that had likewise served to establish Hayward's practice in the south-west of England.[30]

With connections like these, and a family relationship with one of the leading metropolitan architects of the day, perhaps it is the case that Hayward was no ordinary 'local architect'. But until more research is done on those provincial architects who emerged in the 1830s and 1840s, it will not be possible to know for certain how much (if at all) he was the exception rather than the rule.

Henry Goddard, however was an entirely home-grown product.[31] He was the son of Joseph Goddard, who had himself occasionally used the title of architect, but was little more than a surveyor-cum-carpenter who had migrated to Leicester from a nearby village in the last years of the eighteenth century. Henry was apprenticed to his father as a 'carpenter, joiner and cabinetmaker' but the business was much diversified with valuation; surveying and property speculation playing a major part. His earliest surviving architectural work shows him to have been thoroughly conversant both with the plain Georgian vernacular and the simple Tudor Revival modes, the latter especially popular in the late 1830s and 1840s with the gentry and 'squarson' clientele that Goddard came to serve. But, despite the good-quality carpentry which reflected his craft, problems arose with his church restoration work as the standards of reordering that were acceptable to the parish fell short of what was demanded by the grant-awarding ICBS. By the late 1840s Goddard's un-ecclesiological arrangements at East Norton in Leicestershire were so 'very objectionable' that the Society and the parish failed to agree on the terms of a grant, and, as we have seen at Barwell, the Society was still unhappy about the quality of Goddard's work in the mid-1850s.[32]

But Henry Goddard was not an unsophisticated man. He moved his office away from the insalubrious and congested manufacturing quarter of Leicester, where his father had established the firm at the turn of the century, to the professional Georgian quarter near the principal parish (and civic) church. Architects of the calibre of Henry Chamberlain of Birmingham trained in his office. He married into a family that occupied a leading position in the cultural life of the city and was a great collector of pictures, glass, china and furniture. It is one aspect of his collecting that gives the clue to his world picture and helps distinguish him from the younger men of the generation of Hayward — sixteen years his junior. After the establishment of the Leicestershire Architectural and Archaeological Society in the mid-1850s Henry became one of the most enthusiastic exhibitors of strange and wonderful objects, from an early translation of Thomas à Kempis or a 1653 Bible to Chinese curiosities, a Roman vase and some mezzotint portraits. This was the taste of the late eighteenth-century dilettante rather than of the mid-nineteenth-century professional.

Henry Goddard was a general practitioner architect whose clients ranged from manufacturers and tradesmen (for whom he designed shops, dye-houses, factories and public houses) to landed gentry who commissioned houses and stables. Church work formed an important part — but only part — of his output; he received thirteen substantial ecclesiastical jobs during the 1840s, and nine in the following decade.[33] The practice's local dominance in church commissions was not to become secure until the 1860s. During the 1840s and 1850s Goddard faced a number of formidable problems. Extrapolating regional experience from national trends is always fraught with danger, but the slump in the construction industry as a result of the banking crisis of 1846 and the shaky recovery through the early 1850s is reflected in more anecdotal evidence for Leicestershire. Cobbett's scathing observations on the exceptionally miserable dwellings of the county are well enough known, and the situation was not remedied until comparatively late in the century.[34] In the city of Leicester, which was later to gain a respectable reputation for the quality of its housing, demand in the late 1840s and early 1850s was met primarily by subletting and infilling rather than by new-build.[35] Nor was the demand for Anglican church-building in the county particularly brisk. Recent research has shown that in the urban areas of the north Midlands the Anglican church 'was relatively backward in providing places of worship' and in many parts of the countryside over-large medieval churches provided more sittings than there were people to fill them.[36] That this is reflected in the pattern of church-building and restoration on the ground has been demonstrated by Geoff Brandwood; by the end of the 1850s only about 20 per cent of the churches of Leicestershire and Rutland had been thoroughly restored.[37] Even so, the absence of 'thorough' restoration in the remaining 80 per cent of churches did not mean no repair or restoration at all, and such work remained an important activity in Goddard's practice. Goddard's experience bears out Chris Miele's observation in his essay in this volume that church work could sustain a practice through difficult times; during the precarious late 1840s and early 1850s almost all Goddard's recorded commissions were church or church-related work, such as church schools and parsonages. Even so, the surviving day books and ledgers suggest that it was barely enough to sustain the business.

The problems associated with the general economic situation and what appears to have been a slow recovery in Leicestershire were compounded for Goddard by two specific factors. The first of these we have already touched upon — the low esteem in which his church work was held by influential men such as Joseph Clarke of the ICBS; the second was the difficulty Goddard encountered in penetrating the Leicester market.

For much of the 1830s and the 1840s there was little demand in Leicestershire for ecclesiologically sound churches and restorations. Two quite distinct factors help to explain this. Leicester itself became known in the nineteenth century as the 'metropolis of dissent', and this nonconformist ascendancy extended into the surrounding manufacturing villages, especially to the west and south-west of the city. Indeed, Henry Goddard's earliest ecclesiastical work was a plain brick classical Baptist chapel in Leicester (1836). Elsewhere in the county, especially in the south and east, Anglicanism held sway. As has already been noted, the size of many of the medieval churches reduced the need for major new building campaigns, since they provided more than enough seating accommodation — although, as Andrew Saint points out elsewhere in this volume, a rational assessment of need was not always the prime motive behind the erection of new churches. These rural parts of the county had a higher than average number of absentee lords of the manor and, where a lord was resident, he was often of the traditional Old Anglican persuasion that had little interest in ecclesiologically sound restoration work. (A contrasting pattern for south-east Devon is examined in greater detail by Chris Brooks in his essay.) Only in isolated pockets of the county was there any sign of enthusiasm for the new churchmanship and only one Leicestershire clergyman joined the Cambridge Camden Society during the 1840s.[38] The archdeacon of Leicester, T. K. Bonney, was unsympathetic to ecclesiological thinking and it is possible that Ambrose de Lisle's establishment of the Roman Catholic monastery at Mount St Bernard in 1835 administered a further brake on ritualist development in the county.[39] For all these reasons, the influence of the active and liturgically correct Architectural Society of the Archdeaconry of Northampton failed to penetrate the Leicestershire border.

As has already been suggested, Camdenian principles came gradually to influence most Anglican reordering schemes, but Henry Goddard was slow to respond. His first new church, built in 1858 at Kilby in Leicestershire — a modest, granite-faced, Early English design with nave and chancel under a single high-pitched roof — shows some regard for medieval precedent but still no clear grasp of 'the better things which the present day requires in all church work'. The practice's next new church displays quite dramatically the accomplished hand of Henry's son, Joseph. Tur Langton of 1865–66 was (after Butterfield's St Andrew's, Leicester) the most advanced church design of its time in Leicestershire, an exuberant essay in the High Victorian Early French style that one associates with Street [**71**]. The site was donated by one of the practice's old patrons, Sir Charles Isham, who had commissioned Henry to carry out substantial work at Lamport Hall, Northamptonshire, in the early 1840s. But the inspiration is new: Joseph espoused a full-blooded Ruskinian Gothic vocabulary that he used as much in his secular work during the 1860s and 1870s as in his churches. The influence of E. F. Law, the leading Northampton church architect, a major force in the architectural society there, and one of Joseph's sponsors when he was elected an associate of the RIBA, is possible but cannot be confirmed.

By mastering the principles of ecclesiology, the practice of Goddard and

71] Henry and Joseph Goddard, St Andrew's, Tur Langton, Leicestershire, 1865–66; exterior perspective from a contemporary watercolour by the Goddard office

Son established a professional ascendancy in the county, with a marked concentration of work in the south-east where Anglican communicants predominated and where, although accommodation was ample, churches had remained unimproved. Of 78 major restorations in Leicestershire during the 1860s, 24 (nearly 31 per cent) were the work of Goddard and Son; this leading position in the county was maintained albeit at a slightly lower rate (26 per cent) thoughout the rest of the century.[40]

But if the practice were to make serious progress it had to establish a strong position in the expanding Leicester market. Although its office was situated in the city, the Goddards made little headway in securing work there during the critical 1840s and 1850s. For some years the architectural scene in Leicester had been dominated by William Parsons (1796–1857), an almost exact contemporary of Henry Goddard, and past and present members of his office. Pre-eminent among these was William Flint (1801–62). The small group of local architects who came to command the Leicester scene during the last quarter of the century — of which, by this time,

Joseph Goddard was one — included at least eight who had passed through either Parson's or Flint's office. At first it proved difficult to penetrate this professional élite. Even in the 1860s, which saw a dramatic rise of 60 per cent in Leicester's population, Goddard and Son were poorly represented; of 273 references in the buildings regulation registers for that decade only ten (3.6 per cent) were ascribed to the Goddards.[41]

It was not simply a matter of taking advantage of the gross increase in population and the building work that this generated. During the 1860s and beyond, the city strengthened its role not just as a significant industrial centre based primarily on textiles and footwear, but also as the centre of a growing service and professional sector, and the single largest concentration of middle-class wealth in the region. With this came an increasing demand for housing, commercial building and churches.

There were two obstacles which Henry and Joseph Goddard needed to overcome if they were to secure ecclesiastical commissions in the city. One was their Anglicanism. This very likely affected progress in many spheres, not just nonconformist church-building, and to address this, Joseph took into partnership in 1873 A. H. Paget, a member of a leading local Unitarian family and a member of Leicester's Great Meeting. Paget also brought with him a wealth of relevant experience; a period working with Cubitt held him in good stead when the practice won the competition for the single biggest nonconformist church in Leicester, the Melbourne Hall (1880–01), which resembles and was evidently inspired by James Cubitt's Union Chapel, Islington. The other obstacle returns us to a now familiar theme. Local architects involved in Anglican church work in Leicester singularly failed to meet ecclesiological standards; the restoration of St Mary's, Leicester, 'perpetrated by a Mr Flint ... left all the old errors, and added an abundance of new ones' and it was 'distressing to see so much time and money wasted on simply disfiguring an ancient church'.[42] Given views like these, enlightened clergymen and patrons in the city turned almost exclusively during the 1850s, 1860s and 1870s to metropolitan architects such as Scott, Butterfield, Christian and Street.

As suggested earlier in this essay, the route to success for a local architect in the last decades of the century required full integration into the dominant provincial élite. Joseph's stylistic mastery — forged and tempered to meet the wayward demands of local competitions — was but a single aspect of this process.[43] He was a professional to his fingertips and, with a small group of friends and colleagues, used the professional bodies first to establish and then to reinforce something that came close to a local architectural monopoly in Leicester. Founded in 1872, the Leicester and Leicestershire Society of Architects, in which Goddard was a driving force, strengthened bonds with the RIBA and sister organisations in cities like Birmingham and Sheffield. It came to exert considerable influence over the city council, and by the late 1870s very few major commissions, either private or municipal, fell to architects from outside this self-governing group. There were other routes to local influence as well. Goddard's partner, Paget, was a leading light in Leicester's literary and philosophical society, and Joseph himself was a founding member of the city's Museums Committee. He was also involved in the establishment of the Leicester School of Art; significantly, the school came to concentrate on industrial design for artisans, and its courses were well attended by young architects.

As the volume and variety of work increased, so church commissions came to occupy a smaller part in the firm's activities. Even so, they remained important, partly because they were so prestigious, and partly because they meant a lot to the architects. The manuscript sources that survive for Joseph Goddard are very laconic when it comes to declaring personal opinions; nevertheless, his sketchbooks show that he was much moved by Pearson's St Augustine's Kilburn, and the church provided the model for his own St John the Baptist, Leicester (1884–85; [**72**]). His son, Henry Goddard, travelled further afield, to Torcello, to study the great church there before preparing his designs for St James the Greater (1899–1901). But in the main the practice's energies were focused on commercial and domestic work. It is not possible to disentangle Joseph's social and business life; he and his clients shared the same set of cultural and aesthetic values. Much business was settled over the port and the billiard-table. His son remembered large dinner parties at which many of Joseph's client-friends attended as having been characteristic of his father's social life, and bonds here were reinforced when he joined his 'cronies' at the hunt.[44] Moving his household out ever deeper into the suburbs with each wave of middle-class expansion, Joseph finally bought — and remodelled — a seventeenth-century house in the country, became a Justice of the Peace, and died in 1900 as lord of the manor of Newton Harcourt.

72] Joseph Goddard, St John the Baptist, Leicester, 1884–45

Notes

1 *Builder*, LV (part 2), 1888, p. 378.
2 *Ecclesiologist*, II, 1843, p. 23.
3 For such a revisionist historian see, for instance, Nigel Yates, *Buildings, Faith, and Worship: the Liturgical Arrangement of Anglican Churches 1600–1900*, London, 1991, especially chapter 8.
4 Called 'then one of the few architects of repute' in Leicester in the *Report of the Leicester and Leicestershire Society of Architects*, XI, 1883–84, p. 8.
5 Lambeth Palace Library, Incorporated Church Building Society Records (hereafter ICBS), no. 4758 (punctuation emended). Clarke had enquired as to whether Goddard was an architect or builder and the parish authorities had replied that 'He is exclusively an architect of many years standing and of extensive practice.' The quotation is also given in the only published study of the Goddards: Geoff Brandwood and Martin Cherry, *Men of Property: The Goddards and Six Generations of Architecture*, Leicester, 1990, where fuller details of the practice may be found.
6 See, among other works, J. M. Bourne, *Patronage and Society in Nineteenth-Century England*, London, 1986, where many of these issues are usefully discussed.
7 The clergy provides some interesting parallels. Armed with plenty of theological justifications, it too was striving to define itself as a specialist profession; the use of vestments and the adoption of deep chancels can be seen in part as signs of distinction from the laity. However, the clergy, more seriously than the architects, failed to control nominations and entry into the profession. See A. Haig, *The Victorian Clergy*, London, 1984.
8 I am indebted to Dr Chris Brooks for this reference, gathered from the Chudleigh parish records, Devon Record Office, Chudleigh PF7/1. I would like here to register my thanks to Dr Brooks for agreeing to the release of material collected as part of the Devon Nineteenth-Century Churches Project, prior to publication of a fuller story of Devon church-building.
9 These transactions are referred to hereafter as *TEDAS*.
10 The family relationship between Hayward and Barry is easily confirmed, but the reference to his having been a pupil of Barry is rather more obscure; Hayward is described as 'nephew and pupil of Sir Charles Barry' in an article that touches on his work at Pembroke College in *Proceedings of the Oxford Architectural and Historical Society*, new series V, 1883, p. 191.
11 A. Graves, *Royal Exhibition Exhibitors, 1769–1904*, London, 1907, p. 50.
12 Bryan Little, *Birmingham Buildings; the Architectural History of a Midland City*, Newton Abbot, 1971, p. 23 and plate 44.
13 Discussed in A. Barry, *The Life and Works of Sir Charles Barry*, London, 1867.
14 *TEDAS*, I, 1842, pp. 25–6.
15 A complete list is given in R. J. E. Boggis, *A History of the Diocese of Exeter*, Exeter, 1922, pp. 493–5.
16 There is no space here to describe some of the more dramatic manifestations of this, for example the surplice riots, which are covered in G. C. B. Davies, *Henry Phillpotts*, London, 1954, pp. 180ff.
17 Philip C. Delagarde, 'Observations on the present state of church architecture with hints for the regulation of the society', *TEDAS*, I, 1842, p. 112.
18 Delagarde, 'Observations', p. 113.
19 The earliest known reference to a Hayward church design shows him to be even further away from Camdenian ideals than at Tipton. When commenting of Hayward's proposal for a new chapel at Barnstaple in 1835, the archdeacon objected to having 'the pulpit placed immediately before the communion table as being inconsistent with the ordinances of our Church'. The chapel was also designed originally with a cast iron roof, as well as with galleries. Lambeth Palace Library, ICBS no. 1848.
20 *Ecclesiologist*, 1841–42, p. 15. Medley's career is most conveniently summarised in Phoebe B. Stanton, *The Gothic Revival and American Church Architecture: An Episode in Taste, 1840–1856*, Baltimore, 1968, pp. 127ff. The standard biography is W. Q. Ketchum, *The Life and Work of Reverend John Medley, D. D.*, St John, New Brunswick, 1893.
21 The Medley tomb and its background is discussed fully in Chris Brooks and Jo Cox, 'John Bacon junior and the Medley memorial', *Bulletin of the International Society for the Study of Church Monuments*, VII, 1982, pp. 129–33.
22 Yates, *Building, Faith, and Worship*, p. 155.
23 The event was commemorated in W. H. Teale, *Six Sermons Preached at the Consecration of St John the Evangelist Jedburgh*, Edinburgh, 1845. I am grateful to the Revd A.

C. Ryrie, the rector of Jedburgh, for his help.
24 *Ecclesiologist*, III, 1844, p. 113.
25 For Butterfield's involvement, see Paul Thompson, *William Butterfield*, London, 1971, pp. 44, 435, 476, 495.
26 *Ecclesiologist*, II, 1843, p. 21.
27 Douglas Macleane, 'A History of Pembroke College, Oxford', *Oxford Historical Society*, XXXIII, 1897, pp. 433–4. Hayward's first name is mistakenly given here as Charles — presumably a confusion with the London architect Charles Foster Hayward. Jeune may also have used his good offices as Dean of Jersey to get Hayward church-building and restoration work in the Channel Islands, for which see Raoul Lemprière, *Buildings and Memorials of the Channel Islands*, London, 1980.
28 *Ecclesiologist*, new series VIII, 1850, pp. 257–8.
29 *Ecclesiologist*, new series XII, 1854, pp. 214–15, 285.
30 Stanton, *Gothic Revival and American Church Architecture*; chapters 4 and 5 cover Canadian and American developments, and Medley's and Wills's roles in them are treated in detail there.
31 As material on the Goddards and nineteenth-century church-building in Leicester is already available in published or thesis form, it is not intended here to give more than a summary outline of relevant information. Dr Geoff Brandwood is the leading scholar in this field, and I am very grateful to him for discussing many issues raised in this paper and making material from his researches available to me. Brandwood and Cherry, *Men of Property* has already been mentioned. See also Geoff Brandwood, *The Anglican Churches of Leicester*, Leicester, 1984; *Ancient and Modern: Churches and chapels around Market Harborough*, Leicester, 1987; 'Anglican churches before the restorers: a study from Leicestershire and Rutland', *Archaeological Journal*, CXLIV, 1987, pp. 383–408; and his unpublished Ph.D thesis, *Church-building and restoration in Leicestershire and Rutland, 1800–1914*, Leicester Univesity, 1984. See also J. D. Bennet, *Leicestershire Architects 1700–1850*, Leicester, 1968, and R. J. B. Keene, *Architecture in Leicestershire, 1834–1984*, Leicester, 1984.
32 Brandwood and Cherry, *Men of Property*, p. 54.
33 Brandwood and Cherry, *Men of Property*, pp. 15–20, and index of principal works, pp. 106–7.
34 William Cobbett, *Rural Rides*, Everyman edition, 1912, II, pp. 265–6. The situation seems to have been only partly relieved by the time Hunter surveyed conditions for Sir John Simon in the late 1860s; *Royal Commission on the Employment of Children, Young Persons and Women in Agriculture, General Report*, 1867–68.
35 See Malcom Elliott, *Victorian Leicester*, Chichester, 1979.
36 K. D. M. Snell, *Church and Chapel in the North Midlands: Religious Observance in the Nineteenth Century*, Leicester, 1991, particularly pp. 19ff.
37 Brandwood, 'Anglican churches before the restorers', especially pp. 73–6.
38 This was Henry Alford (later Dean of Canterbury), who commissioned Pugin to work on Wymeswold church.
39 An interesting suggestion by Geoff Brandwood; this paragraph is largely derived from his thesis, especially pp. 73–6.
40 These figures appear in Brandwood and Cherry, *Men of Property*, pp. 22, 80.
41 Leicestershire Record Office, Register of Building Regulations; see also Brandwood and Cherry, *Men of Property*, p. 15.
42 *Ecclesiologist*, new series III, 1846, p. 197. Flint wrote a furious riposte in the *Leicester Journal*, accusing the *Ecclesiologist* of 'virulent mendacity' and attacking 'the malevolence of the ecclesiological clique', quoted in *Ecclesiologist*, new series IV, 1847, pp. 35–6.
43 Much of this material appears in Brandwood and Cherry, *Men of Property*, and a more detailed study of the 'provincial cultural élite' is in preparation.
44 H. L. Goddard, 'I remember, a few notes of family matters ... from 1870 onwards', an uncatalogued MS memoir in the possession of Anthony Goddard, Newton Harcourt, Leicestershire.

Chapter 9 · Anthony Symondson

Theology, worship and the late Victorian church

In 1870 English church architecture took a new direction. It did not happen overnight, nor were its causes purely stylistic. Theological, liturgical and social factors determined change. The religious and aesthetic mood of England in the 1870s and 1880s was profundly influenced by the Oxford Movement and Anglo-Catholicism. These movements had stimulated and reawakened a Catholic spirit of sacramental faith and worship.

Catholicism, sacramental theology and the Eucharist

The Oxford Movement was external to the Roman Catholic Church. Its emergence in 1833 was not due to any action on the part of the Catholic Church. The Movement's recovery of Catholic understanding was founded on the Church of England's appeal to the practice and teaching of the undivided church, the Caroline divines and the implications which resulted in terms of sacramental theology, doctrine and worship. It was early realised that the prevailing practice in the Church of England at the beginning of the nineteenth century was far removed from anything which the undivided Church would have recognised. Though the principles of the Movement could have no other logical termination than submission to the Holy See, one of its express aims was to defend the national Church against the claims of Rome.

Catholic principles of church architecture had been anticipated by A. W. N. Pugin and a small trickle of converts in the years before the watershed of J. H Newman's reception into the Roman Catholic Church in 1845. For them Catholicism was synonymous with art. The highest expression of art was the architecture of the Middle Ages. The Catholic Church was seen in romantic terms; Pugin wanted to establish continuity between the Church in the nineteenth century and the fourteenth and fifteenth centuries. It was medieval Catholicism which he and the early converts venerated. It gave expression to his own genius and spiritual desires. The appointment of Pugin as Professor of Ecclesiastical Antiquities at Oscott enabled him to propound his conviction that Catholicism and Gothic art were intimately associated. Catholics had a religious obligation to encourage Gothic architecture and no other; for a time this resulted in a school of zealous clerics eager to put Pugin's precepts into practice.

Integral to the revival of Pugin's architectural innovations was the revival of liturgical purism and scholarship. Parallel ideals were developing in the Church of England, but the main battle of the early years of the Oxford Movement was the recovery of the meaning and value of sacraments, which had ceased to be understood in a Catholic sense. The 1840s and 1850s were dominated by doctrinal controversies on baptism and the Eucharist. It was the second which had major consequences for the development of worship and church planning.

The eucharistic controversy began in the diocese of Bath and Wells. Between 1854 and 1858 George Denison, Archdeacon of Taunton, was unsuccessfully prosecuted in the civil courts for teaching the doctrine of the Real Presence in the Eucharist. The doctrine defines the actual and objective presence of the Body and Blood of Christ in the Sacrament. In contrast, protestant doctrines maintain that the Body and Blood are present only figuratively or symbolically. The doctrine could be defended by appealing to the catechism in the *Book of Common Prayer*, the primitive Church, and Anglican divines from Hugh Latimer onwards; treatises defending the doctrine were published by John Keble and E. B. Pusey.

In 1857 Alexander Penrose Forbes, Bishop of Brechin, delivered a primary charge in which he defended the doctrine. This led to a crack of the crozier from three of his fellow bishops of the Scottish Episcopal Church who, in 1859, put him on a charge for heresy. It led to resistance by parish clergymen in England and Scotland who themselves defended the doctrine through preaching, it encouraged the rise of ritualism as an expression of eucharistic doctrine in ceremonial form and broadened the principles of the Oxford Movement into Anglo-Catholicism.

From 1870 Anglican church architecture was stimulated by Catholic principles analogous to those of Pugin. These principles provided a settled plan and allowed the collaboration of traditional crafts in traditional ornament and furnishing. Five architects were seriously engaged in theological and liturgical issues which established the form of the late Victorian church; all started out as Anglo-Catholics. George Frederick Bodley, Thomas Garner, Gilbert Scott the younger, John Thomas Micklethwaite and John Dando Sedding were intent on building churches for the twentieth century. They believed that the future of the Church of England was Anglo-Catholic and that its worship would be eucharistic.

The rise of liturgiology

Pugin's desire to establish the continuity of the Catholic Church in England with the late medieval Church was reinforced by liturgical study. In England, the study of the origins of worship was then almost unknown. In the Catholic Church the father of liturgical scholarship was Daniel Rock, a recusant priest who was domestic chaplain to the Earl of Shrewsbury and later a canon of St George's Cathedral, Southwark. It was in the seclusion of Alton, where he had gone in 1827, that Rock began to collect material for his treatise on the Mass, published in two volumes in 1833, *Hierugia; or the Holy Sacrifice of the Mass*. Lord Shrewsbury had sent Rock to Rome for two years to enable him to study ancient liturgy in the libraries. The most valuable feature of his work lies in the drawings and scriptural allusions to the Mass taken from evidence he had examined in the catacombs; it was the first time such evidence had been used in liturgical study to demonstrate the customs of the primitive Church and establish their continuity.

Rock's *magnum opus* was the three volumes of the *Church of Our Fathers*, published in 1849–53. It dealt with 'the belief and ritual in England before and after the coming of the Normans', especially as exemplifed by St Osmund's rite for Salisbury Cathedral. *The Church of Our Fathers* contains the fullest and most complete account of the religious observances and worship of the Middle Ages; it is a book of lasting value, republished, with revisions, as late as 1905. Rock's work was not confined to textual comparisons but included accurate descriptions of the ceremonies of the medieval Church, notably those of the late Middle Ages, which Pugin was so zealous to revive. The tangible result of his work was seen, for instance, in the exemplary standards of liturgical practice in St Chad's Cathedral, Birmingham, and in St Marie's, Sheffield. Both were noted for the scrupulous care and solemnity of their ceremonial, their use of plainchant, the beauty and appropriateness of their Gothic architecture and furniture and the full participation of the worshippers in the ceremonial of the people. Ironically, his plea for 'our old majestic chasuble, the aparalled alb, the full flowing surplice' and the revival of Gothic embroidery found greater fulfilment in late Victorian Anglican developments in medieval ceremonial and in the embroidery rooms of Anglican convents, than in the Catholic Church.

Anglican liturgical studies had a different, if partly analogous, source. They were textual rather than preceptory. It would be natural to suppose that their origin lay in the foundation of the Cambridge Camden Society in 1839, embodied in the work of John Mason Neale and the rise of ecclesiology. The source is different. It derives from the days before ecclesiology was born, emanating from Oxford before Keble preached the 1833 assize sermon, and from the teaching of Charles Lloyd (1784–1829).

From 1819 to 1822 Lloyd held the preachership at Lincoln's Inn at the same time as being chaplain to the Archbishop of Canterbury. Lincoln's Inn was close to the Sardinian Embassy Chapel, where French *émigré* priests officiated. The *émigrés* were noticed by him to assemble at stated times for the recitation of the breviary. He was led to enquire into the book, and he found that its structure reminded him of the matins and evensong of the Book of Common Prayer.

When Lloyd took the Divinity Chair at Oxford in 1827 he supplemented his formal discourses by private lectures which were attended by graduates such as R. H. Froude, E. B. Pusey, Frederick Oakeley and J. R. Bloxam, all of whom were to become luminaries of the Oxford Movement. To their surprise he taught that the Prayer Book was the reflection of medieval and primitive devotion, still embodied in its Latin form in the Roman breviary and missal.[1] The effect of Lloyd's teaching on a generation susceptible to Romanticism, which was beginning to see the Church of England in terms of historic continuity and to rediscover historical Christianity, was more influential than has been recognised. Lloyd helped them to discriminate between what was medieval, what was primitive, what was reformed. Dean Church maintained that he planted in their minds the idea of historical connection, and generated spritual sympathy between the modern and the pre-Reformation Church.[2] Lloyd published none of his liturgical work; his notes and annotations were later amplified and published (with his own research) by William Palmer in 1832 in *Origines Liturgicae; or Antiquities of the English Ritual and a Dissertation on Primitive Liturgies*.

Palmer's *Origines Liturgicae* marked a watershed in Anglican liturgical scholarship. Of Lloyd's select group only one went on to study on his own. He was J. R. Bloxam, Newman's curate. A careful and learned ecclesiologist, Bloxam was the real originator of the ceremonial revival of the Church of England; he was also a patron of Pugin and an acquaintance of Rock. Bloxam's method was to make collections of extracts from books and documents on rites and customs, which he printed privately in 1842 as a *Book of Fragments*. Bloxam's work was terminated by the preparation of *Hierurgia Anglicana: Documents and Extracts illustrative of the Ritual of the Church in England after the Reformation*. Started by the Cambridge Camden Society and completed in 1848, it was an antiquarian scrapbook comprising a selective survey of sources (including Puritan criticism) showing the continued use of pre-Reformation ornaments and vestments including incense; the customs of cathedrals and collegiate churches during the Caroline period; and descriptions of independent survivals of cathedral and parish ceremonies. *Hierurgia Anglicana* was the first work which was archaeological and practical, intended to have immediate application. 'Let us endeavour to restore everywhere amongst us the Daily Prayers, and (at the least) weekly Communion; the proper Eucharistic vestments, lighted and vested altars, the ancient tones of Prayer and Praise, frequent Offertories, the meet celebration of Fasts and Festivals (all of which and much more of a kindred nature is required by ecclesiastical statutes).'[3]

The Ecclesiological Society's campaign was reinforced by a surprising statement from the Diocese of Exeter. Bishop Phillpotts declared 'if the churchwardens of Helston shall perform this duty, at the charge of the parish, providing an alb, a vestment, and a cope, as they might in strictness be required to do, I shall enjoin the minister, be he who he may, to use them.'[4] The man responsible for Phillpotts's liturgical opinions was William Maskell, his chaplain. Maskell was a medievalist and High Churchman who was educated at Oxford but was of a half-generation later than Lloyd's pupils. He was appointed chaplain in 1847. While rector of Corscombe, Dorset, he had made two significant contributions to Anglican liturgical studies which were to have repercussions on the ritual movement. Maskell's *Ancient Liturgy of the Church of England according to the Uses of Sarum, Bangor, York and Hereford, and the Modern Roman Liturgy, arranged in parallel* was published in 1844 and *Monumenta Ritualia Ecclesiae Anglicanae* in three volumes in 1846. His work encouraged a movement which attempted to revive ceremonial on English medieval principles. In the 1840s it led to a spate of less scholarly works which set out to encourage similar liturgical objectives, though none remotely equalled Maskell's work. His scholarship, the archaeological and practical objectives of *Hierurgia Anglicana* and its appeal to lawful authority prepared the ground for ritualism. Ritualism was a development which was set on restoring the Eucharist to its historic place as the heart, centre and objective of worship.

The ornaments rubric and ritualism

Ritualism was not a movement for the practice and revival of ceremonial for its own sake. The majority of ritualists, working in hopelessly poor parishes in industrial towns, saw ceremonial as a way of teaching uneducated congregations which otherwise would find it difficult to understand sacramental doctrine. It was the good work that many of them were doing that retained Pusey's reserved support. What he objected to was ceremonial as an end in itself, divorced from social and pastoral application.

The case for ceremonial rested on the scope and legality of the ornaments rubric of the *Book of Common Prayer*. The rubric was first inserted in the *Prayer Book* of 1549 at the beginning of the order for morning and evening prayer; it was re-enacted by Parliament in 1604 and retained in the *Prayer Book* of 1662. The rubric states that 'chancels shall remain as they have in times past' and continues 'Such ornaments of the church, and of the ministers thereof, at all times of their ministration, shall be retained, and be in use as were in this Church of England, by authority of parliament, in the second year of the reign of King Edward the sixth.' Interpretation of the rubric had been a vexed question since the sixteenth century. The greater body of opinion in the early years of the nineteenth century, when liturgical study began and then when incipient signs of ritualism emerged in isolated parishes in the early 1850s, was that it was obsolete. That was Pusey's opinion, later shared by other High Churchmen who did not believe it sustained the heavy weight of evidence for the legal use of sacramentals that was being placed upon it.

In 1858 there sprang upon the Church a work whose title should be given in full: *Directorium Anglicanum; being a Manual of Directions for the Right Celebration of the Holy Communion, for the saying of Matins and Evensong, and for the Performance of other Rites and Cermonies of the Church according to the Ancient Uses of the Church of England. With Plan of Chancel and Illustrations*. It was edited by John Purchas; nothing like it had been published before. Using the ornaments rubric as a source of authority, it was a manual of directions for clergy at the altar. It made provision for a form of High Mass with a priest, deacon and sub-deacon, and gave instructions for servers and the correct appointment of churches. For fifty years the *Directorium* remained the standard work on

Anglican ceremonial. Its claim to accord with the ancient uses of the Church of England was, however, cosmetic and illusory. It depended far more on the translation by Hilarius Dale of Joseph Baldeschi's *Ceremoniario della Basilica Vaticana*, published in 1839, and the *Pontificale Romanum* in the Paris edition of 1664. Roman rubrics were adapted to the Anglican rite. The consequence was the development of a tendency to seek dependence on the liturgical and devotional life of the Catholicism of Western Europe as it had developed since the Reformation on the pretext of applying living rather than dead models. The alternative tendency among the less advanced ritualists was to emphasise the continuity of the Oxford Movement with the pre-Reformation Church and the history of the Church of England since the Reformation, to cling closely to authorised forms of Anglican worship, interpreting them in the most Catholic sense they were able to bear. Architecturally, both tendencies had profound implications for the planning of the late Victorian church.

John Purchas's *Directorium* was published in 1858. In the same year, Bodley was commissioned by Charles Beanlands, a curate of St Paul's, Brighton, to design St Michael and All Angels, Brighton. Bodley and his family worshipped at St Paul's in the 1850s, Bodley being organist. Purchas was appointed as a curate of St Paul's in 1861, the year of St Michael's consecration, and Bodley would have known him. He stayed until 1866, when he was appointed perpetual curate of St James's Chapel, Brighton. The *Directorium* provided plans and illustrations of the sanctuary. What is evident in the sanctuary plan of St Michael's is the setting out of steps on a functional rather than archaeological basis, modelled on Purchas's precepts. St Michael's was soon to become the most advanced ritualistic church in England, outstanding for its magnificent ceremonial, splendid vestments and operatic music. Bodley's subsequent sanctuary plans continued to be determined by the principles laid down in the *Directorium*, as did his liturgical arrangements of the altar with a high gradine and overpowering reredos. It was for this reason that, despite his artistry and mastery of the Gothic style, his liturgical planning and design were anathematised by a later generation of medievalists who condemned him for inauthenticity.

The second edition of the *Directorium*, revised by F. G. Lee in 1865, has illustrations by Edmund Sedding, a 29-year-old architect. Edmund Sedding was to die two years later, but he and his younger brother John, then aged 27, were closely involved in ritualism as a burgeoning movement. Edmund entered G. E. Street's office in 1852, John in 1858. In 1856 John Chambers was appointed perpetual curate of St Mary's, Crown Street, Soho. In 1861 he was joined by a fiery Anglo-Irishman, R. F. Littledale, a close friend of John Mason Neale, co-founder of the Cambridge Camden Society. Under Chambers and Littledale, St Mary's, Crown Street, became a river of ritualistic activity into which many tributaries flowed. The Sedding brothers worshipped there, and lodged with Chambers, during their pupillage to Street. It was Littledale who introduced Edmund Sedding to Purchas, and Purchas who introduced him to Lee; and so resulted the illustrations, 'so full of Catholic feeling and a correct taste for the best form of Christian art', to the second edition of the *Directorium*.

In this way the Roman strand of liturgical influence entered the stream of late Victorian church architecture and planning, coming to fruition in the mature work of John Sedding. The younger Sedding's personal religion was Anglo-Catholic and was shared by the majority of his pupils. Edmund Sedding's association with the *Directorium* also forged a link which, through Littledale, connected Neale with the progressive architectural movements of the late nineteenth century. Neale was a patron of Street; he was also an early patron of Bodley. When the two tendencies, English and Roman, are defined, Neale is associated with Roman developments. Of the remaining founders of the Cambridge Camden Society, national tendencies were expressed by Benjamin Webb at St Andrew's, Wells Street, to which were added the energies of A. J. Beresford Hope.

Modern Gothic

In 1879, in a speech inaugurating the St Paul's Ecclesiological Society, Beresford Hope defined ecclesiology as the 'science of worship' and reminded his audience of the original purpose of the Ecclesiological Society forty years previously. 'It grew up from a desire to see what was the real mission of the parish church of modern days; to realize what were the essential features of it as compared with the old English church; what were the elements which should be declared the absolutely best through changes and reforms, what should necessarily or wisely be dropped, and what were the features of modern times which might most usefully be carried out.'[5] Such aspirations underlay R. C. Carpenter's designs for St Mary Magdalene's, Munster Square (1849–52), which represented the ideal of a town church before All Saints', Margaret Street (1849–59), designed by William Butterfield, superseded it. Both churches provided a model. Of the two St Mary Magdalene's has been less considered, overshadowed by the art-historical interest of All Saints' continental Gothic and polychromy. Yet it was Carpenter who brought Pugin's ideals into the Church of England.

St Mary Magdalene's was modelled upon the Austen Friars church in London, which embodied valuable late-medieval precedent. Beresford Hope in 1879 applied the standards of ecclesiology to Austin Friars. He praised it for its 'singular beauty' and described it as 'very broad, without triforium or clerestory, the arches rising up to the waggon-headed roof of the nave and aisles, the three being of equal height, and lighted by large traceried windows, as one might expect to find in a church built in the fourteenth century'. His admiration was not confined to aesthetics. 'The Austen Friars, like other bodies of preaching friars, had large churches, which were intended for vast masses of people, for sermons and for processions, rather than for conventual services.'[6] Large churches were required for modern urban conditions, so: 'This church had been the type of two churches erected since, viz. Pugin's Cathedral of St George, Southwark [1841–48], and Richard Carpenter's church of St Mary Magdalene, Munster Square ... The noteworthy features of these three churches, the old and the two new, was to give space by enlarging the floor areas. There was … neither triforium nor clerestory in either, only pillars, arches and roof.'[7] Function stimulated the choice of type and style as much as beauty. It was these factors — function, style, and beauty — which were influential on the minds of those who initiated Modern Gothic. Modern Gothic, as it turned out, was synonymous with late Gothic.

The pioneers of Modern Gothic were all, bar one, pupils of Sir Gilbert Scott, united in reaction to his progressive Gothic style. In 1870 Bodley was 43, Garner 31, G. G. Scott the younger 33, T. G. Jackson 35, Micklethwaite 27 and the odd man out from Street's office, J. D. Sedding, 32. With the exception of Bodley, they were young men in a hurry. It is illuminating to know where they worshipped. Bodley's youthful association with St Paul's, Brighton, has been established; in later life he went to All Saints', Margaret Street, (where Street was churchwarden) and to St Alban's, Holborn. Garner and Scott went to St Alban's, Holborn, where Sedding was churchwarden. Micklethwaite went to St Mary Magdalene's, Munster Square. The evidence is instructive. These churches were in the vanguard of Anglo-Catholic advance. St Alban's, Holborn, represented the Roman tendency; St Mary Magdalene's, Munster Square, the English; All Saints', Margaret Street, at this date the least developed, veered in a Roman direction. All Saints' and St Alban's were designed by Butterfield, St Mary Magdalene's by Carpenter. Butterfield and Carpenter came to be regarded in terms of reaction and advance; it was Carpenter who pointed to the future.

Quite apart from aesthetic distaste, mid-Victorian experiments to create a Victorian style, and the adoption of continental Gothic, were tarnished for these young Anglo-Catholic rebels with *odium theologicum*. While Butterfield and Street were, in terms of churchmanship, in a position of unassailable orthodoxy, others were not. E. B. Lamb, Bassett Keeling, S. S. Teulon, and E. L. Blackburne were tainted by protestantism, their clients were Low Churchmen. Their planning, style of decoration and ornament were anathematised and depicted as having moved the Gothic Revival into a cul-de-sac. To Micklethwaite, Scott the younger, Jackson and Bodley their villainy was embodied in 'go'.[8] In 1870 Micklethwaite was invited to contribute a series of articles on church architecture to a short-lived periodical, *The Sacristy*; they were republished in 1874 in *Modern Parish Churches*. Micklethwaite's book is the seminal work for the evolution of the late Victorian church; it launched an attack on pedantic antiquarianism, commercialism and 'go', three elements inimical to good architecture. Church architecture, Micklethwaite maintained, should have utility as its foundation. He advocated a return to Pugin and Carpenter as arbiters of utility and style, and condemned commercialism, perpetrated by the rise of church furnishers and glass-painters. He repudiated the work of his master, Sir Gilbert Scott, and his imitators. '"Go",' Micklethwaite concluded, 'affects originality, but it displays none; the same stale tricks are played over and over again, and their use shows no readiness of invention … In short, "go" is the architectural wearing of his hat on one side, whereby a man imagines he looks very knowing, whilst really he does but mark himself a snob'.[9]

In the literature of the next twenty years, culminating in the opaque prose of Bodley, Micklethwaite's phrases and illustrations were transmitted from one writer to another. The group regarded mid-Victorian Gothic as an aberration, a failed experiment. Micklethwaite also voiced their repudiation of the revival of the dead letter of medievalism, which bore no relation to the liturgical requirements of modern congregations, and in doing so condemned, by inference, Camdenian antiquarianism. He was determined to break the tyranny of correctness. Micklethwaite proposed three ways forward. First, a return to rational church design. Secondly, an appeal to the utilitarian function of worship in determining the plan and purpose of a church. Thirdly, an appeal to the future, a theme he reiterated with increasing urgency as the nineteenth century approached its end. 'And even if we are indifferent to these things ourselves, we build for posterity, and we have no right to entail upon them the result of our carelessness.'[10] Finally he made a case for style, despite his dismissal of the tyranny of styles or stylistic experiment. His appeal to Pugin and Carpenter anticipated late Gothic, as much as his appeal to rational church design returned to Pugin's rediscovery of structural logic. Style was not a matter of period but of function and beauty. 'When we have a building to design, be it a church or anything else, the first thing is to ascertain exactly what are its requirements, both practical and aesthetic; and then, having determined exactly what ought to be done, do it in the most simple, natural and straightforward manner possible.'[11]

Preparing the ground

The late Victorian church was an urban phenomenon. In 1850 Street published a paper in the *Ecclesiologist* on town churches. He advocated the use of brick rather than stone and recommended tall clerestories as the best form of lighting churches in densely-built districts; he pointed to the continent for the great height and length of churches. He proposed large chancels because the opportunities for using them were likelier in the town than the country. Street's principles were influential on the churches of James Brooks in the East End of London, and, in essence, they were as influential on the later architects of the Gothic Revival. The late Victorian use of materials, scale and generosity of planning may be traced to Street's paper, but the interpretation of his principles was different. Social and religious factors were not the same as those faced by Street in 1850. The late Victorian church partly arose from a crisis: the results of Sir Robert Peel's reforming New Parishes Act of 1843, which led to the subdivision of urban parishes into districts, each with a small church, were considered disastrous.

Subdivision was seen by Gilbert Scott the younger as counter-productive. Addressing the Leeds Church Congress in 1872 he said:

> I cannot but think ... although it is almost heresy to say so in Leeds, that the sub-division of parishes has been carried a great deal too far. We have pushed the parochial system to an extreme. Everywhere one sees little churches, little parsonages, little schools, where, to meet the real wants of the day, everything should be large. What we want are large churches, serviced by a numerous

clergy, and not these miniature churches each with its own incumbent and perhaps a single curate, with which the Ecclesiastical Commission are providing our towns.[12]

Scott maintained that small churches reinforced class divisions and provided for 'respectable people' to 'pay their Sunday tribute to propriety'. For him the main object of church-building was 'to act upon the people at large, upon the artisans and mechanics, the labourers and the poor, who constitute the bulk of the nation'. If that was to be achieved 'we need quite another kind of building'.[13] Like Street he appealed to the continent, but for amplified reasons. Fundamental to Anglo-Catholic doctrine was equality before God in the Eucharist.

> In French and Belgian churches, it is common enough to see the poorest and the richest worshipping in the same church; you may see the beggar, the strolling musician, the working man in his blouse, and the fine lady, all assisting at the same mass, without the slightest inconvenience, simply because the church is large enough to give everyone plenty of room. It is only in large buildings that persons of all ranks can be brought together with mutual satisfaction. Small churches will always be, I am convinced, the monopoly of the respectable classes ... In a French, a Belgian, or an Italian church the whole thing is quite different ... The church there is a public place, where one man has just as much right as another, and until we can get that feeling about our own churches, our national Church will never be, in reality, the Church of the nation.[14]

The modern church

In 1870 two churches sharing the same dedication to St Augustine were designed by Bodley and Garner and by J. L. Pearson. They were built for urban congregations, one at Pendlebury, in Manchester, the other at Kilburn, in London. Pendlebury was built by a rich industrialist, E. S. Hayward, for his mill-hands. Kilburn rose under the guidance of an Anglo-Irish, Anglo-Catholic clergyman, R. C. Kirkpatrick, for a disaffected and largely eclectic north London middle-class congregation. They shared a common precedent, Albi Cathedral.

No medieval cathedral had more influence upon the late Victorian church than Albi [**73**]. A red brick cell on a monumental scale, a parallelogram undivided inside by structural compartments, reinforced by internal buttresses forming bays used as chapels, vaulted throughout, polychromatically decorated within, Albi's principles provided a solution to the problem of accommodating large congregations with maximum room to give them a clear, unobstructed view of the high altar. Earlier experiments to accomplish the same purpose had been attempted by John Prichard at St Andrew's, Cardiff in 1859–63, by Street at All Saints', Clifton in 1863–72, and by Bodley in 1865–68 at St Salvador's, Dundee. The inspiration for these churches was Gerona Cathedral, which has spatial affinities with Albi. It provided a broad nave, lit by a tall clerestory, with canted bays at the east end from which an apsidal chancel opened. Spaciousness was provided in the nave, combined with width in the sanctuary; visibility was given to the worshippers. Albi extended the principle of spacious accommodation and visibility.

73] Albi Cathedral, 1277–1512

Bodley and Garner's adaptions were different from those of Pearson. St Augustine's, Kilburn (1870–80), designed in severe early Gothic, followed Albi by resembling an unbroken cell. It differed in its internal spatial articulation by marking the divisions between nave and chancel by shallow transepts, and providing an apsidal chapel which flows from the south transept. The nave adopted Albi's system of internal buttressing. A triforium was provided within the bays formed by the buttresses, intended for additional seating for the sisters and residents of two religious communities that worked in the parish. Kilburn is a virtuosic exercise in terms of structure and space, creating an impression of great size, unified by vaulting. But despite its brilliance, the plan is relatively conventional.

At St Augustine's, Pendlebury (1870–74; [**74**]) Bodley and Garner applied the Albi principle in a purer form but translated the Cathedral's severe style into late English Gothic. They developed a more radical plan [**75**] and broke new ground. The parallelogram of Albi, its internal buttresses, huge scale and unbroken internal space, was translated into a church with a single span, with internal passages pierced through the buttresses at ground level to form narrow passage aisles. The plan gave the worshippers an unbroken view of the altar, which could not be said of Pearson's adaption at Kilburn; the aisles in the buttresses gave access to the congregation going to and from their seats. It was the first, most radical, church to emerge from Bodley and Garner's partnership and had far-reaching consequences.

With the building of St. Augustine's, Pendlebury, what the Victorians regarded as the modern church was born: a nave of wide span, narrow passage aisles, clean lines, unbroken wall surfaces, and height. Externally, Bodley and Garner combined red brick and freestone with greater sophistication and texture than Pearson's hard use of brick in Kilburn. Inside they also achieved a different result. Pearson had left unpainted surfaces exposed in yellow brick; Bodley and Garner plastered the wall surfaces of the nave, leaving exposed the stone arches of the bays and aisles. Colour played a significant part. Plaster surfaces were left to be painted in flowing diaper patterns but, until decorated, were limewashed. A wooden wagon-vault, painted and decorated, replaced the stone vault of Albi. Painted wainscot panelling ran round the lower wall almost to the springing of the arches at the base of the buttresses. Albi's painted interior was translated into a unified statement of muted half-tones, accomplished by patterns and broad planes of colour. All unnecessary features were avoided. The result was secured by line, proportion and disposition of light and shade, with the continuous vault giving dignity of effect. One result of the Pendlebury model was that churches could achieve height and dignity for lower cost: doing without a chancel arch made for a cheaper building as well as allowing the creation of a high, unbroken vault. Yet there were disadvantages as well. Visibility of the altar was achieved at the expense of audibility and warmth; the modern church was difficult for preaching and difficult to heat.

Liturgical planning

It was Gilbert Scott the younger who rescued modern church planning from the exclusive influence of Albi. Scott had married in 1872, and by that time so had Bodley and Garner. They all knew each other as assistants or pupils of Sir Gilbert Scott, and Bodley was related to Scott by marriage. In the early 1870s they took houses in Church Row, Hampstead, became neighbours and shared a common drawing office, independent of their official premises. Bodley, Garner and Scott cannot entirely be seen as individuals, each responsible for his own work. Even apart from their establishment of the church furnishers, Watts & Co., formed in 1874 to execute the partners' designs under their complete artistic control,[15] they shared ideas which were brought to bear on their work. Into this group, Scott the

74] Bodley and Garner, St Augustine's, Pendlebury, Manchester, 1870–74

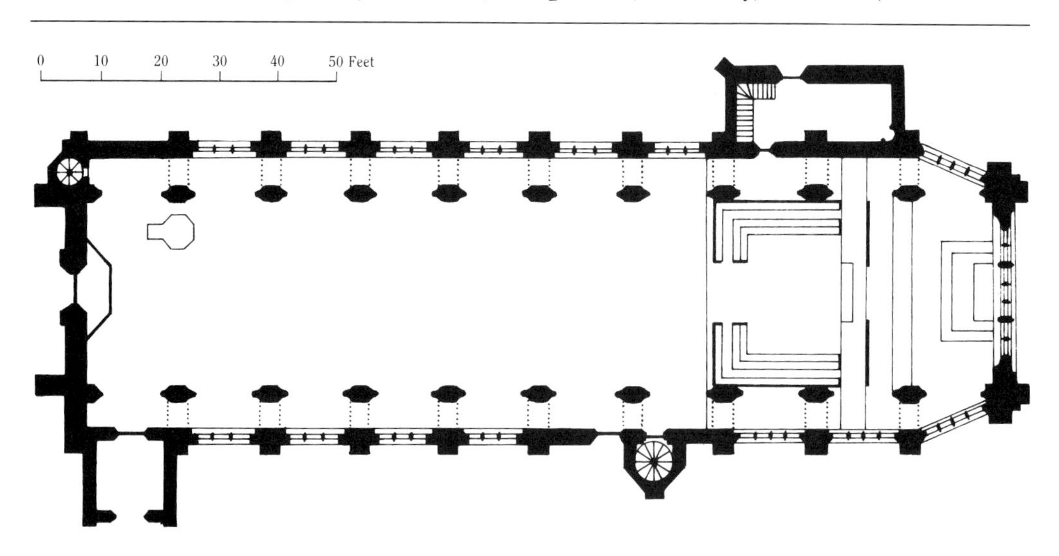

75] St Augustine's, Pendlebury. Ground plan

younger brought John Dando Sedding, though he was not as integrally associated with them on a professional or social basis. In later papers given by Bodley, Scott and Sedding so many ideas and phrases are repeated that a synoptic problem is created. Many of them must have originated in that shared drawing office in Church Row as much as in the shared churchmanship of the protagonists.

Scott's first church, St Agnes's, Kennington Park (1874–91; [**76**]), became, after St Augustine's, Pendlebury, the most influential church of the late nineteenth century. When his design was published in the *Building News* in 1875 it provoked criticism because it was in the debased Perpendicular style, later than Bodley and Garner's adoption of flowing Decorated. Walter Millard described the effect it had in Street's office, where he was an improver:

76] Gilbert Scott the younger, St Agnes's, Kennington Park, 1874–91

> A new thing, truly, were we shown in this said design ... Whereupon up went a howl of derision amongst us. For in the first place, the design savoured of the end of the fourteenth or the beginning of the fifteenth century; and in those early days we were much disposed to ask, can any good thing come out of so 'late' a period in Gothic Architecture as that? ... Yet somehow we couldn't help turning to this odd 'new' thing again — more than once; whilst, by and by, a stray few of us even began to suggest that, after all, there was something in it, that the man apparently possesed ability and that he seemed to know just a little about what he was driving at — erratic though it might be.[16]

Scott designed a group consisting of a church, vicarage and school in banded red brick, admired for its gradation of colour, with stone dressings. What critics objected to was St Agnes's low-pitched gables, square-headed windows, mannered buttresses and unexpected plan. St Agnes's was plastered internally and designed as a receptable for beautiful late Gothic furniture and ceremonial. But its aesthetic was in no way soft. 'St Agnes' wrote Gavin Stamp, 'combined sensitive refinement with the best of mid-Victorian "hard" Gothic tradition.'[17] J. N. Comper analysed St Agnes's architectural qualities and weaknesses:

> Taken by themselves the very noble proportions of the arches and vaulting and window traceries and their refined mouldings are English enough; but the panelled bases of the piers level with the high panelling on the walls, which were originally a quiet red ... and the wide spans of the arches are much more suggestive of a Continental church. Like Butterfield's All Saints, Margaret Street, these large parts are a fine feature, but the church somehow hardly looks in reality the size it is. Great height — something like two-and-a-half times the width of the nave — is obtained by the steep pointed barrel ceiling tied by irons; but this, and the very square clerestory windows and abruptly ending stone pilasters are the weakest part of the design and not worthy of the rest.[18]

St Agnes's had a deceptively simple plan [**77**] which masked its liturgical innovations: nave, aisles and chancel under one roof; diminutive transepts which did not project, equal in width to one bay of the nave; chapels at the east ends of both aisles. Admiration for the furniture and painted decoration, much of which was carried out under the direction of C. E. Kempe, was primarily confined to its beauty of design and execution. Kempe also provided a unified scheme of stained glass. It is the furniture's functional qualities that are remarkable; the tall, heavily carved, rood-screen had a loft which was designed to be used liturgically, either by singers or for chanting the Passion Gospel in Holy Week; the chapels were enclosed in parclose screens; the steps of the sanctuary were carefully designed for ceremonial. The high altar was raised to eye-level and had a triptych of wood, carved, painted and gilded, based on fifteenth-century German models; it was set forward several feet in advance of the east window in order to emphasise the sanctuary and give an impression of great length from east to west. No architect since Pugin had a more assured understanding of the liturgical function of Gothic church furniture than Scott until the arrival of Comper fifteen years later. In comparison with Scott, Bodley and Garner seem graceful but dilettantish.

Nothing could have been achieved at Kennington if the church had not

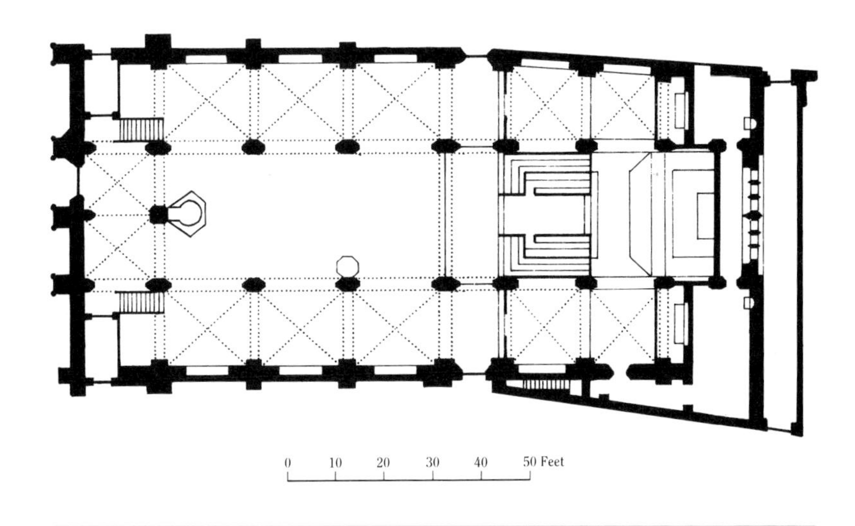

77] St Agnes's, Kennington Park. Ground plan

been founded as an Anglo-Catholic parish. Like St. Augustine's, Kilburn, it was the result of a faction which had broken away from another parish due to an attempt to suppress ritualism. Canon T. B. Dover, the founder, was a medievalist. St Agnes's became the centre of the revival of pre-Reformation ceremonial, as far as it was then understood, based upon the Sarum Missal. Plainsong accompanied the Solemn Eucharist; processions formed a conspicuous feature (explaining the height of the aisles, designed freely to accommodate banners); the celebrating ministers wore embroidered vestments designed by Kempe. Kempe's workshop manager, William Tate, was sacristan. Curates shared these medieval ideals, and three of them became Comper's early patrons. St Agnes's, Kennington Park, was a seed-bed for later developments that continued the principles of liturgical planning well into the twentieth century.

Living churches for living men

J. D. Sedding's two major contributions to town church design were even more startling than Scott's: Our Holy Redeemer, Clerkenwell (1887–95) and Holy Trinity, Upper Chelsea (1888–90). Undergirding Sedding's faith was a passionate belief in the Incarnation. Defending the use of imagery at the Portsmouth Church Congress in 1885, Sedding declared, 'If "the Word made flesh and dwelling among us" may be portrayed at all, you will agree with me that, as a matter of principle, you cannot exclude any part of His earthly life and ministry from the sphere of art.'[19] He saw religious art in Catholic terms, as a central part of European civilisation, integral to the conversion of the masses. Art was divine; the Catholic artist held order from above. Above all, art had a redemptive purpose for the poor:

> The face of English society is smeared all over with defilement; the wear and tear of existence increases, and the conditions of life are well-nigh unbearable.

> The smoke hangs over six counties; the green fields fade yearly farther away from the children's feet; and men, women and children lie huddled together in our hideous towns in one dark surging mass of misery and crime, hunger and despair. Yet priest and artist make no sign; they do not bring beautiful pictorial art to the churches, where beauty alone can be seen by the poor man without envy or despair.[20]

Sedding's ideas were more emotional than scientific. Their appeal to feeling explains the powerful influence he had on young architects and artists. From the Incarnation flowed the sacraments, God working in and through matter, reaching their fulfilment in the sacrament of the altar, the centre of Christian worship. Sedding's incarnational faith and its sacramental application explain his desire to build 'living churches for living men' and create 'modern art for modern people'. Christ was in art and architecture 'all in all, or not at all'.[21]

Sedding was a master of spatial and liturgical design. He broke new and controversial ground in his design for Our Holy Redeemer, Clerkenwell, by adopting the style of the early Italian Renaissance, considered unthinkable for Anglican church architecture until very late in the nineteenth century. Our Holy Redeemer was founded as a new parish to serve a poor district; it did not have a factional origin. Sedding saw in the Renaissance an opportunity of applying his ideal of bringing pictorial art to the poor and placing the worshippers in direct visual relationship to the high altar without the intervention of screen or choir. The nave ended at the foot of the sanctuary; the altar was placed beneath a baldacchino in a ritual enclosure; the organ and choir were situated in a west gallery. He achieved this by placing a cross within a square, much as Wren had done in the City churches. Although Sedding described the church as 'broadly Italian', his application of the Renaissance was as much English as Italian. The liturgical life of Our Holy Redeemer was from the start as Italian as the architecture; hence the application of direct liturgical emphasis, unhampered by medievalism or ecclesiology. Liturgically, Our Holy Redeemer returned to first principles.

At Holy Trinity, Upper Chelsea [**78**], the principle of direct visibility was carried further. Most writers on Holy Trinity have concentrated on Sedding's experiments with style and his attempt to design a church decorated and furnished by the leading artists of the day. He had nursed this ambition since delivering a paper on 'Modern Ecclesiastical Art' to the St Paul's Ecclesiological Society in 1885. In 1880 he had delivered another paper to the same society on 'Architecture of the Perpendicular Period'. In it we find the seeds of his solution to development, which was to 'take up the threads of Gothic tradition where they were left in the fifteenth century and weave them into the weft of modern need and thought'.[22] Stylistically, Sedding's experiments led to what became known as late Gothic freely treated. As free and innovative, however, were the liturgical experiments he attempted at Holy Trinity.

One reason why they have not been recognised is that they have never been properly tested. For the greater part of its history Holy Trinity has had a conventional Anglican life. It was built with Anglo-Catholic intentions, and the arrested development of the church's Anglo-Catholic life, and alterations made to Sedding's original design for the high altar, have masked its liturgical ingenuity. In essence the plan of Holy Trinity is a free rendering of Gerona Cathedral, without an apse and structural divisions at

78] John Dando Sedding, Holy Trinity, Upper Chelsea, 1888–90. Sedding's original conception of the interior, as drawn by Gerald Horsley

the east end. The broad nave is contained within a single cell of five bays beneath a ribbed vault. The nave is doubled to the north to contain a chapel, enclosed in transverse barrel vaults; on the south it is confined to a passage aisle. In the chancel the choir-stalls are kept low and divided by a broad pavement raised on marble steps, effortlessly leading to a long high altar which commands the church and which originally was to be completed by a carved and gilded triptych. A low screen separates chancel from nave. Medievalism was abandoned as fully as at Our Holy Redeemer. Holy Trinity was designed for the ceremonial of High Mass taken from the *Pontificale Romanum*, the living ceremonial of the Catholic Church. For Sedding it was the ceremonial of the mainstream of Catholic tradition which fulfilled the demands of modern worship and which he believed would continue until the end of time.

It is in the Lady Chapel that he provided a liturgical surprise, the implications of which have never, as far as I know, been recognised. Sedding intended the high altar to be a combination of classic and Gothic; the mensa and gradine were classical, the reredos was Gothic. The altar in the chapel is Early Christian. Raised on steps in its own imposing sanctuary, it stands beneath a classical baldacchino carried on four Ionic columns of red marble. The arrangement of the altar anticipates reservation of the Blessed Sacrament; the marble gradine has in the centre a blind panel which with no difficulty could be adapted as a tabernacle. The subject of the painted altar frontal is the homage of the nineteenth century to the Saviour and His Mother, before whom kneel figures of 'Gordon as soldier; Damien as martyr; Selwyn as bishop; Browning as poet; Lowder as priest'.[23] The Blessed Sacrament would give the iconography objective application. Sedding was the first Anglican architect of the late nineteenth century to design a baldacchino for an altar.[24] He did not arrive at this solution by accident. To see how he reached it we need to look at the current state of liturgiology.

Liturgiology and the altar

In 1880 Gilbert Scott the younger was received into the Catholic Church. In the following year he published *An Essay on the History of English Church Architecture prior to the Separation of England from the Roman Obedience*. Scott applied a new approach to architectural history; he put English church architecture into a context of historic continuity and demonstrated that the roots of church architecture are to be found in the plans of the basilicas in Rome. He illustrated ancient plans, the basilicas themselves and reconstructions of early Christian altars protected by a baldacchino. Scott developed a thesis which showed that the liturgical use of basilicas dictated the plan and that liturgical function was decisive in the evolution of architectural form and style.

In 1879 a group of Catholic laymen founded the Guild of St Gregory and St Luke 'for the purpose of promoting the study of Christian antiquities and of propagating the principles of Christian art'. The Guild's promoter was W. H. James Weale, an authority on Flemish art, bibliophile and liturgical scholar, newly returned to England after twenty-three years in Bruges. There he had been a leading member, with Baron Béthune, of the Belgian Guild of St Thomas and St Luke, which he had helped to found in 1864. Conspicuous among the founder members of the new Guild were Edmund Bishop, the liturgiologist, and Everard Green, the Somerset Herald, both converts. Weale, Bishop and Green were medievalists, uncritically devoted to Pugin. Liturgy was a major preoccupation: practically in terms of the conduct of the laity in church; textually in the examination of liturgical manuscripts; historically in the investigation of early Christian, medieval and early recusant practices.

In 1880 Bishop read a paper on the history, character, design and position of the high altar. This was a turning point in the Guild's history. Several architects were members and began to introduce their Catholic colleagues. They included J. F. Bentley, J. A. Hansom, F. A. Walters, J. H. Eastwood and Leonard Stokes. All were involved in hard practical discussion on technical points of church design. The improvements noticeable in Catholic church-building in the late nineteenth century are traceable to these debates. Bishop contributed his unique knowledge and understanding of the historical evolution of styles and forms, notably in a paper on the baldacchino in 1881.[25]

A serious problem for Catholic architects was rubricism. Strict regulations, enforced by the Sacred Congregation of Rites, governed the appointments of the altar, limiting freedom of expression in all but decoration. Similar limitations were applied to the plan of Catholic churches which were subject to Counter-Reformation models. One of Pugin's most surprising achievements had been the translation of English Catholic architecture from a classical to a Gothic language. His successors more surprisingly translated Baroque liturgical models into Gothic terms. For these reasons Catholic churches in Britain appear less progressive than their Anglican counterparts. This does not imply that there was no movement.

In 1886 F. A. Walters designed the Sacred Heart, Wimbledon. It is one of the largest and most impressive Catholic churches in Greater London and was built for the Society of Jesus. Conspicuous in Walters' perspective is a design for a baldacchino above the high altar. Bishop was insistent that a baldacchino was a necessary part of the Christian altar. At the Sacred Heart, Walters applied principles that had formed a conspicuous part of the Guild's discussion to the design of a liturgically pure altar translated into Gothic terms. The Sacred Heart, Wimbledon is the sole instance of English Jesuit involvement in liturgical purism, and Walters' baldacchino made it a landmark in liturgical development in England. Other members of the Guild were responsible for designing much of the furniture and stained glass. It was a model church, summing up their liturgical aspirations. In the same year, 1886, Bentley designed Corpus Christi, Brixton, for the vice-warden of the Guild, a Belgian priest, Father Hendrik van Doorne. Corpus Christi survives as a noble fragment of what would have been Bentley's largest church, Westminister Cathedral excepted. Even in its present form, confined to chancel and transepts, it is possible to see what it owes in style and materials to Scott, Bodley and

Garner. Its greatest debt to the Guild is the cohesion of the high altar which, though faithful to rubrics, is free of the domination of a structural exposition throne and cumbersome ornament.

What is noticeable about these churches is their conservative plans. Both designs made provision for aisles to accommodate large numbers, and the nave arcades obstructed the altar from the aisles. Among Catholics, it was Stokes who first combined liturgical purism with the radical planning of the modern church, enabling visual participation, at St Clare's, Sefton Park, Liverpool, (1888–90). Here the Albi principle, as it was interpreted by Pearson at Kilburn, was applied in the flowing Decorated style of Bodley and Garner at Pendlebury, making St Clare's seem more dependent on them than Pearson. Triforia run through the internal buttresses and aisles lead to chapels. The nave — large, long and wide — enables visual participation in the Mass.

These strands came to fulfilment in Bentley's design for Westminster Cathedral in 1892. The structural principles of Albi, as interpreted by Pearson, were translated into Byzantine terms on a scale and level of spatial freedom which surpassed all earlier attempts. Despite its ostensible style, Westminster Cathedral is the fulfilment of the Gothic Revival in terms of planning, detail, materials, building and spatial clarity, surpassing Sir Giles Scott's Anglican cathedral at Liverpool. Bishop and Green disliked Bentley's design — though it was supported by Weale — and would have preferred a Gothic cathedral. Even so, the direct impact of the Guild of St Gregory and St Luke is apparent in the baldacchino above the high altar; a modern interpretation of an early Christian precedent, it conforms to the principles thrashed out by the Guild at successive meetings in 1880–81. That it was built at all was a triumph for Bishop over Bentley's instinctive suspicions. Bishop afterward recalled, 'I was hammering at that, for months together ... for J. F. Bentley's behoof. He was as obstinate as only that obstinate "he" *could* be. I pelted him with texts and examples ... of all ages'.[26] In a letter to Green, however, Bishop expressed his disappointment in the cathedral as a whole. 'My own summing up of the building is that it spells ... the end of that romanticism which has carried so many of us to "Rome" and a good many to Romanism'. Westminster Cathedral marked for him the end of Puginian hope. He was, he said, 'simply "Goth" and "Roman" both, and never got over the "Romanticism" and enthusiasms of the days long since departed, and the hopes along with them'.[27]

Radical medievalism

The Anglican equivalent of the Guild of St Gregory and St Luke was the St Paul's Ecclesiological Society. It was founded in the same year, 1879, by J. Wickham Legg, with the obscure object of 'the non-professional study of ecclesiology'. Ostensibly it was a revival of the defunct Ecclesiological Society, but Legg had wider ambitions. It is necessary to put them in context and identify the difference between late and early nineteenth-century liturgical scholarship.

Fr Henry Thurston SJ, in an introduction to a revised edition of *The*

Mass, by Adrian Fortescue, made a surprising declaration. 'We need not hesitate to declare that the modern revival of liturgical studies, in an attempt to obtain fuller light on the origins of the Mass, owes a great deal to English example.' He pointed to the publications of the Henry Bradshaw Society as a collection of liturgical documents without parallel in any other country.[28] The Society was founded for the publication of rare liturgical texts. It was named after Henry Bradshaw, librarian of the University of Cambridge from 1867 to 1886, who was a pioneer in editing medieval texts. The prime mover was Legg. In 1889 he sought the support of Edmund Bishop and Dom Aidan Gasquet, who were known to have transcriptions of valuable manuscripts. From the Society's foundation it had an ecumenical dimension which, though uneasily sustained, brought together Catholic and Anglican liturgical scholars. Edmund Bishop was the most erudite and influential scholar of his time, a historical positivist who distinguished sharply between the theological and scientific, or critical, attitude to history. Liturgical texts, the evolution of worship, historical enquiry were to be approached scientifically, and the conclusions that emerged were to be accepted as evidence of truth, however much they overturned presuppositions. 'Work with a rope round your neck', Bishop advised. He was for a time a member of the Benedictine community at Downside and retained close associations with the Abbey; it was there that he met Dom Gasquet with whom he collaborated in the research upon which Gasquet's reputation rests.

Bishop had begun life as a civil servant, Legg as a physician. Legg's active life was divided into two distinct periods; his medical career from 1866 to 1887, and his liturgical studies, pursued from 1887 until his death in 1921. To the study of liturgy he brought the accurate scientific training which had made his reputation as a physician. Legg had the same scientific approach to documents as Bishop but he was less objective; he applied the scientific method for the sake of a thesis, using classical methods of textual criticism for the purpose of underpinning Anglo-Catholicism. Like Bishop, Legg was a medievalist with strong architectural interests. He, too, was uncritically devoted to Pugin, but for different reasons. Legg was emphatic about the full implications of the ornaments rubric as it applied in the second year of the reign of King Edward VI, 1548–49:

> I am sure we must raise the cry of *Back to Pugin*, to the principles which Pugin advanced; we must throw away the worldly spirit of the Renaissance, and take our inspiration from the Middle Ages, remembering the direction of the Prayer Book that the chancels shall remain as in times past, and holding fast to a mediaeval liberty of practice as contrasted with the attempts of the Congregation of Rites to establish all over the world the iron uniformity which is the aspiration in most things of the nineteenth century.[29]

Against Anglo-Catholic pragmatism of the school nurtured on the *Directorium Anglicanum* Legg attempted to persuade the Church of England that 'all that is Roman is not ancient, and all that is English is not Puritan'.[30] His campaign was radical, practical and scholarly.[31]

In 1879, when Legg founded the St Paul's Ecclesiological Society, who was capable of designing churches that would embody his medievalist ideals? Scott was about to become a Catholic, so he was eliminated. Bodley and Garner, despite their poetic command of the Gothic style and their limpid church interiors, were anathema to Legg; of the two, Bodley was considered the worse culprit. He was condemned for creating a snare and delusion by representing altars in Gothic terms, heavily dependent upon the dispositions of the *Directorium Anglicanum*. Legg saw them as Counter-Reformation arrangements embellished in a German late Gothic manner. They were modelled upon contemporary continental precedents which were incorrectly thought to have a continuous medieval tradition. Worse, he saw in Bodley and Garner's evolution of the single-cell church a recrudescence of the Oratorian idea of a church as 'a big hall with an altar at one end', a plan he believed to be destructive of scientific ecclesiology.[32] Sedding was out of the question. It was Micklethwaite who, in the 1880s, came closest to achieving what was considered to be genuine liturgical authenticity. He was in sympathy with Legg's intentions and himself published papers on the revival and application of medieval ceremonial, untainted by modern Rome. Few of Micklethwaite's churches fulfilled the hopes he had for them; many remained unfinished and unfurnished. The most complete, and closest to Micklethwaite's aspirations, is St Paul's, Wimbledon Park (1888–96; [**79**]): this is influenced by the Austin Friars church, making the arcade its principal internal feature, and is richly furnished and glazed by Kempe. Like Holy Trinity, Upper Chelsea, St Paul's has had a conventional Anglican life and never developed ceremonially.

The architect who fulfilled Legg's ideals was Bodley's pupil, J. N. Comper; it was he who identified the problem with Bodley's altars. On Christmas Day, 1892, he had gone to Matins and the Missa Cantata at St Barnabas', Pimlico. In a letter to his mother Comper wrote:

> They were singularly beautiful services — that is to say as far as music was concerned for they kept throughout to the simple and unspeakably lovely old English music and hymns. Mr Bodley's reredos which I saw for the first time seemed to me to belong to a different order of things. Splendid as it is (it cost £1,000 or more) and from the aesthetic (only too aesthetic in the abused sense of the word) point of view, faultless; it has not the old Gothic ring about it, nor has it the grave and real character of the 'Tractarian' church of which St Barnabas was *the* example and is no longer.[33]

Earlier in the same year Comper had designed a Gothic altar for the chapel of St Matthew's Clergy House, Westminster. Pugin had made attempts to design a similar altar but had never succeeded in returning to the essential simplicity of the original. Modelled on late medieval precedent, which Comper had established by studying medieval manuscripts and Flemish panel paintings, the altar had four riddel posts, hung with curtains suspended by silk cords looped in split rings, supporting gilded figures of kneeling angels holding tapers. There were no gradines, or shelves, for a crucifix and candlesticks, simply a plain altar with the ornaments standing directly upon it. Suspended from above, the Blessed Sacrament was reserved in a pyx beneath a conical tent painted blue and green. Nothing like it had been erected in an Anglican or Catholic church since the Reformation.

79] J. T. Micklethwaite, St Paul's, Wimbledon Park, 1888–96

A. E. Maidlow Davis, Secretary of the Society of St Osmund, contested Comper's interpretation and invited him to address a meeting of the Society in 1893. Comper's paper was entitled *Practical Considerations on the Gothic or English Altar and Certain Dependent Ornaments*. Present were Micklethwaite and W. H. St John Hope, an antiquary, who had come to hear it with the intention of demolishing Comper's case. They were surprised by its unexpected orthodoxy. Micklethwaite and Hope gave a good report to Legg who, in the autumn of the same year, heard Comper repeat the same talk in Aberdeen. He went in a pessimistic frame of mind, thinking that nothing good could come from Bodley, but he was converted; he invited Comper to give the paper for a third time before the St Paul's Ecclesiological Society. Two years later Legg gave Comper a commission to design the Scottish Episcopal church of St Margaret, Braemar. This church realised all that Legg was striving for, and he considered it the best of Comper's early churches. When he started the *English Churchman's Kalendar* in 1899 he asked Comper to allow him to illustrate it with photographs of his work because it exemplified his ideals. The *Kalendar* familiarised the Church of England with Comper's designs and did a great deal to establish his success.

Legg and Comper did not apply medievalism for its own sake. For Legg it provided a solution to the problem of interpreting the ornaments rubric in national and historical terms consistent with the evolution of the

Oxford Movement. For Comper the primary appeal of the late Middle Ages was motivated by a direct response to beauty mediated in Eucharistic terms. Legg and Comper were men of knowledge and taste, and it was these qualities which did much to commend their ideas to the educated. Both considered that a return to 'the old Gothic ring' and the plan of the fifteenth-century Perpendicular churches of East Anglia met the needs of the modern age. Nevertheless, criticism of Legg's campaign early took the form of of accusing it of reviving antiquarianism, of perpetrating British Museum religion.

The church that embodied these experiments is St Cyprian's, Clarence Gate, St Marylebone (1902–03; [**80**]). For many years it was considered the most liturgically satisfactory church in London. It is best to let Comper describe the church's liturgical motivation himself.

> The new St Cyprian's follows the fully developed type of the English parish church ... Its aim is different from that of the cathedral, monastic or collegiate church, in which the high altar is for private use and is, accordingly, enclosed by solid screens ... The parish church has no such requirements ... its need is to make the high altar public to the whole body of worshippers ... and to do this in such a manner as shall not grossly violate the earlier tradition of the Christian Church which veiled the altar from view. In the late mediaeval and Elizabethan periods this tradition survived ... but its theory ... was preserved at all times by the open chancel screens which, seen against the silver and jewels of the painted glass, greatly enrich the beauty of the altar but obstruct the view of it no more than a lantern hides the light it is made to contain ... By these various means the fabric is prepared for the greater dignity and prominence of the altar, that is the holy table upon which the Divine Mysteries are celebrated ... By the richness of its coverings, no less than by its size and austere isolation, it expresses its supreme and august importance. It is not treated as a mere base for some erection above it ... nor for an overpowering reredos ... It is the emphasis of the table of the altar which is of real consequence; and the reredos and curtains around it and the canopy over it are solely for the purpose of giving dignity to [it].
>
> This was the ideal of the English parish church before and after the introduction of the Book of Common Prayer, and it is for the realisation of this ideal that the new church of St Cyprian is prepared. Its design neither seeks nor avoids originality: still less is its aim to reproduce any period of the past, but only to fulfil these and other needs which are ours today, and to do so in the last manner of English architecture which for us in England is the most beautiful manner of all.

St Cyprian's was designed as a 'lantern, and the altar is the flame within it'.[34]

In 1905 Garner completed the noble choir of Downside Abbey. It had reawakened Edmund Bishop's romantic hopes. Writing to Dom Bede Camm he said, 'Much time is spent — or wasted, if you will — in the bare rising choir ... I shall never have such another chance again of seeing a building such as this rising and growing now rapidly to completion ... a dreamlike realization of a dream — and yet there is the hard stone, all concrete and material ... and in a manner better, nobler than had been first conceived. — *I do not get over my wonder.*'[35] Garner had worked

80] J. N. Comper, St Cyprian's, Clarence Gate, 1902–03

closely with Bishop on his design; together they discussed plans for the future. 'He was some two hours with me, and the half a dozen plans on the table before us.'[36] Garner died in 1906 and none of these plans came to fruition. Bishop did not appreciate what replaced them.

In 1896 Comper had designed a Gothic altar for the lady chapel at Downside. In 1913 it was replaced by a richer version. The altar was given by Comper's early patron, A. S. Barnes, who had been received into the Church a year before Garner.[37] It was a votive offering for his conversion. The design fulfilled all that Pugin, and those influenced by him, considered to be late medieval perfection. Here at Downside, in an unfettered Catholic context, the fullest expression of Pugin's and Comper's medieval ideal was achieved without struggle or compromise. With the nobility of

Garner's choir, it embodied the aspirations of this school of liturgical scholarship in an expression of faultless artistry of such authenticity and conviction that it was equal, in design and workmanship, to the original.

Conclusion

The story might end here, but to conclude it with St Cyprian's, Clarence Gate, Downside Abbey and Pugin *revividus* would not only distort history but would not allow the development of the strands I have tried to identify. The radical medievalism of Legg and Comper took liturgically informed church planning and arrangement into a siding. Its purity was compromised by Percy Dearmer, who popularised and plagiarised their ideas in *The Parson's Handbook* in 1899. He removed the sting from their fervent Anglo-Catholicism, trivialised their principles and opened the door to commercialism. The strands flowing from Bodley and Garner, Gilbert Scott the younger and Sedding met with greater success. It was Bodley's and Sedding's liturgical principles, taken from Roman sources, which ultimately ruled Anglo-Catholic design for the greater part of the twentieth century.

The Great War sapped the economic foundations of major church-building. Of the generation of Bodley and Garner's, Scott's and Sedding's pupils two only continued the originality of planning, strength, conviction and ideals of their masters. Comper alone maintained serious engagement with theological and liturgical issues; Temple Moore brought the architectural developments initiated by Scott to maturity. '[Moore's] designs', wrote Goodhart-Rendel, 'are indistinguishable in kind from those of the Middle Ages and as independent of exact precedent as they.'[38] Moore was a better architect than Comper, better than any of his contemporaries from Bodley and Garner's and Sedding's offices, better than his own pupils, Giles and Adrian Scott. Temple Moore stands alone in the history of English church architecture of the twentieth century in his emancipation from stylism, theory and restrictive convention. But as a liturgical planner, as opposed to a planner of churches, he contributed little that he had not learned from Scott. The brilliance and ingenuity of his plans for churches on difficult sites were an architectural rather than liturgical response.

From 1911 Comper abandoned medievalism for an inclusive application of the Christian architectural tradition. It was Comper's planning which first drew John Betjeman to consider his work among the moderns. He believed that what Voysey and Baillie Scott had done for houses, Comper had achieved for churches, and considered him the most daring church planner working in England in the twentieth century.[39] Style came to mean less to Comper as he moved away from medievalism. He continued to use precedent but he adapted and refined it to his own purposes, as he had from the start. The church which draws together the threads of late nineteenth-century Anglo-Catholic aspiration, the fruit of liturgiology, the incarnational principle of theology, the indebtedness of the Christian tradition to history, and the primacy of beauty in the service of God is Comper's masterpiece, St Mary's, Wellingborough (1904–31; [**81**]).

81] J. N. Comper, St Mary's, Wellingborough, Northamptonshire 1904–31

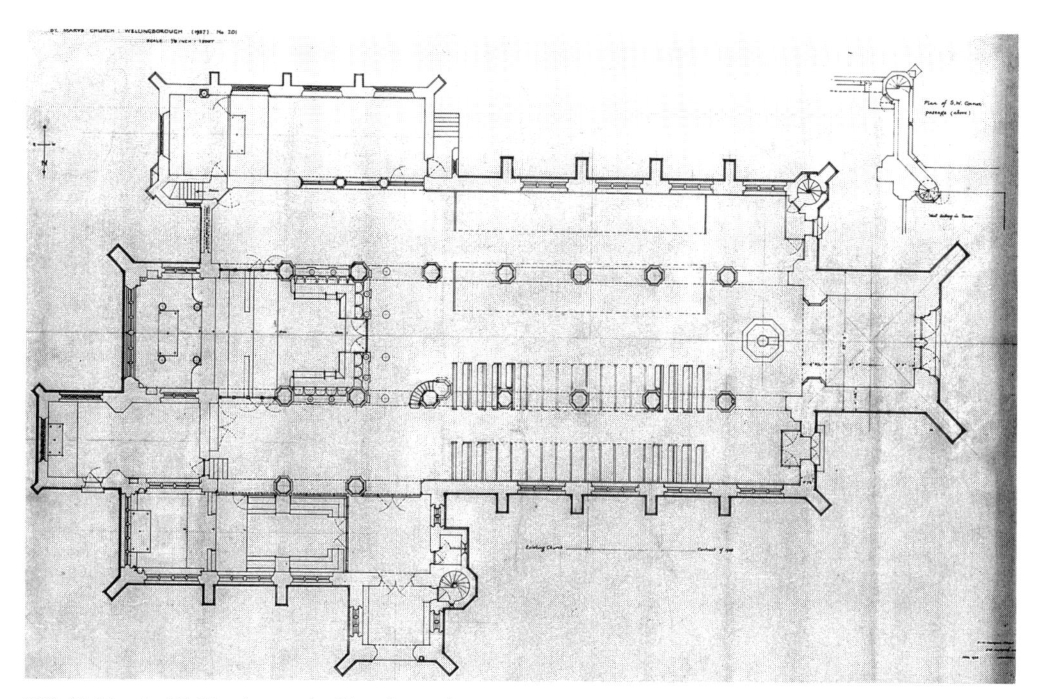

82] St Mary's, Wellingborough. Plan drawn by Comper in 1927

No church built in England in the twentieth century owes more to the accretive legacy of the European tradition than St Mary's. For Comper it was an expression of unity rather than a museum of precedent. The plan [**82**] owes its origin to St Patrice, Rouen, a fifteenth-century church composed of a nave with a chancel enclosed in the centre of five aisles. These gave Comper the idea of space which would bring more worshippers round the high altar. St Mary's was originally intended to have five aisles at the east end. The plan was forestalled by the Bishop of Peterborough who declined permission for a fifth aisle on the south side of the chancel because he did not want to encourage multiplication of altars. The large scale of St Mary's presented problems for the prominence of the altar; a long, low Gothic altar would look insignificant. Edmund Bishop had sent Comper an off-print of an article 'On the History of the Christian Altar' which had been published in 1905 in the *Downside Review*. In it Bishop set out evidence for the indispensability of the baldacchino (or ciborium as Comper preferred to call it) placed above the high altar in advance of the east window. Every detail thereafter took its heightening from the altar. St Mary's as a whole embodied Scott's theory of architectural evolution set out in his *Essay*. It incorporates the Christian tradition from the third century to modern times. The furniture has its own functional value. No detail was wasted on superfluous ornament that did not express a constructional purpose; the fan pendants became lighting fittings. St Mary's could not have been built at any time other than the twentieth century; it is a modern church, yet Comper proudly boasted, 'Only to its contemporaries does the church owe nothing.'[40]

Historically, so much reached fulfilment here: the ecclesiology of the Cambridge Camden Society and its successors; liturgical clarity; a solution to the mid-Victorian battle of the styles, where Comper combined classic and Gothic in one; the understanding of history and the doctrinal convictions of the Oxford Movement; the purity, aspiration, beauty and refinement of the flowering of the Gothic Revival; the understanding of the Church of England as national, yet international, in what Anglo-Catholics believed was its inherent Catholicism. Most of all, perhaps, St Mary's celebrates the hard-won battle for eucharistic worship in triumphant terms; dominated by a figure of the Pantokrator, the Almighty, the Ruler and Creator of all things, the eternal Christ for ever young, majesty and grace are fused in one.[41]

Notes

I am indebted to the following librarians for their assistance: James Bettley, British Architectural Library; Stephen Gregory, Sion College; Christina Mackwell, Lambeth Palace; Bríd O'Brien, Milltown Institute of Theology and Philosophy, Dublin; Adrian James, Society of Antiquaries; Michael Walsh, Heythrop College, University of London. I must also thank Paul Joyce and Geoffrey Fisher for help with plans and illustrations, and Stephen Dykes Bower, Peter Howell, Andrew Saint and Gavin Stamp for information and illuminating discussion.

1 J. Wickham Legg, 'Notes on the Marriage Service in the Book of Common Prayer of 1549', *Transactions of the St Paul's Ecclesiological Society*, III, 1895, p. 173.
2 R. W. Church, *The Oxford Movement: Twelve Years, 1833–1845*, London, 1891, p. 41.
3 Quoted in S. Gaselee, 'The aesthetic side of the Oxford Movement', in N. P. Williams and Charles Harris (eds), *Northern Catholicism*, London, 1933, pp. 426–7.
4 Gaselee, 'The aesthetic side of the Oxford Movement', p. 427.
5 A. J. B. Beresford Hope, *Transactions of the St Paul's Ecclesiological Society*, I, 1881, p. iii.
6 Beresford Hope, *Transactions*, I, p. ii.
7 Beresford Hope, *Transactions*, I, p. ii.
8 By inference William Burges and his followers were vilified for the adoption of early French Gothic.
9 J. T. Micklethwaite, *Modern Parish Churches*, London, 1874, p. 266.
10 Micklethwaite, *Modern Parish Churches*, p. 266.
11 Micklethwaite, *Modern Parish Churches*, p. 269–70.
12 G. G. Scott, 'Church Architecture', *Report of the Church Congress held at Leeds*, London, 1872, p. 83.
13 G. G. Scott, 'Church Architecture', p. 84.
14 G. G. Scott, 'Church Architecture', p. 84.
15 A. Symondson, 'Wallpapers from Watts and Co.', *The Connoisseur*, CCIV, 1980, pp. 114–21.
16 Walter Millard, 'Notes on some works of the late Geo. Gilbert Scott M.A., F.S.A. — Gilbert Scott the Younger', *Architectural Review*, V, 1898, p. 59. St Agnes's was destroyed by enemy action in 1941.
17 Gavin Stamp, 'George Gilbert Scott Junior', in R. Dixon (ed.), *Sir Gilbert Scott and the Scott Dynasty, South Bank Architectural Papers*, Polytechnic of the South Bank, London, n.d., p. 42.
18 J. N. Comper, 'The Architects and the Churches', unpublished MS, Comper's private papers, private collection.
19 J. D. Sedding, 'Religion and Art — their influence on each other', in C. Donnelly (ed.), *Report of the Church Congress held at Portsmouth*, London, 1885, pp. 176–7.
20 Sedding, 'Religion and Art', p. 180
21 Sedding, 'Religion and Art', p. 177
22 Henry Wilson, 'Some considerations of John Sedding's work', republished in Alastair Service (ed.), *Edwardian Architecture and its Origins*, London, 1975, p. 277.
23 T. Francis Bumpus, *London Churches Ancient and Modern*, 2 vols, London, 1904, II, pp. 368–9.

24 In 1869 Sir Arthur Blomfield designed St Barnabas's, Oxford, in an Italian Romanesque style under the influence of Thomas Combe, Printer to the University. Combe wanted a basilica. A baldacchino was designed in *trecento* Gothic. The church was not approved by ecclesiologists, who accused it of antiquarianism.
25 Nigel Abercrombie, *The Life and Work of Edmund Bishop*, London, 1959, pp. 76–9; Winifred de l'Hôpital, *Westminster Cathedral and its Architect*, 2 vols, London, 1919, II, pp. 664–7.
26 Abercrombie, *Edmund Bishop*, p. 350.
27 Abercrombie, *Edmund Bishop*, p. 282.
28 Henry Thurston SJ, 'Introduction' to Adrian Fortescue, *The Mass: a Study of the Roman Liturgy*, London, 1937, p. lx.
29 J. Wickham Legg, 'On some ancient liturgical customs now falling into disuse', *Transactions of the St Paul's Ecclesiological Society*, II, 1886–90, p. 129.
30 Legg, 'On some ancient liturgical customs', p. 129.
31 The radical medievalist movement was advanced in 1890 by the foundation by Martin Briggs of the Plainsong and Medieval Music Society to apply accurate plainsong notation to Anglican liturgical texts. It followed the leadership of Dom Joseph Pothier (1835–1923), of Solesme. Of greater consequence for architecture was the Alcuin Club, founded by Legg in 1897 'to encourage and assist in the practical study of ceremonial, and the arrangement of churches, their furniture and ornaments, in accordance with the rubrics of the *Book of Common Prayer*, strict obedience to which is the guiding principle of the Club.' It proved a fissile body; within six months Legg and other founding members had resigned.
32 Legg, 'On some ancient liturgical customs', p. 129.
33 J. N. Comper to Mrs John Comper, 26 December 1892, Comper's private papers, private collection. Comper's departure from Bodley's aestheticism and his independence of the Arts and Crafts Movement are discussed in Anthony Symondson, 'Art Needlework in Ireland: J. N. Comper and the Royal Irish School of Art Needlework', *Irish Arts Review Year Book*, 10, 1994, pp. 126–35.
34 J. N. Comper, *Further Thoughts on the English Altar: or Practical Considerations on the Planning of a Modern Church*, London, 1933, pp. 31–2.
35 Abercrombie, *Edmund Bishop*, p. 350; Dom Augustus James, *The Story of Downside Abbey Church*, Stratton on the Fosse, 1961, p. 51.
36 Abercrombie, *Edmund Bishop*, p. 351.
37 Garner became a Roman Catholic as a result of Pope Leo XIII's condemnation of Anglican Orders.
38 H. S. Goodhart-Rendel, 'Temple Lushington Moore', *D. N. B. 1912–1921*, p. 385.
39 A. Symondson, 'John Betjeman and the cult of J. N. Comper', *Journal of the Thirties Society*, VII, 1991, pp. 3–13, 52.
40 J. N. Comper, *Further Thoughts*, p. 32.
41 A. Symondson, *Sir Ninian Comper, the Last Gothic Revivalist*, London, 1988, pp. 25–8.

Index

Index

Index